Careers in Transportation

Careers in Transportation

SALEM PRESS
A Division of EBSCO Information Services, Inc.
Ipswich, Massachusetts

GREY HOUSE PUBLISHING

Cover photo: World map with logistic network distribution on background. Image by thitivong (iStock Images).

Copyright © 2019 by EBSCO Information Services, Inc., and Grey House Publishing, Inc.

Careers in Transportation, published by Grey House Publishing, Inc., Amenia, NY, under exclusive license from EBSCO Information Services, Inc.

All rights reserved. No part of this work may be used or reproduced in any manner whatsoever or transmitted in any form or by any means, electronic or mechanical, including photocopy, recording, or any information storage and retrieval system, without written permission from the copyright owner. For permissions requests, contact proprietarypublishing@ebsco.com.

∞ The paper used in these volumes conforms to the American National Standard for Permanence of Paper for Printed Library Materials, Z39.48 1992 (R2009).

Publisher's Cataloging-In-Publication Data
(Prepared by The Donohue Group, Inc.)

Title: Careers in transportation.
Other Titles: Careers in--
Description: [First edition]. | Ipswich, Massachusetts : Salem Press, a division of EBSCO Information Services, Inc. ; Amenia, NY : Grey House Publishing, [2019] | Includes bibliographical references and index.
Identifiers: ISBN 9781642653038 (hardcover)
Subjects: LCSH: Transportation--Vocational guidance--United States. | Aerospace industries--Vocational guidance--United States. | Transport workers--Vocational guidance--United States. | Regional planners--Vocational guidance--United States.
Classification: LCC TA1160 .C37 2019 | DDC 388.023--dc23

First Printing

PRINTED IN THE UNITED STATES OF AMERICA

CONTENTS

Publisher's Note vii

Introduction ix

Transportation and Material-Moving Occupations by Industry 1

Aerospace Engineers 27

Air Traffic Controllers 43

Aircraft Mechanics 58

Airline and Commercial Pilots 74

Automotive Technician 89

Bus Drivers 103

Cartographers and Photogrammetrists 118

Computer Programmers 133

Computer Systems Analysts 146

Construction Equipment Operators 157

Delivery Truck Drivers and Driver/Sales Workers 174

Dispatchers 187

Flight Attendants 197

Hand Laborers and Material Movers 211

Heavy and Tractor-Trailer Truck Drivers 223

Industrial Designers 237

Industrial Engineers 253

Information Technology Project Managers 270

Logisticians 287

Material-Moving Machine Operators 301

Material Recording Clerks 316

Ship Loader 328

Software Developer 337

Taxi Drivers, Ride-Hailing Drivers, and Chauffeurs 349

Urban and Regional Planner 363

Water Transportation Workers 378
Appendix A: Holland Code 397
Appendix B: Bibliography...401
Index 403

PUBLISHER'S NOTE

Careers in Transportation contains a thorough introduction to the field of transportation and logistics, one of the fastest-growing career options in the United States and across the globe. This volume begins with an overview of the various career opportunities in a variety of industry sectors such as Rail, Water, and Truck Transportation; Scenic and Sightseeing, Couriers and Messengers; and Support Services. The book also includes twenty-six occupational profiles, including Aerospace Engineers; Cartographers and Photogrammetrists; Dispatchers; Logisticians; Taxi Drivers, Ride-Hailing Drivers, and Chauffeurs; Urban and Regional Planners; and Water Transportation Workers. These career profiles offer details about a particular career path by providing:

Snapshot details including the most current data about
- Median Pay
- Typical Entry-Level Education
- On-the-Job Training
- Number of Jobs
- Job Outlook
- Employment Change

Career Overview includes a description of the career in terms of its
- Duties
- Examples of titles for positions in that specific career
- Work environment
- Work schedules

Each profile provides details about **How to become...** that explain how to begin and grow a career within a specific career profile by describing
- Important qualities
- Education
- Licenses, certifications, and registrations that may be required
- Advancement opportunities

Profiles also include the most current details about pay compared to other career clusters as well as a look at pay by industry as well as a description of **Similar Occupations** that lists specific jobs that are related in some way to the protective service career being profiled.

Job Outlook and **Job Prospects** describe current and anticipated rate of growth for a specific career, and compares the rate to other jobs in areas in the same career cluster, as well as to career growth taken as a whole.

Each profile concludes with **More Information** to direct readers to additional resources such as specific associations or certifying bodies for further details.

Merging scholarship with occupational development, this single comprehensive guidebook provides students passionate about finding a career in transportation with the necessary insight into the wide array of options available in this diverse and dynamic field. The book offers guidance regarding what job seekers can expect in terms of training, advancement, earnings, job prospects, working conditions, relevant associations, and more. Careers in Transportation is specifically designed for a high school and undergraduate audience and is edited to align with secondary or high school curriculum standards.

Scope of Coverage

Understanding the wide scope of jobs, settings for providing care, and industries where nurses typically work is important for anyone preparing for a career in protective services, from government to nonprofits, to private industry.

Careers in Transportation is enhanced with numerous charts and tables, including projections from the U.S. Bureau of Labor Statistics, and median annual salaries or wages for those occupations profiled. Enhancements, like Fun Facts, Famous Firsts, and dozens of photos, add depth to the discussion. Additional highlights in the book include twenty-one interviews—**Conversation With...**—featuring a professional working in a related job who can offer insight into specific areas of transportation such logistics, computer programming, bus drivers, truck drivers, ride-sharing services, industrial design and engineering. Various industry sectors and subsectors are also considered, including air transportation, water transportation, sightseeing and tour guides, and more. The respondents share their personal career paths, detail potential for career advancement, offer advice for students, and include a "try this" for those interested in embarking on a career in their profession.

Special Features

Several features continue to distinguish this reference series from other career-oriented reference works. The back matter includes:
- **Appendix A: Guide to Holland Code.** This discusses John Holland's theory that people and work environments can be classified into six different groups: Realistic; Investigative; Artistic; Social; Enterprising; and Conventional. See if the job you want is right for you!
- **Appendix B: General Bibliography.** This is a collection of suggested readings, organized into major categories.
- **Subject Index:** Includes people, concepts, technologies, terms, principles, and all specific occupations discussed in the occupational profile chapters.

Acknowledgments

Thanks are due to Allison Blake, who took the lead in developing "Conversations With," with help from Alicia Banks and Cynthia Hibbert, as well as to the professionals who communicated their work experience through interview questionnaires. Their frank and honest responses provide immeasurable value to *Careers in Transportation*. The contributions of all are gratefully acknowledged.

INTRODUCTION

Careers in Transportation have been receiving a great deal of interest in the past decades. From truck drivers to ride-sharing, air travel to logistics, materials moving to warehousing, getting people and goods from point A to point B is one of the most challenging and rewarding careers of our time. As autonomous cars and advances in artificial intelligence change the landscape of how people and goods move, corresponding changes are happening in the vehicles and transportation machines we use, the infrastructure we build, and the expectations we have. This book examines a selection of career opportunities with profiles that range from drivers and pilots to computer systems analysts and information technology (IT) project management.

About the Industry

Every day, people and goods move throughout the United States. Workers in the transportation and warehousing industry help to get them where they need to go. The transportation and warehousing industry helped to get goods like toothpaste or your shoes to you from across the country or from around the world.

The North American Industry Classification System identifies 11 subsectors in transportation and warehousing. In May 2015, the U.S. Bureau of Labor Statistics (BLS) counted about 4.8 million jobs in 10 of these subsectors. Employment in transportation and warehousing has climbed steadily over the past several decades; in recent years.

Truck drivers account for about one of every five jobs in the transportation and warehousing industry, according to the BLS. But this industry employs workers in many other occupations, too, such as ship captains, cargo and freight agents, and avionics technicians. And as these workers know, there are lots of reasons to consider a career in this industry, chief among them the fact that these jobs are not something that can be outsourced overseas.

What the Industry Does

The biggest segment of the transportation and warehousing industry involves moving goods. Each year, about 63 tons of freight per person is shipped in the United States, according to the Bureau of Transportation Statistics. Trucks carry the most freight. Trains, pipelines, boats, and ships also transport large amounts of freight. Airplanes carry much smaller amounts. Another large segment of this industry involves moving people, which includes air transportation and related support activities, transit and ground transportation, and scenic and sightseeing transportation. There's some overlap in the work of transporting goods and transporting people. Trains and airplanes, for example, transport both.

Between production and sale, goods are kept in warehousing and storage facilities (also called distribution centers). These establishments also may provide logistics services, such as packaging, inventory control, and transportation arrangement.

Job Outlook—and Opportunity

BLS projects employment in transportation and warehousing to grow by about 7 percent between 2016 and 2026, or as fast as average compared to the overall growth rate projected for all industries during that time. Projections vary by industry subsector. New jobs are projected in truck, water, scenic and sightseeing, and transit and ground transportation; support activities for transportation; and warehousing and storage. However, employment declines are projected in rail, air, and pipeline transportation and for couriers and messengers. The postal service also is projected to lose jobs. But even in industry subsectors that are projected to have declines, job openings are expected to arise from the need to replace workers who retire or leave their occupation for other reasons. Employers report that they are having difficulty finding people who are qualified. With workers retiring, the transportation industry finds itself competing with other industries for the same candidates.

That combination—difficulty in recruiting and loss of workers through retirement—makes the industry ripe for opportunity. Transportation and warehousing is an industry with many career options from the dock to the boardroom, making it likely that you can find a fit that makes you happy, whether you prefer to focus on more physical work, people skills, technology, or management.

Individuals who work transportation and warehousing occupations typically do one or more of the following:
- operate vehicles;
- move or track materials;
- help customers;
- support operations;
- maintain and repair vehicles and equipment;
- manage or provide business or financial expertise; or
- other work.

Operating Vehicles

If you've ever heard the call of the open road—or rail, water, or airway—consider a vehicle operator career. Vehicle operators usually travel to one or more destinations, following a set route or making assigned stops as they transport goods or people. They may plan their routes using satellite tracking systems, handheld computers, or other technology. Depending on the job, workers may also load and unload vehicles, interact with customers, or perform minor repairs and maintenance.

Each type of operator has his or her own expertise. For example, harbor pilots must be familiar with the tides and conditions of the waterway in which they work, and driver sales workers must be knowledgeable about the products and services they provide. Some of these workers, such as tractor-trailer truck drivers, may travel long distances when operating vehicles; others, such as delivery services drivers, may have routes closer to home.

Some people in these occupations work for themselves, which usually requires that they buy and operate their own vehicles. For example, occupations such as taxi drivers and chauffeurs, ship and boat captains, and truck drivers had higher percentages of self-employed workers than some other occupations in the industry. Transportation and warehousing is the largest industry employer of vehicle operators.

Moving or Tracking Materials

Jobs in these occupations might involve lots of lifting or carrying: loading and unloading items or retrieving them from shelves or other places. A worker in these occupations may identify and track item locations using handheld scanners or other technology. Workers may also inspect items for damage, compile reports, or do minor equipment repairs.

Some of these workers operate forklifts or other machinery to move pallets, boxes, or other containers. Others unload and move materials by hand. Still others keep records of materials, working in, for example, a stockroom or shipping and receiving department.

Although wages in some of the largest material-moving and tracking occupations are relatively low, supervisory positions may offer higher pay. Even without supervisory duties, some workers might advance to higher wages: The top-earning 10 percent of crane and tower operators in the industry, for example, had wages higher than $89,760, compared with a median of $55,620 for all crane and tower operators. Transportation and warehousing is among the largest industry employers of material-moving and tracking occupations.

Helping Customers

Answering questions and resolving problems related to travel or transportation is a big part of the job for many of these workers. They might also assist with purchases, such as for postage, tickets for travel, or onboard beverages. Some ensure the comfort and safety of passengers.

In some of these occupations, workers travel frequently. For example, flight attendants, railroad conductors, and tour and travel guides usually accompany passengers on their trips. For many of these customer helpers, transportation and warehousing is the largest industry of employment.

Supporting Operations

Efficient movement of people and goods requires lots of workers who provide assistance. These workers make sure that transportation systems and equipment are safe and running smoothly. Operations support workers may provide vehicle operators with critical information, such as schedules or routes. And they inspect people, vehicles, and goods for potential hazards.

Particulars of the work vary. For example, an air traffic controller might communicate with pilots so that planes can safely take off, fly, and land. A sailor might keep watch for boats or debris in the water that could obstruct a vessel. The equipment differs by occupation, too. Pumping station operators use pumps or compressors to direct the flow of oil, gas, or other fluids; railroad switch operators use track switches to reroute train cars. Some of these support occupations have most of their employment in transportation and warehousing, but others have large numbers of jobs in government—or, in the case of pumping station operators, in mining and oil and gas extraction.

Maintaining and Repairing Vehicles and Equipment

Maybe you have a curiosity for understanding how things work—or a knack for fixing them when they break. If so, a career in maintenance and repair might be a good fit. Workers in these occupations keep vehicles and equipment running properly. In addition to doing regular maintenance, these workers diagnose problems, replace defective parts, and keep records of their work. They might also update systems or equipment, such as by installing new technology in trucks or planes. Some of these workers specialize. For example, avionics technicians repair electronic instruments in airplanes. Other workers, such as general maintenance and repair workers, have a broader focus.

Transportation and warehousing is the largest industry of employment for many of these maintenance and repair occupations. For industrial machinery mechanics and general maintenance and repair workers, however, manufacturing and other industries account for greater shares of employment.

Managing or Providing Business or Financial Expertise

Every business needs workers who can lead its employees and oversee its funds. Workers in these occupations plan and guide both day-to-day and long-term business functions. They make sure that resources are being used efficiently and that finances are in order.

Many of the occupations are managers, who direct a business or department and its employees. Managers often develop budgets, set policies, and oversee others' work, sometimes focusing on a particular task, such as sales. Other occupations specialize in areas related to business operations, such as logistics, human resources, or training and development. Still others have duties related to financial operations, such as accounting.

Transportation and warehousing is the largest industry of employment for transportation, storage, and distribution managers. However, there are large numbers of jobs in other industries.

Other Work

Whatever your interest—computers, engineering, or something else—you might find a way to pursue it by working in the transportation and warehousing industry. For example, database administrators help to store and organize large amounts of information related to the movement of people and goods, such as customer shipping records. And industrial engineers assist companies in running more efficiently.

Pros and Cons

Whether on land, at sea, or in the air, workers in transportation and warehousing don't always have a smooth ride. But there's still a lot that they like about their jobs. Transportation jobs keep some workers on the go, and the constant motion has its benefits. Many workers like the fact that each day on the job is different. Workers who travel get to see the sights, but being away from home for long periods can be difficult. And their jobs may require night, weekend, or holiday work. Workers also must endure all types of weather conditions, from heat waves to blizzards. In addition, the work can be physically difficult—or dangerous. Safety is a top priority, say workers, but injuries do occur. Even as workers focus on safety, however, timeliness still matters.

A stressful reality for many of these workers is that material goods—or people's lives—may depend on the safety of transportation vehicles, equipment, and routes. Whether delivering the mail, driving children to school, or coordinating distribution, transportation and warehousing workers develop relationships with regular customers and meet new people all the time. And that's something a lot of workers enjoy.

Prospects, Pay—and More

Job opportunities are often good for workers in this industry. Benefits, such as health insurance or retirement plans, are often generous, too. But for many workers, compensation is not their motivation.

Getting Started

You can usually qualify for many entry-level jobs in transportation and warehousing with a high school diploma or less education. Most of the occupations also involve on-the-job training. Depending on the specific job you apply for, you may need to pass a background check and a drug test, have a valid driver's license and minimal or no moving violations, or meet other criteria before you are hired. In some occupations, experience gained in the military is good preparation for the work and may be accepted in place of other entry requirements.

When they evaluate job applicants, employers in transportation and warehousing often look for people who are enthusiastic about the industry and willing to learn. The specific skills and abilities that are required vary by occupation. Some workers, for example, must be able to stand for long periods of time or to lift heavy objects. Others need mechanical ability or good people skills. Nearly all transportation and warehousing workers, however, should be dependable and have good judgment. Good communication, teamwork, and problem-solving skills are also helpful, as is being able to adapt to new technologies and practices.

Typical education requirements for entering occupations in this industry range from less than a high school diploma to a bachelor's degree. Sometimes, work experience may substitute for education. Other times, employers prefer to hire an applicant who has a higher level of education than what is typically required at the entry level.

If you don't have a high school diploma, you might qualify for some entry-level occupations. Among the occupations that typically require this level of education to enter are hand laborers and material movers, industrial truck and tractor operators, and stock clerks. Many of occupations in this industry typically require a high school diploma for entry. These include delivery services drivers, transportation security screeners, and bus and truck mechanics.

Some occupations require a certificate or an associate's degree for employment. For example, heavy or tractor-trailer truck drivers need a certificate, which takes about three months to earn, from a professional truck driving school, to qualify for entry-level jobs. Aircraft mechanics also typically must earn a certificate, usually from an aviation maintenance technician school approved by the Federal Aviation Administration (FAA). And avionics technicians and air traffic controllers usually need an associate's degree from an FAA-approved school.

Higher-paying occupations in transportation and warehousing typically require a bachelor's degree to enter. Ship pilots, for example, typically need a bachelor's degree from a maritime academy. And many entry-level business and financial, computer, and engineering workers usually must have a bachelor's degree in a subject related to their job.

Employer-provided training is a key way for workers in this industry to learn the work. New entrants might learn from experienced employees or attend formal training programs. In many occupations, regular safety training is also provided. Maintenance and repair workers have some of the longest training periods to become fully competent in their occupation. Other occupations that require on-the-job training include flight attendants and pumping station operators.

Some occupations require special credentials. Bus drivers and tractor-trailer truck drivers, for example, need a commercial driver's license issued by their state and may need endorsements, such as for transporting schoolchildren. Locomotive engineers and conductors may need to be certified by the Federal Railroad Administration.

Workers can enter many occupations in transportation and warehousing without having experience in a related occupation. But employers in this industry, as in many others, frequently promote from within. The more involved you are in transportation and warehousing, the better your chances of getting a job—or of moving into a higher-paying one.

TRANSPORTATION AND MATERIAL-MOVING OCCUPATIONS BY INDUSTRY

Employment of transportation and material-moving occupations is projected to grow 6 percent from 2016 to 2026, about as fast as the average for all occupations, adding 634,300 new jobs. Material-moving workers are expected to be needed to move materials in nearly all sectors of the economy. Additionally, the economy depends on truck drivers to transport freight and keep supply chains moving.

Occupation	Job Summary
Airline and Commercial Pilots	Airline and commercial pilots fly and navigate airplanes, helicopters, and other aircraft.
Air Traffic Controllers	Air traffic controllers coordinate the movement of aircraft to maintain safe distances between them.
Bus Drivers	Bus drivers transport people between various places—including work, school, and shopping centers—and across state or national borders. Some drive regular routes, and others transport passengers on chartered trips or sightseeing tours.
Delivery Truck Drivers and Driver/Sales Workers	Delivery truck drivers and driver/sales workers pick up, transport, and drop off packages and small shipments within a local region or urban area. They drive trucks with a gross vehicle weight (GVW)—the combined weight of the vehicle, passengers, and cargo—of 26,000 pounds or less. Most of the time, delivery truck drivers transport merchandise from a distribution center to businesses and households.
Flight Attendants	Flight attendants provide routine services and respond to emergencies to ensure the safety and comfort of airline passengers while aboard planes.
Hand Laborers and Material Movers	Hand laborers and material movers manually move freight, stock, or other materials. Some of these workers may feed or remove material to and from machines, clean vehicles, pick up unwanted household goods, and pack materials for moving.

Occupation	Job Summary
Heavy and Tractor-Trailer Truck Drivers	Heavy and tractor-trailer truck drivers transport goods from one location to another. Most tractor-trailer drivers are long-haul drivers and operate trucks with a GVW capacity—that is, the combined weight of the vehicle, passengers, and cargo—exceeding 26,000 pounds. These drivers deliver goods over intercity routes, sometimes spanning several states.
Material-Moving Machine Operators	Material-moving machine operators use machinery to transport various objects. Some operators move construction materials around building sites or excavate earth from a mine. Others move goods around a warehouse or onto container ships.
Railroad Workers	Workers in railroad occupations ensure that passenger and freight trains run on time and travel safely. Some workers drive trains, some coordinate the activities of the trains, and others operate signals and switches in the rail yard.
Taxi Drivers, Ride-Hailing Drivers, and Chauffeurs	Taxi drivers, ride-hailing drivers, and chauffeurs transport people to and from the places they need to go, such as airports, homes, shopping centers, and workplaces. These drivers must know their way around a city to take passengers to their destinations.
Water Transportation Workers	Water transportation workers operate and maintain vessels that take cargo and people over water. The vessels travel to and from foreign ports across the ocean and to domestic ports along the coasts, across the Great Lakes, and along the country's many inland waterways.

About the Transportation and Warehousing Sector

The transportation and warehousing sector is part of the trade, transportation, and utilities supersector.

The transportation and warehousing sector includes industries providing transportation of passengers and cargo, warehousing and storage for goods, scenic and sightseeing transportation, and support activities related to modes of transportation. Establishments in these industries use transportation equipment or transportation-related facilities as a productive asset. The type of equipment depends on the mode of transportation. The modes of transportation are air, rail, water, road, and pipeline.

The transportation and warehousing sector consists of these subsectors:

- Air Transportation
- Rail Transportation
- Water Transportation
- Truck Transportation
- Transit and Ground Passenger Transportation
- Pipeline Transportation
- Scenic and Sightseeing Transportation
- Support Activities for Transportation
- Postal Service
- Couriers and Messengers
- Warehousing and Storage

Air Transportation Subsector

Industries in the air transportation subsector provide air transportation of passengers and/or cargo using aircraft, such as airplanes and helicopters. The subsector distinguishes scheduled from nonscheduled air transportation. Scheduled air carriers fly regular routes on regular schedules and operate even if flights are only partially loaded. Nonscheduled carriers often operate during nonpeak time slots at busy airports. These establishments have more flexibility with respect to choice of airport, hours of operation, load factors, and similar operational characteristics. Nonscheduled carriers provide chartered air transportation of passengers, cargo, or specialty flying services. Specialty flying services establishments use general-purpose aircraft to provide a variety of specialized flying services.

The air transportation subsector consists of these industry groups:

- Scheduled Air Transportation
- Nonscheduled Air Transportation

EMPLOYMENT BY OCCUPATION

	Employment, 2018
Aircraft mechanics and service technicians	39,760
Airline pilots, copilots, and flight engineers	74,180
Cargo and freight agents	7,590
Reservation and transportation ticket agents and travel clerks	67,740

Source: Occupational Employment Statistics

EARNINGS BY OCCUPATION

	Wages, 2018			
	Hourly		Annual	
	Median	Mean	Median	Mean
Aircraft mechanics and service technicians	$38.69	$37.16	$80,470	$77,300
Airline pilots, copilots, and flight engineers	(1)	(1)	$146,880	$172,270
Cargo and freight agents	$21.46	$22.07	$44,630	$45,910
Reservation and transportation ticket agents and travel clerks	$24.37	$22.78	$50,680	$47,390

Footnotes
(1) Wages for some occupations that do not generally work year-round, full time, are reported either as hourly wages or annual salaries depending on how they are typically paid.

Source: Occupational Employment Statistics

Conversation With... LAURIE HEIN DENHAM

CTL, CAE
Senior Director
Logistics & Supply Chain Academic Relations
American Production and Inventory Control Society
Supply Chain Profession, 14 years

1. What was your individual career path in terms of education/training, entry-level job, or other significant opportunity?

I graduated from the University of Tennessee with a BS in education and a minor in psychology. I went on to earn a master's degree in social work at the same school. I couldn't find a job in my field so I worked for a staffing company. Three years later, I opened my own staffing company and we served a lot of nonprofit associations. I sold the company to take the position of Executive Director of the American Society of Transportation and Logistics (AST&L).

I was hired by an individual I met through a professional network who knew I'd had my own business; at that time, fourteen years ago, my field of expertise was business, not logistics. My logistics training has been on the job.

However, all of my schooling helped in my position. As executive director of a small association I wore a lot of hats: I oversaw governance with our Board of Directors and Board of Examiners as well as membership, certification, marketing, and business development. I worked with academics who wrote the exams for our certifications. I learned to ask a lot of questions, when to listen, and how to get people to work collaboratively.

I was really impressed with the quality of people in the logistics industry. It's a relational business. You must have strong relationship skills to get goods moved; you must work together.

AST&L has now merged with APICS and my new role is to work with universities and K-12 schools globally to build awareness of the supply chain logistics industry. There are really good and plentiful jobs in logistics, and the industry does not have enough talent.

For instance, we worked with twelve high schools in the state of Florida to implement an entry-level credential program, the Global Logistics Associate (GLA). Through grant funding, we provided curriculum. At the end of their senior year, students took their GLA exam. Those who passed the exam received twelve hours of college credit to any state college in Florida. We'd like to see other states offer similar credit for industry credentials.

This is a fast-paced, always-changing business. There isn't anything that logistics doesn't touch. You could be a crane operator at a port, or do logistics analysis scanning data and trying to determine what mode of transportation will be most effective moving goods. You can negotiate for services, or sell services.

2. What are the most important skills and/or qualities for someone in your profession?

Agility and flexibility, because no day is the same. Soft skills are also very important because there's a lot of customer service involved and you're dealing with relationships. Analytical skills are also important.

3. What do you wish you had known going into this profession?

I wish something like the GLA program had been around because it offers a birds'-eye overview of the industry that would have been helpful to me.

4. Are there many job opportunities in your profession? In what specific areas?

Recent statistics put logistics at the twenty-fourth fastest-growing career; U.S. News & World Report says this is the twelfth best business career with a $73,870 median salary. We're working to better define the jobs so the public better understands the field's career opportunities, because you could be a logistics manager in seven different companies and have seven different titles. Right now, logisticians are second to engineers as the most sought after graduates.

5. How do you see your profession changing in the next five years? What role will technology play in those changes, and what skills will be required?

I see huge growth in this profession. It's a global economy, and people are going to be moving goods. Manufacturing is returning to the United States and jobs are opening up because baby boomers are retiring. Technology is very important and changes rapidly. People worry that more robots will do their work, but advanced manufacturing will still need people to build and repair robots and people to make the parts. There are still going to be plenty of jobs.

6. What do you enjoy most about your job? What do you enjoy least about your job?

I enjoy that I get to work with academics, industry and students to have the necessary conversations to develop programs so students will have the skills and knowledge that employers need.

I least enjoy sitting at my desk but that's a necessary part of almost any job.

7. Can you suggest a valuable "try this" for students considering a career in your profession?

Check YouTube for videos that show the logistics process, starting with raw goods. Also, we have chapters all over the world so, working through them, you can find informational interviews, ask for a facilities tour, or attend an APICS event through our student scholar program. Many universities offer summer camps for a week that focus on the supply chain logistics industry, as well as advanced manufacturing.

Note: This interview first appeared in *Careers in Manufacturing & Production* © 2016.

About the Rail Transportation Subsector

Industries in the rail transportation subsector provide rail transportation of passengers and/or cargo using railroad rolling stock. The railroads in this subsector primarily either operate on networks, with physical facilities, labor force, and equipment spread over an extensive geographic area, or operate over a short distance on a local rail line.

The rail transportation subsector consists of a single industry group, Rail Transportation.

EMPLOYMENT BY OCCUPATION

	Employment, 2018
Locomotive engineers	33,420
Railcar repairers	13,350
Rail-track laying and maintenance equipment operators	7,620
Railroad brake, signal, and switch operators	11,830
Railroad conductors and yardmasters	37,690

Source: Occupational Employment Statistics

EARNINGS BY OCCUPATION

	Wages, 2018			
	Hourly		Annual	
	Median	Mean	Median	Mean
Locomotive engineers	$29.97	$32.34	$62,330	$67,270
Railcar repairers	$29.72	$29.49	$61,810	$61,350
Rail-track laying and maintenance equipment operators	$26.93	$26.64	$56,010	$55,400
Railroad brake, signal, and switch operators	$28.33	$28.94	$58,920	$60,200
Railroad conductors and yardmasters	$30.60	$32.16	$63,650	$66,890

Source: Occupational Employment Statistics

About the Water Transportation Subsector

The water transportation subsector is part of the transportation and warehousing sector. Industries in the water transportation subsector provide water transportation of passengers and cargo using watercraft, such as ships, barges, and boats. The subsector is composed of two industry groups: (1) one for deep sea, coastal, and Great Lakes; and (2) one for inland water transportation. This split typically reflects the difference in equipment used.

The water transportation subsector consists of these industry groups:

- Deep Sea, Coastal, and Great Lakes Water Transportation
- Inland Water Transportation

EMPLOYMENT BY OCCUPATION

	Employment, 2018
Captains, mates, and pilots of water vessels	17,720
General and operations managers	1,100
Laborers and freight, stock, and material movers, hand	1,710
Sailors and marine oilers	14,420
Ship engineers	3,920

Source: Occupational Employment Statistics

EARNINGS BY OCCUPATION

	Wages, 2018			
	Hourly		Annual	
	Median	Mean	Median	Mean
Captains, mates, and pilots of water vessels	$34.51	$41.03	$71,790	$85,350
General and operations managers	$54.30	$67.36	$112,950	$140,100
Laborers and freight, stock, and material movers, hand	$16.43	$17.51	$34,170	$36,430
Sailors and marine oilers	$19.30	$22.76	$40,150	$47,330
Ship engineers	$36.49	$38.95	$75,910	$81,010

Source: Occupational Employment Statistics

About the Truck Transportation subsector

Industries in the truck transportation subsector provide over-the-road transportation of cargo using motor vehicles, such as trucks and tractor-trailers. The subsector is subdivided into general freight trucking and specialized freight trucking. This distinction reflects differences in equipment used, type of load carried, scheduling, terminal, and other networking services. General freight transportation establishments handle a wide variety of general commodities, generally palletized, and transported in a container or van trailer. Specialized freight transportation is the transportation of cargo that, because of size, weight, shape, or other inherent characteristics require specialized equipment for transportation.

The truck transportation subsector consists of these industry groups:

- General Freight Trucking
- Specialized Freight Trucking

EMPLOYMENT BY OCCUPATION

	Employment, 2018
Bus and truck mechanics and diesel engine specialists	53,200
Laborers and freight, stock, and material movers, hand	114,080
Truck drivers, heavy and tractor-trailer	880,710
Truck drivers, light or delivery services	48,080

Source: Occupational Employment Statistics

EARNINGS BY OCCUPATION

	Wages, 2018			
	Hourly		Annual	
	Median	Mean	Median	Mean
Bus and truck mechanics and diesel engine specialists	$20.99	$21.56	$43,660	$44,840
Laborers and freight, stock, and material movers, hand	$15.26	$16.19	$31,730	$33,660
Truck drivers, heavy and tractor-trailer	$21.64	$22.23	$45,000	$46,230
Truck drivers, light or delivery services	$18.83	$19.48	$39,170	$40,520

Source: Occupational Employment Statistics

About the Transit and Ground Passenger Transportation Subsector

Industries in the transit and Ground Passenger Transportation subsector include a variety of passenger transportation activities, such as urban transit systems; chartered bus, school bus, and interurban bus transportation; and taxis. These activities are distinguished based primarily on such production process factors as vehicle types, routes, and schedules.

The transit and ground passenger transportation subsector consists of these industry groups:

- Urban Transit Systems
- Interurban and Rural Bus Transportation
- Taxi and Limousine Service
- School and Employee Bus Transportation
- Charter Bus Industry
- Other Transit and Ground Passenger Transportation

EMPLOYMENT BY OCCUPATION

	Employment, 2018
Bus and truck mechanics and diesel engine specialists	13,890
Bus drivers, school	199,190
Bus drivers, transit and intercity	71,500
Dispatchers, except police, fire, and ambulance	18,900
Taxi drivers and chauffeurs	83,490

Source: Occupational Employment Statistics

EARNINGS BY OCCUPATION

	Wages, 2018			
	Hourly		Annual	
	Median	Mean	Median	Mean
Bus and truck mechanics and diesel engine specialists	$23.09	$23.65	$48,020	$49,190
Bus drivers, school	$16.31	$16.78	$33,930	$34,910
Bus drivers, transit and intercity	$17.51	$18.32	$36,420	$38,110
Dispatchers, except police, fire, and ambulance	$16.13	$17.19	$33,550	$35,760
Taxi drivers and chauffeurs	$12.84	$13.90	$26,710	$28,910

Source: Occupational Employment Statistics

About the Pipeline Transportation Subsector

Industries in the Pipeline Transportation subsector use transmission pipelines to transport products, such as crude oil, natural gas, refined petroleum products, and slurry. Industries are identified based on the products transported (i.e., pipeline transportation of crude oil, natural gas, refined petroleum products, and other products).

The pipeline transportation of natural gas industry includes the storage of natural gas because the storage is usually done by the pipeline establishment and because a pipeline is inherently a network in which all the nodes are interdependent.

The pipeline transportation subsector consists of these industry groups:

- Pipeline Transportation of Crude Oil
- Pipeline Transportation of Natural Gas
- Other Pipeline Transportation

EMPLOYMENT BY OCCUPATION

	Employment, 2018
Control and valve installers and repairers, except mechanical door	1,960
Gas compressor and gas pumping station operators	1,460
Gas plant operators	4,790
Industrial machinery mechanics	3,380
Petroleum pump system operators, refinery operators, and gaugers	6,210

Source: Occupational Employment Statistics

EARNINGS BY OCCUPATION

	Wages, 2018			
	Hourly		Annual	
	Median	Mean	Median	Mean
Control and valve installers and repairers, except mechanical door	$30.62	$30.03	$63,690	$62,460
Gas compressor and gas pumping station operators	$32.70	$31.87	$68,020	$66,290
Gas plant operators	$33.95	$34.11	$70,610	$70,950
Industrial machinery mechanics	$30.24	$30.15	$62,890	$62,710
Petroleum pump system operators, refinery operators, and gaugers	$34.28	$34.15	$71,310	$71,030

Source: Occupational Employment Statistics

About the Scenic and Sightseeing Transportation Subsector

Industries in the scenic and sightseeing transportation subsector utilize transportation equipment to provide recreation and entertainment. These activities have a production process distinct from passenger transportation carried out for the purpose of other types of for-hire transportation. This process does not emphasize efficient transportation; in fact, such activities often use obsolete vehicles, such as steam trains, to provide some extra ambience. The activity is local in nature, usually involving a same-day return to the point of departure.

The scenic and sightseeing transportation subsector consists of these industry groups:

- Scenic and Sightseeing Transportation, Land
- Scenic and Sightseeing Transportation, Water
- Scenic and Sightseeing Transportation, Other

EMPLOYMENT BY OCCUPATION

	Employment, 2018
Bus drivers, transit and intercity	3,560
Captains, mates, and pilots of water vessels	3,040
Reservation and transportation ticket agents and travel clerks	2,340
Sailors and marine oilers	2,210

Source: Occupational Employment Statistics

WAGES BY OCCUPATION

	Wages, 2018			
	Hourly		Annual	
	Median	Mean	Median	Mean
Bus drivers, transit and intercity	$16.05	$17.39	$33,380	$36,170
Captains, mates, and pilots of water vessels	$22.65	$25.36	$47,120	$52,760
Reservation and transportation ticket agents and travel clerks	$13.43	$14.91	$27,930	$31,010
Sailors and marine oilers	$13.77	$16.18	$28,650	$33,650

Source: Occupational Employment Statistics

About the Support Activities for Transportation Subsector

Industries in the support activities for transportation subsector provide services that support transportation. These services may be provided to transportation carrier establishments or to the general public. This subsector includes a wide array of establishments, including air traffic control services, marine cargo handling, and motor vehicle towing.

The support activities for the transportation subsector consists of these industry groups:

- Support Activities for Air Transportation
- Support Activities for Rail Transportation
- Support Activities for Water Transportation
- Support Activities for Road Transportation
- Freight Transportation Arrangement
- Other Support Activities for Transportation

EMPLOYMENT BY OCCUPATION

	Employment, 2018
Aircraft mechanics and service technicians	38,160
Cargo and freight agents	59,100
Dispatchers, except police, fire, and ambulance	15,500
Laborers and freight, stock, and material movers, hand	76,830
Truck drivers, heavy and tractor-trailer	64,530

Source: Occupational Employment Statistics

EARNINGS BY OCCUPATION

	Wages, 2018			
	Hourly		Annual	
	Median	Mean	Median	Mean
Aircraft mechanics and service technicians	$26.14	$26.51	$54,360	$55,150
Cargo and freight agents	$20.70	$22.26	$43,050	$46,300
Dispatchers, except police, fire, and ambulance	$17.01	$18.71	$35,380	$38,910
Laborers and freight, stock, and material movers, hand	$14.90	$17.27	$31,000	$35,930
Truck drivers, heavy and tractor-trailer	$18.59	$20.10	$38,670	$41,800

Source: Occupational Employment Statistics

Conversation With...
DAVID CORRELL
Research Scientist
Massachusetts Institute of Technology (MIT)
Center for Transportation and Logistics, Cambridge, MA
Supply Chain Industry, 10+ years

1. What was your individual career path in terms of education/training, entry-level job, or other significant opportunity?

I was interested in Russia and the countries of the former Soviet Union, so I went to Siberia as a high school exchange student. Then I went to The George Washington University in Washington, DC and earned a BA in International Relations and Affairs. Through that experience, I became interested in international commodity flows, especially energy. After college, I worked for the U.S. Department of Energy as an economist, then I went to New York City and worked as an analyst for Horizon Client Access, where I basically analyzed the Russian oil and gas sector.

About this time, I wanted to go home to Iowa, so I went to graduate school at Iowa State University and studied renewable energy and agriculture and earned an MS. That research led me to a real interest in the logistics network for alternative fuels. I started to build models to understand transportation networks. I went on to earn a PhD in Logistics, Materials and Supply Chain Management.

I then became an assistant professor of operations management at Clark University in Worcester, Massachusetts, teaching and doing research there, then an opportunity came up here at MIT. I wear two hats: I teach and do research.

Right now, I'm doing research on American truck drivers, working with new, large data sets that are the result of a recently passed law that requires drivers to electronically log all working hours. Using new analytical techniques, I'm trying to find out how drivers use their time, how their time is wasted, and am looking at how to predict if a driver might quit. We're finding that how drivers' time is utilized or wasted on weekends matters a lot. Drivers get paid a certain number of cents per mile. Some distribution centers are very respectful of drivers' time, while others make them wait.

It's hard to find qualified people to carry all the loads our economy generates. A lot of trucking companies have 100 percent turnover from year to year. Companies are interested in the research we're doing so they can make necessary changes to accommodate drivers.

2. What are the most important skills and/or qualities for someone in your profession?

Curiosity and critical thinking. To have a career in research you have to be very interested in learning and very excited about interesting questions. The best researchers are very curious, and also disciplined thinkers. If you stick too tightly to your idea of what a study's answer might be, you may not see what your research is telling you.

3. What do you wish you had known going into this profession?

A career in teaching and research means you are unlikely to be able to choose the location where you live. You go where the opportunities are. Also, I didn't start with a strong interest in computer science but you want to be strong with those skills so you have the toolbox to explore the questions that interest you.

4. Are there many job opportunities in your profession? In what specific areas?

Yes, and I think more are coming. More and more data are available to companies and they really want people who can make sense of that data to help them make better decisions. Data science and research in the transportation space don't necessarily require a PhD. A lot of opportunities are available at the master's level, including at independent research centers.

5. How do you see your profession changing in the next five years? How will technology impact that change, and what skills will be required?

Many companies are talking to me and people in my position about making more data-driven transportation decisions. Maybe longer term, self-driven trucks on certain components of routes will change how we design our transportation routes. I think more data-driven planning will enable us to be much more efficient. People are surprised by how much leading companies struggle with an estimated time of arrival for their trucks. We will get better at harmonizing the supply chain with the integration of data.

6. What do you enjoy most about your job? What do you enjoy least about your job?

As a researcher, I enjoy discovering something interesting and sharing it with clients. Typically, the least exciting part of my work is the 60 to 90 percent of project time spent cleaning the data. You need to go through the dataset to see if entries are correct or complete and it take a lot of time and is not very fun. But you have to take cleaning seriously because otherwise you're analyzing nonsense.

7. Can you suggest a valuable "try this" for students considering a career in your profession?

Next time you or a friend buys something online, try to think about the whole chain of events involved in getting that product to your house. Individual pieces had to come to a factory, were assembled—perhaps on the other side of the world—and arrived at your door in a way that costs so little that you weren't scared away. To orchestrate that is a complicated and interesting project. If you like thinking about that, maybe you would like working in this area.

About the Postal Service Subsector

The postal service subsector includes the activities of the National Post Office and its subcontractors operating under a universal service obligation to provide mail services, and using the infrastructure required to fulfill that obligation. These services include delivering letters and small parcels. These articles can be described as those that can be handled by one person without using special equipment. This allows the collection, pick-up, and delivery operations to be done with limited labor costs and minimal equipment. Sorting and transportation activities, where necessary, are generally mechanized. The restriction to small parcels distinguishes these establishments from those in the transportation industries. These establishments may also provide express delivery services using the infrastructure established for provision of basic mail services.

The postal service subsector consists of a single industry group, postal service.

EMPLOYMENT BY OCCUPATION

	Employment, 2018
First-line supervisors/managers of transportation and material-moving machine and vehicle operators	
Postal service clerks	78,830
Postal service mail carriers	342,410
Postal service mail sorters, processors, and processing machine operators	103,830
Postmasters and mail superintendents	13,730

Source: Occupational Employment Statistics

EARNINGS BY OCCUPATION

	Wages, 2018			
	Hourly		Annual	
	Median	Mean	Median	Mean
First-line supervisors/managers of transportation and material-moving machine and vehicle operators				
Postal service clerks	$26.58	$24.45	$55,280	$50,860
Postal service mail carriers	$26.54	$24.89	$55,210	$51,780
Postal service mail sorters, processors, and processing machine operators	$28.26	$24.64	$58,770	$51,250
Postmasters and mail superintendents	$36.53	$37.05	$75,980	$77,060

Source: Occupational Employment Statistics

About the Couriers and Messengers Subsector

Industries in the couriers and messengers subsector provide intercity and/or local delivery of parcels and documents (including express delivery services) without operating under a universal service obligation. These articles can be described as those that may be handled by one person without using special equipment. This allows the collection, pick-up, and delivery operations to be done with limited labor costs and minimal equipment. Sorting and transportation activities, where necessary, are generally mechanized. The restriction to small parcels partly distinguishes these establishments from those in the transportation industries. The complete network of courier services establishments also distinguishes these transportation services from local messenger and delivery establishments in this subsector. This includes the establishments that perform intercity transportation as well as establishments that, under contract to them, perform local pick-up and delivery. Messengers, which usually deliver within a metropolitan or single urban area, may use bicycle, foot, small truck, or van.

The couriers and messengers subsector consists of these industry groups:

- Couriers
- Local Messengers and Local Delivery

EMPLOYMENT BY OCCUPATION

	Employment, 2018
Couriers and messengers	21,920
Customer service representatives	9,480
Dispatchers, except police, fire, and ambulance	6,800
Truck drivers, light or delivery services	211,120

Source: Occupational Employment Statistics

EARNINGS BY OCCUPATION

	Wages, 2018			
	Hourly		Annual	
	Median	Mean	Median	Mean
Couriers and messengers	$13.45	$14.75	$27,980	$30,680
Customer service representatives	$18.92	$19.92	$39,350	$41,440
Dispatchers, except police, fire, and ambulance	$20.69	$21.70	$43,040	$45,140
Truck drivers, light or delivery services	$23.50	$24.27	$48,880	$50,480

Source: Occupational Employment Statistics

About the Warehousing and Storage Subsector

Industries in the warehousing and storage subsector are primarily engaged in operating warehousing and storage facilities for general merchandise, refrigerated goods, and other warehouse products. These establishments provide facilities to store goods. They do not sell the goods they handle. These establishments take responsibility for storing the goods and keeping them secure. They may also provide a range of services, often referred to as logistics services, related to the distribution of goods. Logistics services can include labeling, breaking bulk, inventory control and management, light assembly, order entry and fulfillment, packaging, pick and pack, price marking and ticketing, and transportation arrangement. However, establishments in this industry group always provide warehousing or storage services in addition to any logistic services. Furthermore, the warehousing or storage of goods must be more than incidental to the performance of services, such as price marking.

The warehousing and storage subsector consists of a single industry group, warehousing and storage.

EMPLOYMENT BY OCCUPATION

	Employment, 2018
Industrial truck and tractor operators	183,350
Laborers and freight, stock, and material movers, hand	329,540
Shipping, receiving, and traffic clerks	59,880
Stock clerks and order fillers	99,770
Transportation, storage, and distribution managers	11,380

Source: Occupational Employment Statistics

EARNINGS BY OCCUPATION

	Wages, 2018			
	Hourly		Annual	
	Median	Mean	Median	Mean
Industrial truck and tractor operators	$16.96	$17.44	$35,270	$36,280
Laborers and freight, stock, and material movers, hand	$14.58	$15.71	$30,320	$32,680
Shipping, receiving, and traffic clerks	$15.85	$16.96	$32,970	$35,280
Stock clerks and order fillers	$15.35	$16.20	$31,920	$33,690
Transportation, storage, and distribution managers	$43.76	$46.35	$91,030	$96,410

Source: Occupational Employment Statistics

Aerospace Engineers

Snapshot

Career Cluster(s): Manufacturing, Science, Technology, Engineering & Mathematics

Interests: Engineering, mathematics, physical sciences, flight, jet propulsion

Earnings (Median Pay): $115,220

Employment & Outlook: As Fast as Average Growth Expected

OVERVIEW

Sphere of Work

Aerospace engineers design, develop, test, maintain, and assist in the manufacture of different types of aircraft, missiles, spacecraft, and other technologically advanced modes of transport. Aerospace engineers in the field of aeronautical engineering work on civilian and military aircraft, which may include helicopters, airliners, fighter jets, missiles, and other airborne craft. Aerospace engineers in the field of astronautical engineering work with satellites, rockets, and similar space-bound technologies. Aerospace engineers focus on aerodynamics, propulsion, hull composition, communications networks, and electrical systems.

Work Environment

Aerospace engineers typically work in government or business offices, where they manage administrative tasks, design models and schematics, and write reports. They also spend time working in laboratories, industrial plants, and manufacturing facilities, where they work with other technicians to assemble systems and aircraft. Those engineers who work in astronautical engineering also work at launch facilities, while aeronautical engineering typically requires spending time at noisy airfields. Aerospace engineers generally work in several complex and busy locations over the course of a project, with many separate activities taking place simultaneously. They work a regular 40-hour workweek, although longer hours may be required as deadlines draw near.

Profile

Interests: Data, Things
Working Conditions: Work Inside
Physical Strength: Light Work
Education Needs: Bachelor's Degree, Master's Degree, Doctoral Degree
Licensure/Certification: Required for Professional Engineers (PEs)
Physical Abilities Not Required: Not Climb, Not Kneel
Opportunities for Experience: Internship, Apprenticeship, Military Service, Part-Time Work
Holland Interest Score: IRE

* See Appendix A

Occupation Interest

Aerospace engineers are part of an exciting industry, one that helps develop high-speed trains, deep-sea vessels, missiles/rockets, commercial airliners, and many other large aircraft and spacecraft. They use the most advanced technology to design, build, test, and maintain these vehicles. Because they have expertise unique to their field and area of specialization, aerospace engineers receive highly competitive salaries. The job market for aerospace engineers is continuously growing, thanks to the sales of new aircraft and missiles, as well as growth in the commercial airline construction industry.

A Day in the Life—Duties and Responsibilities

There are two basic types of aerospace engineers: aeronautical engineers (who focus on aircraft, missiles, and other "earthbound" technologies) and astronautical engineers (who focus on spacecraft and space exploration technologies). Both aeronautical and astronautical engineers further specialize in certain types of products or product features. Aerospace engineers create conceptual designs of aeronautical or astronautical vehicles, instrumentation, defense systems, guidance and navigation systems, and propulsion systems according to the specifications of the client. They also improve the structural design of existing aircraft and spacecraft. Some engineers specialize in innovating more sophisticated production methods. All of these design and development processes include practical steps such as analyzing production costs, developing quality control standards, and testing methodologies, as well as establishing timelines for project development and completion. During the course of construction and/or assembly, aerospace engineers travel to the production site and conduct inspections and tests on the systems to ensure that they are operating efficiently and according to the needs of the client. Many aerospace engineers assist in the production phase, integrating systems and examining components as they are being built.

When production is complete, the aerospace engineer creates performance and technical reports so that customers have a full knowledge of the vehicle's capabilities. He or she retains copies of such reports for future reference. In the event that the vehicle or a vehicular system malfunctions, aerospace engineers play an important role in the investigation, examining damaged parts and reviewing performance reports and other documentation to determine the cause of the malfunction.

Duties and Responsibilities

- **Designing and developing aircraft**
- **Overseeing the manufacture of prototypes (models)**
- **Testing prototypes to evaluate their operation**
- **Estimating the time and cost to complete projects**

OCCUPATION SPECIALTIES

Aeronautical Engineers

Aeronautical Engineers design, develop, and test aircraft, space vehicles, and missiles. They test models to study how they operate under a variety of conditions in order to make the equipment safe.

Aerodynamists

Aerodynamists analyze the suitability and application of designs for aircraft and missiles. They also plan and evaluate the results of laboratory and flight-test programs.

Field Service Engineers

Field Service Engineers study performance reports on aircraft and recommend ways of eliminating the causes of flight and service problems in airplanes.

Aeronautical Research Engineers

Aeronautical Research Engineers conduct research in the field of aeronautics.

Stress Analysts

Stress Analysts study the ability of airplanes, missiles, and components to withstand stress during flight.

Aeronautical Test Engineers

Aeronautical Test Engineers plan and supervise the performance testing of aerospace and aircraft products.

Aeronautical Design Engineers

Aeronautical Design Engineers develop basic design concepts used in the design, development and production of aeronautical/aerospace products and systems.

Value Engineers

Value Engineers plan and coordinate engineering activities to develop and apply standardized production requirements for parts and equipment used in aircraft and aerospace vehicles.

Aeronautical Project Engineers

Aeronautical Project Engineers direct and coordinate activities of personnel who design systems and equipment for aeronautical and aerospace products.

Aeronautical Drafters

Aeronautical Drafters draft engineering drawings and other equipment and scale models of prototype aircraft that is planned by engineers.

WORK ENVIRONMENT

Immediate Physical Environment

Aerospace engineers spend long hours working at drawing boards in offices but also spend significant amounts of time working in laboratories, manufacturing facilities, test facilities, and airfields. These locations are generally clean, very well organized, and well ventilated. There are physical risks when working with or in close proximity to machines, electricity, manufacturing chemicals, and engines, so safety protocols are strictly enforced.

Human Environment

Aerospace engineers work with many other professionals, including engineers with different specialties. They interact with electricians, technicians, construction personnel, forklift and other heavy machinery operators, physicists, chemists, and project managers.

Transferable Skills and Abilities

Communication Skills
- Speaking effectively
- Writing concisely

Interpersonal/Social Skills
- Working as a member of a team

Organization & Management Skills
- Paying attention to and handling details
- Performing duties that change frequently

Research & Planning Skills
- Using logical reasoning

Technical Skills
- Applying the technology to a task
- Performing scientific, mathematical, and technical work

Technological Environment

Aerospace engineers use a variety of analytical tools and sophisticated technology in their daily work. Computer-aided design (CAD) and computer-aided manufacturing (CAM) software, as well as a variety of computer modeling and design programs, are used for planning and design. Analytical and scientific software help aerospace engineers to examine thermal patterns, complex mathematical formulas, and other aspects of systems engineering. At test facilities, engineers use such tools as flow meters, lasers, and vibration testing equipment.

EDUCATION, TRAINING, AND ADVANCEMENT

High School/Secondary

High school students who intend to become aerospace engineers should study mathematics, including algebra, applied mathematics, trigonometry, calculus, and geometry. Physics, chemistry, and other laboratory sciences are equally important. Computer science courses expose high school students to design and analytical software, while industrial arts courses expose them to mechanical equipment, such as engines and electrical systems. High school students interested in the field of aerospace engineering must apply to related college or university programs.

Suggested High School Subjects
- Algebra
- Applied Communication

- Applied Math
- Applied Physics
- Blueprint Reading
- Calculus
- Chemistry
- College Preparatory
- Composition
- Computer Science
- Drafting
- Electricity & Electronics
- English
- Geometry
- Mathematics
- Physics
- Science
- Statistics
- Trigonometry

Related Career Pathways/Majors

Manufacturing Cluster
- Manufacturing Production Process Development Pathway

Science, Technology, Engineering & Mathematics Cluster
- Engineering & Technology Pathway

Famous First

The first unmanned aircraft system was launched and recovered from a U.S. Coast Guard icebreaker on August 18, 2014. The test was conducted while under sail in the Arctic Ocean, by an AeroVironment Puma AE, which was launched from the flight deck of the Coast Guard Cutter Healy by a team consisting of AeroVironment employees and researchers from the Coast Guard and National Oceanic and Atmospheric Administration (NOAA). Harsh weather conditions, including icing, fog, and high winds, added a degree of difficulty to the test, but after several attempts the crew were able to land the aircraft on the ship deck. Two primary purposes of testing the aircraft under difficult conditions were to ascertain its usefulness in tracking oil spills and in remote search and rescue missions.

Source: "Transportation." *Famous First Facts*, Salem, 2016. *Salem Online*, https://online.salempress.com

Postsecondary

Entry-level aerospace engineers usually need a bachelor's degree. High school students interested in studying aerospace engineering should take courses in chemistry, physics, advanced math, and computer programming and computer languages.

Bachelor's degree programs include classroom, laboratory, and field studies in subjects such as general engineering principles, propulsion, stability and control, structures, mechanics, and aerodynamics, which is the study of how air interacts with moving objects.

Some colleges and universities offer cooperative programs in partnership with regional businesses, which give students practical experience while they complete their education. Cooperative programs and internships enable students to gain valuable experience and to finance part of their education.

At some universities, a student can enroll in a five-year program that leads to both a bachelor's degree and a master's degree upon completion. A graduate degree will allow an engineer to work as an instructor at a university or to do research and development.

Programs in aerospace engineering are accredited by the Accreditation Board for Engineering and Technology (ABET).

Related College Majors
- Aerospace, Aeronautical & Astronautical Engineering
- Drafting, General
- Engineering Design
- Mechanical Drafting

Adult Job Seekers

Qualified aerospace engineers may apply directly to aerospace companies, such as aircraft manufacturers and commercial airlines, or on government agencies, such as the National Aeronautics and Space Administration (NASA). In many cases, applicants to government positions must pass a civil service examination. Many other candidates apply to universities, consulting firms, and research and design companies. Professional associations, such as the Aerospace Industries Association (AIA) and the American Institute of Aeronautics and Astronautics (AIAA), provide networking opportunities.

Professional Certification and Licensure

Licensure for aerospace engineers is not as common as it is for other engineering occupations, nor it is required for entry-level positions. A Professional Engineering (PE) license, which allows for higher levels of leadership and independence, can be acquired later in one's career. Licensed engineers are called professional engineers (PEs). A PE can oversee the work of other engineers, sign off on projects, and provide services directly to the public. State licensure generally requires:

- A degree from an ABET-accredited engineering program
- A passing score on the Fundamentals of Engineering (FE) exam
- Relevant work experience, typically at least 4 years
- A passing score on the Professional Engineering (PE) exam.

The initial FE exam can be taken after earning a bachelor's degree. Engineers who pass this exam are commonly called engineers in training (EITs) or engineer interns (EIs). After meeting work experience requirements, EITs and EIs can take the second exam, called the Principles and Practice of Engineering.

Each state issues its own licenses. Most states recognize licensure from other states, as long as the licensing state's requirements meet or exceed their own licensure requirements. Several states require continuing education for engineers to keep their licenses.

Additional Requirements

Aerospace engineers must have strong analytical and research skills, with an exceptional ability to understand and solve complex problems. They should be experienced with computer systems and design software. Aerospace engineers must have an eye for detail and scientific and mathematical approach to solving issues. Finally, they must have strong communications skills to coordinate with other professionals and customers.

Aerospace engineers who work on projects that are related to national defense may need a security clearance. U.S. citizenship may be required for certain types and levels of clearances.

Fast Fact

There was never an actual historical popular belief that the Moon is made of green cheese. It was typically used as an example of extreme credulity, a meaning that was clear and commonly understood as early as 1638.

Source: en.wikipedia.org

EARNINGS AND ADVANCEMENT

Earnings depend on the individual's education, experience, field of specialization and job duties. The median annual wage for aerospace engineers was $115,220 in May 2018. The lowest 10 percent earned less than $71,640, and the highest 10 percent earned more than $164,210.

In May 2018, the median annual wages for aerospace engineers in the top industries in which they worked were as follows:

Research and development in the physical, engineering, and life sciences	$124,430
Navigational, measuring, electromedical, and control instruments manufacturing	$119,970
Federal government, excluding postal service	$119,640
Aerospace product and parts manufacturing	$113,840
Engineering services	$110,200

Aerospace engineers typically work full time. Engineers who direct projects must often work extra hours to monitor progress, to ensure that designs meet requirements, to determine how to measure aircraft performance, to see that production meets design standards, and to ensure that deadlines are met.

Aerospace engineers may receive paid vacations, holidays, and sick days; life and health insurance; and retirement benefits. These are usually paid by the employer.

EMPLOYMENT AND OUTLOOK

There were approximately 69,600 aerospace engineers employed nationally in 2016. Employment of aerospace engineers is expected to grow as fast as average for all occupations through the year 2026, which means employment is projected to increase 6 percent. New designs and new technologies involved in the creation of commercial and military aircraft will encourage demand for aerospace engineers.

Employment opportunities should be favorable for those trained in software, such as C++, or with education and experience in stress and structural engineering. Finally, the aging of workers in this occupation should help to create openings in it over the next decade.

Related Occupations
- Ceramic Engineer
- Electrical & Electronics Engineer
- Mechanical Engineer

Related Military Occupations
- Aerospace Engineer
- Space Operations Officer

Conversation With...
JOHN ROSE
Chief of Staff, Boeing Defense Space and Security
Huntington Beach, CA
Aerospace Engineer, 17 years

1. **What was your individual career path in terms of education/training, entry-level job, or other significant opportunity?**

   I've always loved aviation and spaceflight, and originally wanted to be an astronaut. By high school, I knew I wanted to be an aerospace engineer and took advanced placement (AP) courses in chemistry and physics. My physics class got to visit the Space Academy in Huntsville, Alabama, which was my second visit there.

   I got my BS in aerospace from Cal Poly Pomona. In college, I worked part time on the attractions in the Disneyland Resort and spent a summer interning with Disney's Ride & Show Engineering, Inc., where I later spent two years of my career. I also did two other internships.

   As graduation approached, Rockwell International, the builder of the Space Shuttle, asked me to interview. I was thrilled, since working on the Space Shuttle was THE job I wanted. So, my first full-time job in the aerospace industry was in a group supporting the Space Shuttle and International Space Station.

   A benefit of working for a large company like Rockwell (which became Boeing) is that they may pay for your advanced degrees. I got my MS in aerospace, also from Cal Poly Pomona, and my MBA from the University of Southern California.

   I've always leveraged the opportunities at Boeing. In my current role, in the Office of the Vice President of Engineering, Mission Assurance and Product Support, I'm working with top leadership to develop global strategy on our defense side.

2. **What are the most important skills and/or qualities for someone in your profession?**

   Aerospace, particularly defense, can be cyclical, so you need to be adaptable. Contracts come and go, sometimes without much notice. Also, new graduates need to recognize that the way something is done in industry may not be how they learned it in class. Inquisitiveness and passion are also important. In addition, the aerospace industry is typically risk averse, so experience is a highly valued commodity. This means younger engineers must be patient; there isn't always a lot of support for putting untested or inexperienced individuals in a critical role.

3. What do you wish you had known going into this profession?

Aerospace products are a prime target for cybersecurity threats and must be protected from being taken offline or taken control of. Had I known cybersecurity would develop into such an important area, I would have taken related coursework.

Also, I had to learn that it's easy to slip through the cracks at a large company and that it isn't a bad thing to ask about opportunities if they aren't presenting themselves.

4. Are there many job opportunities in your profession? In what specific areas?

Companies like Boeing or Lockheed Martin offer jobs in a wide variety of areas, including business development, finance, software development, manufacturing, structural design, systems engineering, and computer science.

Unmanned aerial vehicles (UAVs) are fueling a major evolution. Pilotless vehicles can remove human physiological limitations on what a vehicle can do (for example, making sharper turns or diving deeper) as well as spare humans from some dangerous missions. UAVs are adding a new commercial aspect to the industry because they can be made by smaller companies.

5. How do you see your profession changing in the next five years? What role will technology play in those changes, and what skills will be required?

The fact that most products will be tied to the internet will change how we design and build them, as well as how we approach vulnerabilities relative to such systems as flight controls. Air traffic management is becoming satellite-based, and that's a quickly evolving area of cybersecurity where we need to respond to threats.

Additive manufacturing, or (three-dimensional) 3D printing, is revolutionizing how things are built. Small, portable machines are building pieces used in rocket engines. The concept is also being used on the International Space Station where a 3D computer-aided design and drafting (CADD) model for a specific part or tool can be designed on earth, emailed up to the International Space Station (ISS), and "printed" out.

Immersive development—which is kind of a virtual reality that allows us to try out a repair procedure or do a virtual walkaround of a product without the time and expense of travel—will be a bigger part of the design of and customer support for products.

Systems thinking—being able to conceptualize all of the moving pieces and influencers, versus focusing on one piece—will be valuable.

6. **What do you enjoy most about your job? What do you enjoy least about your job?**

   I really love the amazing products that our industry produces. I love going to an airshow with my son and seeing them. I also love that many of our products support our armed forces. And I have amazing opportunities to work on projects in different parts of the United States and the world.

   But I also have to deal with nontechnical, administrative issues like coordinating meetings that are necessary but not exciting. Another downside is the cyclical nature of being tied to defense and space budgets.

7. **Can you suggest a valuable "try this" for students considering a career in your profession?**

   Try to find an internship. Also, get to an airshow—seeing all the products and watching them fly is great exposure to the amazing things we build.

Note: This interview first appeared in *Careers in Science & Engineering* © 2015.

MORE INFORMATION

Aerospace Industries Association (AIA)
1000 Wilson Boulevard, Suite 1700
Arlington, VA 22209
703.358.1000
www.aia-aerospace.org

American Institute of Aeronautics and Astronautics (AIAA)
12700 Sunrise Valley Drive
Suite 200
Reston, VA 20191-5807
800.639.2422
www.aiaa.org

Hosts annual design competitions:
www.aiaa.org/content.cfm?pageid=210

Offers scholarships for university-level aerospace studies:
www.aiaa.org/content.cfm?pageid=211

National Aeronautics and Space Administration (NASA)
300 E. Street SW, Suite 5R309
Washington, DC 20546-0001
202.358.0001
www.nasa.gov

Provides internship opportunities for high school and college engineering students:
www.nasa.gov/centers/glenn/education/LERCIP_GRC.html

Society of Automotive Engineers International (SAE)
400 Commonwealth Drive
Warrendale, PA 15096-0001
724.776.4841
www.sae.org

Sponsors awards for aerospace leadership and achievement:
www.sae.org/news/awards/industry/aerospace.htm

Michael Auerbach/Editor

Air Traffic Controllers

Snapshot

Career Cluster(s): Transportation, Distribution & Logistics
Interests: Monitoring planes, making decisions quickly, juggling many tasks, gathering information, communicating with others
Earnings (Yearly Average): $124,540
Employment & Outlook: Slower Than Average

OVERVIEW

Sphere of Work

Air traffic controllers regulate air traffic in and in around airports for the purposes of safety and efficiency. Some air traffic controllers monitor planes while in flight, guiding them to airports, assigning landing strips, and directing them to the proper terminals; others oversee the entire air traffic control system from a monitoring center in Virginia. Air traffic controllers make quick decisions about information gathered from radar screens to coordinate with pilots, regional traffic control centers, and ground crews and ensure the safe and efficient movement of air traffic throughout geographical sectors. They also

manage the airport's ground traffic, including emergency vehicles, luggage and fuel trucks, and taxiing planes.

Work Environment

Air traffic controllers generally work a 40-hour week in rotating shifts at airports of all sizes. Major and regional airports, as well as the towers in which controllers work, are extremely busy and complex environments, with many flights arriving and departing during a typical day. The constant activity and decision making required can place a great deal of stress on air traffic controllers, as they are expected to keep traffic flowing efficiently and safely in all weather conditions, day and night. Most air traffic controllers never even see the planes with which they are working, relying instead on radar screens and radio communication to guide planes into and out of airports.

The majority of air traffic controllers work for the Federal Aviation Administration (FAA) or the Department of Defense, although some work at smaller, private airports as well.

Profile

Interests: Data, People Things
Working Conditions: Work Inside
Physical Strength: Light Work
Education Needs: On-the-Job Training, Bachelor's Degree
Licensure/Certification: Required
Physical Abilities Not Required: Not Climb, Not Kneel
Opportunities for Experience: Military Service
Holland Interest Score: SCE; SER

* See Appendix A

Occupation Interest

Air traffic controllers are essential to modern air travel, and those who work at major international airports are responsible for the safety of hundreds of flights per day as well as the safety of millions of travelers, airport visitors, and personnel. The daily life of air traffic controllers is rarely boring—these individuals are constantly monitoring flights and ground activities. Furthermore, air traffic controllers enjoy highly competitive salaries to compensate for the stress inherent to their jobs and have opportunities for advancement. Although the total amount of air traffic is expected to rise sharply, air traffic controller job openings are not expected to increase at the same rate, due to the fact that planes are being developed with new safety technologies.

A Day in the Life—Duties and Responsibilities

Air traffic controllers' primary concern is safety, but they also must direct aircraft efficiently to minimize delays. They manage the flow of aircraft into and out of the airport airspace, guide pilots during takeoff and landing, and monitor aircraft as they travel through the skies. Air traffic controllers use radar, computers, or visual references to monitor and direct the movement of the aircraft in the skies and ground traffic at airports.

The daily tasks of air traffic controllers vary based on the particular area in which they are working. For example, terminal controllers monitor and manage all planes traveling in an airport's airspace, while ground controllers manage all plane and vehicle movement on the tarmac. Radar controllers, meanwhile, only use radar screens to monitor air traffic, while tower flight data controllers use a series of computer programs to sequence flight arrivals and departures. Meanwhile, tower flight data controllers receive flight plans and enter them into the airport's computer records for use by other air traffic controllers and tower personnel. TRACON (terminal radar approach control room) controllers do not work in control towers but direct air traffic from remote terminals.

In general, air traffic controllers maintain and operate a vast network within the airport and its airspace. They coordinate with planes both on the ground and in flight, issuing meteorological reports, receiving and relaying emergency information, offering guidance on altitude changes, clearing takeoffs and landings, and directing alternate routes. They also coordinate with regional air traffic centers, handing off and receiving flights from those centers as flights enter and leave their airspace. As required by federal law, air traffic controllers conduct frequent inspections of airport systems, such as radar and lighting equipment, and maintain detailed logs and records of daily activities and events.

Controllers usually manage multiple aircraft at the same time and must make quick decisions to ensure the safety of aircraft. For example, a controller might direct one aircraft on its landing approach while providing another aircraft with weather information.
Most air traffic controllers work full time, and some work additional hours. The FAA regulates the hours that an air traffic controller may

work. Controllers may not work more than ten straight hours during a shift and must have nine hours' rest before their next shift.

Controllers may rotate shifts among day, evening, and night, because major control facilities operate continuously. Controllers also work weekend and holiday shifts. Less busy airports may have towers that do not operate on a 24-hour basis. Controllers at these airports may have standard work schedules.

Duties and Responsibilities

- Organizing the flow of air traffic in and out of an airport
- Answering radio calls from arriving and departing aircraft
- Issuing landing and takeoff instructions
- Directing pilots as to which runway they should use
- Giving pilots readings on the velocity and direction of the wind and the visibility
- Accepting control of arriving flights from the control center
- Notifying air route control centers to take over as planes leave airport jurisdiction

OCCUPATION SPECIALTIES

Air-Traffic Control Specialists, Tower

Air-Traffic Control Specialists, Tower control the air traffic on and within the vicinity of the airport. They issue instructions to landing and departing planes.

Air-Traffic Control Specialists, Center

Air-Traffic Control Specialists, Center direct air traffic operating under instrument flight rules beyond airport control tower areas and between tower jurisdictions.

Air-Traffic Control Specialists, Station

Air-Traffic Control Specialists, Station receive and transmit flight plans, meteorological, navigational, and other information in an air traffic control station to perform preflight service for airplane pilots.

Chief Controllers

Chief Controllers coordinate and supervise the activities of air traffic controllers in traffic control towers and centers.

Dispatchers

Dispatchers authorize, regulate, and control commercial airline flights according to government and company regulations.

WORK ENVIRONMENT

Immediate Physical Environment

Air traffic controllers work in airport towers or at off-site control facilities (since many airports do not have control towers) and centers. Approach and departure controllers often work in semidark rooms. The aircraft they control appear as points of light moving across their radar screens, and a well-lit room would make it difficult to see the screens properly. These environments are highly complex, with many individuals acting independently yet cooperatively to manage a large number of flights as they enter and depart the airport's vicinity. The intensity of such environments can be both exhausting and stressful.

Human Environment

Air traffic controllers work regularly with other airport personnel, flight crews, and government officials. They consistently maintain contact with incoming and outgoing pilots and flight crews, regional air traffic personnel, and ground crews. Air traffic controllers also work with emergency personnel. Air traffic controllers must react quickly and efficiently while maintaining maximum concentration. The mental stress of being responsible for the safety of aircraft and their passengers can be tiring. As a result, controllers retire earlier than most workers. Those with 20 years of experience are eligible to retire at age 50, while those with 25 years of service may retire earlier than that. Controllers are required to retire at age 65.

Transferable Skills and Abilities

Interpersonal/Social Skills
- Being able to work independently
- Working as a member of a team

Organization & Management Skills
- Making decisions
- Managing time
- Meeting goals and deadlines
- Paying attention to and handling details

Research & Planning Skills
- Analyzing information
- Determining essential information
- Developing evaluation strategies

Technical Skills
- Performing scientific, mathematical, and technical work

Work Environment Skills
- Working in a noisy atmosphere

Technological Environment

Air traffic controllers must work with computers and sophisticated electronic equipment, including radar-based tracking and guidance systems and multicenter traffic management software. They should also be skilled in the use of communications systems, including high-frequency, ultra high-frequency, and very high-frequency radios. They should be capable of using a wide array of guidance systems, including distance-measuring equipment and the Wide Area Augmentation System (WAAS).

EDUCATION, TRAINING, AND ADVANCEMENT

High School/Secondary

High school students should study mathematics, including algebra and geometry. They will also need training in physics, electronics, and computer science. Because communication is so crucial to an air traffic controller's job, courses that build this skill are very important.

Suggested High School Subjects
- Algebra
- Applied Math
- Applied Physics
- College Preparatory
- Electricity & Electronics
- English
- Geometry
- Physics

Related Career Pathways/Majors

Transportation, Distribution & Logistics Cluster
- Transportation Operations Pathway
- Transportation Systems/Infrastructure Planning, Management & Regulation Pathway

Famous First

The first planned nationwide shutdown of air traffic took place on September 10, 1960, while the North American Aerospace Defense Command conducted a military exercise called Sky Shield. No civil aircraft were allowed in the air for six hours, starting at 2:00 a.m., while fighter planes repelled a simulated attack by Soviet bombers.

Source: "Transportation." *Famous First Facts*, Salem, 2016. *Salem Online*, https://online.salempress.com

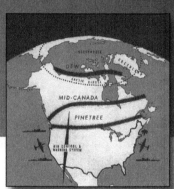

Postsecondary

There are several different paths to becoming an air traffic controller. A candidate must have either three years of progressively responsible work experience, a bachelor's degree, a combination of postsecondary education and work experience totaling three years, or obtain a degree through a Federal Aviation Administration (FAA)-approved Air Traffic Collegiate Training Initiative (AT-CTI) program.

Additionally, to become an air traffic controller, candidates must:

- be a U.S. citizen;
- pass a medical evaluation, including drug screening, and background checks;
- pass the FAA preemployment test, which includes a biographical assessment;
- pass the Air Traffic Controller Specialists Skills Assessment Battery (ATSA); and
- complete a training course at the FAA Academy (and start it before turning 31 years of age).

The biographical assessment, also known as a biodata test, is a behavioral consistency exam that evaluates a candidate's personality fitness to become an air traffic controller. For more information, see the Office of Personnel Management (OPM) page on biodata tests. Applicants who pass both the ATSA and the biographical assessment are eligible to enroll in the FAA Academy.

Controllers also must pass a physical exam each year and a job performance exam twice per year. In addition, they must pass periodic drug screenings.

Some learn their skills and become air traffic controllers while in the military.

Related College Majors
- Air Traffic Controller Training
- Aviation & Airway Science

Adult Job Seekers

Qualified air traffic controllers who have completed all government-mandated education and work experience requirements may apply directly to the FAA, which posts openings on its website. Air traffic controllers may also network through professional trade associations such as the National Air Traffic Controllers Association (NATCA).

Professional Certification and Licensure

All civilian air traffic controllers should complete the AT-CTI and pass the FAA Pre-Employment Test. They must also complete the twelve-week academy program and receive further training at an air traffic control center as "developmental controllers" working in situations that simulate real events.

Additional Requirements

Air traffic controllers must be decisive and able to organize complex and stressful issues in their minds and act swiftly and calmly. They should have exceptional communication skills and technical skills, and should be adept at mathematics and fast information assessment. Previous professional experience in aviation is helpful, since it allows the applicant to bypass a portion of the FAA training that is a prerequisite to interviewing for an air traffic controller job. Because of the stressful and fast-paced nature of the work, air traffic controllers must be in excellent physical and psychological health. Those who want to enter this profession must speak English well enough to be understood clearly over radio and other communications systems.

Fast Fact

The Federal Aviation Administration first required registration for unmanned aircraft systems—mostly drones—on December 14, 2015. Up until the first week of February 2017, weekly registration averaged between 5,000 and 7,000. Hobbyists only need to register once, even if they have more than one aircraft.

Source: faa.gov

EARNINGS AND ADVANCEMENT

Both air traffic controllers' job responsibilities and the complexity of the particular facility determine earnings. For example, air traffic controllers who work at the FAA's busiest facilities earn higher pay. Median annual earnings of air traffic controllers were $124,540 in

May 2018. The lowest 10 percent earned less than $68,090, and the highest 10 percent earned more than $178,650.

Median annual wages, May 2018

Air traffic controllers: $124,540

Air transportation workers: $74,530

Total, all occupations: $38,640

Note: All Occupations includes all occupations in the U.S. Economy.
Source: U.S. Bureau of Labor Statistics, Occupational Employment Statistics

In May 2018, the median annual wages for air traffic controllers in the top industries in which they worked were as follows:

Federal government	$129,180
Professional, scientific, and technical services	$97,690
Support activities for air transportation	$80,750

Depending on length of service, air traffic controllers receive 13 to 26 days of paid vacation and 13 days of paid sick leave each year, life insurance, and health benefits. In addition, air traffic controllers can retire at an earlier age and with fewer years of service than other Federal employees. Air traffic controllers are eligible to retire at age 50 with 20 years of service or after 25 years of active service at any age. There is a mandatory retirement age of 56 for air traffic controllers. However, Federal law provides for exemptions to the mandatory age of 56, up to age 61, for air traffic controllers having exceptional skills and experience.

EMPLOYMENT AND OUTLOOK

There were approximately 24,900 air traffic controllers employed in 2016. Employment of air traffic controllers is projected to grow 3 percent from 2016 to 2026, slower than the average for all occupations.

Although air traffic is projected to increase in the next decade, the satellite-based Next Generation Air Transportation System (NextGen) is expected to allow individual controllers to handle more air traffic. As a result, the demand for additional air traffic controllers should be limited over the next 10 years.

Competition for air traffic controller jobs is expected to be very strong, with many people applying for a relatively small number of jobs. Those with military experience as an air traffic controller may have an advantage.

Most employment opportunities will result from the need to replace workers who are expected to retire or leave the occupation.

Most air traffic controllers work full time, and some work additional hours. The FAA regulates the hours that an air traffic controller may work. Controllers may not work more than 10 straight hours during a shift and must have nine hours' rest before their next shift.

Controllers may rotate shifts among day, evening, and night, because major control facilities operate continuously. Controllers also work weekend and holiday shifts. Less busy airports may have towers that do not operate on a 24-hour basis. Controllers at these airports may have more normal work schedules.

Related Occupations
- Dispatcher

Related Military Occupations
- Air Traffic Control Manager
- Air Traffic Controller
- Flight Operations Specialist
- Special Operations Force

Conversation With . . .
PETER F. DUMONT
President and CEO
Air Traffic Control Association, Alexandria, VA
Air Traffic Control, 44 years

1. What was your individual career path in terms of education/training, entry-level job, or other significant opportunity?

I grew up on Cape Cod, where the service industry dominates. My Cub Scout pack took a field trip to the Hyannis Airport, and we toured the air traffic control tower. I had never known anything about air traffic control, but I decided that's what I wanted to do.

I joined the U.S. Navy right out of high school. Like all sailors, I went to boot camp. I then went to basic air traffic control schooling. As a Navy ATC, you're not just in a tower. You also control airplanes on ships. I was 18. Aircraft carriers are challenging, with 5,000 persons on board with an average age of 22. It's an airport at sea: There's one runway, it's short, and it moves. That certainly increases the challenge.

While in the Navy, I earned a BS in professional aeronautics from Embry-Riddle Aeronautical University. I was stationed at a number of different posts, including on the USS *Midway*. I operated a control tower at Naval Air Station Moffett Field in California, a RADAR approach control at NAS Cubi Point in the Philippines, and controlled the airspace of the coast for special air operations at the Fleet Area Control and Surveillance Facility in Jacksonville, Florida. I operated a major approach control facility at NAS Lemoore, California. I also taught advanced air traffic control.

I retired from the Navy after twenty years and took a position at Serco, Inc., a military subcontractor, to convert military air traffic control towers to civilian use. I served as vice president of aviation, then chief operating officer. I was there 9½ years, and during that time, I earned an MS in aeronautical science in aviation/aerospace management.

As I was considering my next move, I got into a conversation one day with the chairman of the board of the Air Traffic Control Association (ATCA), which at that time was having trouble with management and was on the verge of bankruptcy. He asked if I'd be interested in doing a turnaround of the organization. After interviewing with the hiring committee and board, I was offered the job. I thought it would be a two- or three-year gig but it's lasted thirteen years. I recently completed another MS from Embry-Riddle, this one in unmanned systems and small unmanned aircraft systems.

Introducing unmanned aircraft into the airspace system is probably the most difficult integration we've tried to do since the advent of ATC. The airspace isn't designed for them, and a lot of challenges are coming up for both industry and regulators. We are talking about unmanned systems, which includes small drones for the surveillance of agriculture, disaster management, and law enforcement. Millions are being deployed into our system, and they fly at a relatively low altitude. At the same time, we have common space with rockets and high-altitude aircraft and balloons launching 60,000 feet and above. Getting them up there may be slow but they pass through commercial aircrafts' airspace. Safely controlling the space between the floor of controlled airspace to the upper limits is very challenging.

The ATCA serves a global membership of nearly 4,000 in all segments of the air traffic control and air traffic management community. Among my many roles is membership on Federal Aviation subcommittees, as well as its Unmanned Aircraft Safety Team and Aviation Rulemaking Advisory Committee.

2. What are the most important skills and/or qualities for someone in your profession?

Most air traffic controllers have a Type A personality. They are focused, able to handle stress, and love that it's difficult work. They are proud of what they do.

3. What do you wish you had known going into this profession?

Air traffic controlling does not give you that work-life balance. Your weekends go away, your holidays go away. You work weekends or evenings like nurses or firefighters do. When you're 18, that's fine but when you're 50, it's different because you miss birthdays, family holidays, and wedding anniversaries.

4. Are there many job opportunities in your profession? In what specific areas?

Tremendous opportunities are available, and the earlier you know about them, the more prepared you can be as you go further along in your career. People think you're not an ATC if you're not sitting at the scope controlling airplanes, but think of all the things that go into the national airspace. Right now, there's unmanned systems, equipment manufacturing, engineering, or airspace design. The FAA's William J. Hughes Technical Center in New Jersey, a major technical development laboratory for air transportation, has opportunities. There are ATC instructors and university professors. Cybersecurity and computer science plug very neatly into aviation.

5. How do you see your profession changing in the next five years? How will technology impact that change, and what skills will be required?

Nobody can read the future, but the writing is on the wall that we are going to need systems and procedures to interact in a way that doesn't rely on how we do things now. I see more automation tools in the future. For aircraft with pilots, a text-based system so you reduce voice congestion on airwaves is in the final stages of implementation.

We are talking about managing airspace instead of individual airplanes. There are remote ATC towers with cameras and capabilities to zoom cameras for 360-degree views. The idea is, it's less expensive than building a control tower and you put it in places people don't want to live. I see tremendous opportunity for that type of technology.

6. What do you enjoy most about your job? What do you enjoy least about your job?

Being an air traffic controller brings instant gratification. You work hard, provide a service, and, if you do it right, people are safe. The downside is there is no work-life balance.

In the position I occupy now, I like being engaged in activities that makes a difference in the aviation industry by providing my insights and collaborating to better improve the system. I least like that the innovation that's available is slow to be embraced. Hitting a wall in the regulatory process is frustrating, although that's starting to morph.

7. Can you suggest a valuable "try this" for students considering a career in your profession?

Visit an air traffic control facility. (It takes a little doing, but they'll tell you how to gain access.) Talk to them. Also, ATC simulation games give you an idea of what talking to airplanes is like.

MORE INFORMATION

Air Traffic Control Association (ATCA)
1101 King Street, Suite 300
Alexandria, VA 22314
703.299.2430
info@atca.org
www.atca.org

Federal Aviation Administration (FAA)
800 Independence Avenue, SW
Washington, DC 20591
866.835.5322
www.faa.gov

National Air Traffic Controllers Association (NATCA)
1325 Massachusetts Avenue, NW
Washington, DC 20005
202.628.5451
www.natca.org

Michael Auerbach/Editor

Aircraft Mechanics

Snapshot

Career Cluster(s): Manufacturing, Transportation, Distribution & Logistics

Interests: Aerodynamics, machinery, mechanics, mechanical engineering, aircraft, large engine repair

Earnings (Median Pay): $56,625

Employment & Outlook: Slower Than Average Growth Expected

OVERVIEW

Sphere of Work

Aircraft mechanics work to ensure the safety and efficiency of private and commercial air travel. To this end, they perform scheduled maintenance, conduct Federal Aviation Administration (FAA)–mandated inspections, and make repairs on airplanes, helicopters, and other aircraft. Some aircraft mechanics specialize in one particular area, such as engine repair, while at smaller airports, mechanics are typically expected to work on all aspects of the planes housed there. This includes testing and repairing brakes, ventilation and air conditioning systems, radios, landing gear, and instruments. When operating

issues arise, aircraft mechanics determine the cause, select the proper tools and equipment, and repair or replace the malfunctioning systems while maintaining detailed logs of those repairs.

Work Environment

Aircraft mechanics work in airport hangars, repair areas, and flight lines. Airports, in general, are very busy environments, with planes and other vehicles, as well as people, constantly moving from place to place. Mechanics frequently work with heavy equipment and perform physically challenging work, often in potentially dangerous or uncomfortable locations, such as on an airplane's wing or on top of its fuselage (the main body). The work areas can be extremely noisy, and when working outside of a hangar, aircraft mechanics are exposed to all types of weather. Aircraft mechanics generally work 40-hour weeks, but due to the essential nature of the work, some late night and holiday shifts may be required. There is pressure for this work to be done quickly and correctly, which adds an element of stress to the job.

Profile

Interests: Manufacturing, Transportation, Distribution & Logistics
Working Conditions: Work both Inside and Outside
Physical Strength: Medium Work
Education Needs: On-the-Job Training, Junior/Technical/Community College, Apprenticeship
Licensure/Certification: Required
Physical Abilities Not Required: N/A
Opportunities for Experience: Apprenticeship, Military Service, Part-Time Work
Holland Interest Score: REI; RIE

* See Appendix A

Occupation Interest

A career as an aircraft mechanic appeals to detail-oriented people who enjoy working with their hands and repairing a variety of complex machines. Aircraft mechanics frequently have to solve mechanical problems under strict time constraints, so workers must excel in fast-paced environments.

A Day in the Life—Duties and Responsibilities

Daily responsibilities for aircraft mechanics vary based on the type of aircraft in need of maintenance or the area of specialization in which they work. In general, aircraft mechanics conduct routine inspections of systems and equipment, make repairs when necessary, and handle any emergency mechanical problems that may occur. They check gauges and instruments for operating difficulties and perform routine preflight maintenance as needed. When issues arise, aircraft mechanics make repairs in a hangar or along the flight line, sometimes climbing on top of the fuselage or wings in order to fix or replace malfunctioning equipment.

In addition to mechanical work, aircraft mechanics are responsible for logging the results of their FAA-mandated equipment inspections, as well as keeping records of maintenance performed. They may also participate in the ordering and tracking of inventory.

Airframe and powerplant (A&P) mechanics are certified generalist mechanics who can independently perform many maintenance and alteration tasks on aircraft. A&P mechanics repair and maintain most parts of an aircraft, including the engines, landing gear, brakes, and air-conditioning system. Some specialized activities require additional experience and certification.

Maintenance schedules for aircraft may be based on hours flown, days since the last inspection, trips flown, or a combination of these factors. Maintenance also may need to be done at other times to address specific issues recognized by mechanics or manufacturers.

Mechanics use precision instruments to measure wear and identify defects. They may use x rays or magnetic or ultrasonic inspection equipment to discover cracks that cannot be seen on a plane's exterior. They check for corrosion, distortion, and cracks in the aircraft's main body, wings, and tail. They then repair the metal, fabric, wood, or composite materials that make up the airframe and skin.

After completing all repairs, mechanics test the equipment to ensure that it works properly and record all maintenance completed on an aircraft.

Avionics technicians are specialists who repair and maintain a plane's electronic instruments, such as radio communication devices and equipment, radar systems, and navigation aids. As the use of digital technology increases, more time is spent maintaining computer systems. The ability to repair and maintain many avionics and flight instrument systems is granted through the Airframe rating, but other licenses or certifications may be needed as well.

Designated airworthiness representatives (DARs) examine, inspect, and test aircraft for airworthiness. They issue airworthiness certificates, which aircraft must have to fly. There are two types of DARs: manufacturing DARs and maintenance DARs.

Inspection authorized (IA) mechanics are mechanics who have both Airframe and Powerplant certification and may perform inspections on aircraft and return them to service. IA mechanics are able to do a wider variety of maintenance activities and alterations than any other type of maintenance personnel. They can do comprehensive annual inspections or return aircraft to service after a major repair.

Repairmen certificate holders may or may not have the A&P certificate or other certificates. Repairmen certificates are issued by certified repair stations to aviation maintenance personnel, and the certificates allow them to do specific duties. Repairmen certificates are valid only while the mechanic works at the issuing repair center and are not transferable to other employers.

Airframe mechanics work on all parts of the aircraft aside from the instruments, engines, and propellers, while powerplant mechanics work with engines and some propeller systems. Avionics technicians specialize in navigation, radio, radar, and other flight control systems. Many mechanics who work at small regional airports or with private jets and smaller planes, are combined airframe and powerplant (A&P) mechanics, fulfilling dual roles.

Duties and Responsibilities

- Repairing, replacing, and assembling aircraft parts and frames
- Maintaining or replacing hydraulic units, oxygen systems, fuel and oil systems, fire extinguisher systems, and electrical systems
- Repairing electronic systems, such as computerized controls
- Maintaining and replacing aircraft engines, propeller pumps and fuel, oil and water injection systems
- Certifying aircraft that is ready for operation

OCCUPATION SPECIALTIES

Aircraft Maintenance Supervisors

Aircraft Maintenance Supervisors supervise and coordinate the activities of airframe-and-power-plant mechanics. They train employees in work methods and procedures and inspect work to maintain specified standards and quality.

Experimental Aircraft Mechanics

Experimental Aircraft Mechanics inspect, test, and are responsible for the maintenance and servicing of experimental and prototype aircraft, engines and components, as specified by the government agency or customer requirements.

Reclamation Workers

Reclamation Workers dismantle wrecked and other decommissioned aircraft and salvage parts and equipment and retain any usable parts, cleaning them in solvents and preservatives.

WORK ENVIRONMENT

Immediate Physical Environment

Aircraft mechanics work primarily at airports and airfields, working in hangars as well as outdoor repair areas and flight lines. The work environment is busy and often very loud, and mechanics are frequently expected to work in all types of weather conditions. Mechanics may perform maintenance and repairs while on top of an aircraft's fuselage or wings or in tight spaces within the fuselage.

Human Environment

Aircraft mechanics frequently work in collaboration with their fellow mechanics, some of whom may specialize in particular areas. They may also interact with members of the airport staff, pilots and other flight crew members, and government officials.

Technological Environment

In addition to the handheld tools used to maintain and replace equipment, aircraft mechanics use metal cutters, mechanical lifts and test stands, electrical test equipment, X-ray machines, and magnetic inspection equipment. They must also use mobile computers to log completed maintenance, manage inventory, and analyze engine performance, among other tasks.

Transferable Skills and Abilities

Organization & Management Skills
- Paying attention to and handling details
- Performing duties that change frequently

Technical Skills
- Performing scientific, mathematical, and technical work
- Working with machines, tools, or other objects

Unclassified Skills
- Being physically active

EDUCATION, TRAINING, AND ADVANCEMENT

High School/Secondary

High school students should study industrial arts, including welding and metalworking, engine repair, machine repair, and electronics. Math courses, such as trigonometry and geometry, are also highly useful. Classes in physics and chemistry provide aspiring aircraft mechanics with an understanding of the effects of environmental conditions on a plane's external skin and internal systems.

Suggested High School Subjects
- Algebra
- Applied Math
- Applied Physics

- Blueprint Reading
- Chemistry
- Electricity & Electronics
- English
- Machining Technology
- Trigonometry
- Welding

Related Career Pathways/Majors

Manufacturing Cluster
- Maintenance, Installation & Repair Pathway

Transportation, Distribution & Logistics Cluster
- Facility & Mobile Equipment Maintenance Pathway

Famous First

The first jet airplane used for commercial transport that was built in the United States was the Boeing Stratoliner Model 707, first tested July 15, 1954, by Alvin M. Johnston at Renton, WA, where it was built by the Boeing Airplane Company. It had four Pratt and Whitney J-57 engines with more than 10,000 pounds of thrust. It weighed 190,000 pounds and cost about $20 million. It was designed to carry about 150 passengers across the Atlantic Ocean at a speed of 550 miles per hour. The first transport was delivered on August 16, 1958, to Pan American Airways.

Source: "Transportation." *Famous First Facts*, Salem, 2016. *Salem Online*, https://online.salempress.com

Postsecondary

Some aircraft mechanics and service technicians enter the occupation with a high school diploma or equivalent and receive on-the-job training to learn their skills and to be able to pass the FAA exams. Aviation maintenance personnel who are not certified by the FAA work under supervision until they have enough experience and knowledge and become certified.

Aircraft mechanics and service technicians typically enter the occupation after attending a Part 147 FAA-approved aviation maintenance technician school. These schools award a certificate of completion that the FAA recognizes as an alternative to the experience requirements stated in regulations. The schools also grant holders the right to take the relevant FAA exams.

Avionics technicians typically earn an associate's degree before entering the occupation. Aircraft controls, systems, and flight instruments have become increasingly digital and computerized. Workers who have the proper background in aviation flight instruments or computer repair are needed to maintain these complex systems.

Related College Majors:
- Aircraft Mechanics Airframe
- Aircraft Mechanics Powerplant
- Aviation Systems & Avionics Maintenance Technology.

Adult Job Seekers

Qualified aircraft mechanics may apply directly to positions listed online or in print. Professional trade associations such as the Professional Aviation Maintenance Association (PAMA), as well as regional and international unions, can provide information about available positions and present valuable networking opportunities.

Professional Certification and Licensure

The FAA requires that working aircraft mechanics either be certified or work under a certified mechanic. Mechanics must be at least 18 years of age, be fluent in English, and have 30 months of experience to qualify for either the A or the P rating or both (the A&P rating). Completion of a program at a Part 147 FAA-approved aviation maintenance technician school can substitute for the experience requirement and shorten the time requirements for becoming eligible to take the FAA exams.

Applicants must pass written, oral, and practical exams that demonstrate the required skills within a timeframe of two years.

To keep their certification, mechanics must have completed relevant repair or maintenance work within the previous 24 months. To fulfill this requirement, mechanics may take classes from their employer, a school, or an aircraft manufacturer.

The Inspection Authorization (IA) is available to mechanics who have had their A&P ratings for at least three years and meet other requirements. These mechanics are able to review and approve many major repairs and alterations.

Avionics technicians typically are certified through a repair station for the specific work they perform on aircraft, or they hold the Airframe rating to work on an aircraft's electronic and flight instrument systems. An Aircraft Electronics Technician (AET) certification is available through the National Center for Aerospace & Transportation Technologies (NCATT). It certifies that aviation mechanics have a basic level of knowledge in the subject area, but it is not required by the FAA for any specific tasks. Avionics technicians who work on communications equipment may need to have the proper radiotelephone operator certification issued by the Federal Communications Commission (FCC).

Additional Requirements

Aircraft mechanics must be skilled in working with complex mechanical systems and equipment. Computer skills are also beneficial. Mechanics must be energetic, motivated, and able to quickly diagnose problems. Heavy lifting, climbing to high points on large aircraft, and working in tight spaces are often part of the job, so mechanics must be physically fit and possess a full range of motion. They must also be effective communicators, able to clearly explain maintenance issues to individuals from different professional backgrounds.

Fast Fact
One windshield or window frame of a Boeing 747-400's cockpit costs as much as a BMW car.
Source: confessionsofatrolleydolly.com

EARNINGS AND ADVANCEMENT

Earnings depend on the employer, geographic location, union affiliation and mechanic's training, experience, seniority and responsibilities. Earnings of aircraft mechanics generally are higher than other types of mechanics. As aircraft mechanics gain experience, they may advance to lead mechanic, lead inspector, or shop supervisor. Opportunities to advance may be best for those who have an inspection authorization (IA). Mechanics with broad experience in maintenance and repair may become inspectors or examiners for the FAA.

Median annual earnings of aircraft mechanics were about $62,920 in May 2018. The lowest 10 percent earned less than $36,760, and the highest 10 percent earned more than $97,820.

In May 2018, the median annual wages for aircraft mechanics and service technicians in the top industries in which they worked were as follows:

Scheduled air transportation	$83,870
Aerospace product and parts manufacturing	$64,510
Federal government, excluding postal service	$59,530
Nonscheduled air transportation	$59,020
Support activities for air transportation	$54,350

In May 2018, the median annual wages for avionics technicians in the top industries in which they worked were as follows:

Scheduled air transportation	$81,160
Aerospace product and parts manufacturing	$72,420
Professional, scientific, and technical services	$71,650
Federal government	$58,420
Support activities for air transportation	$57,210

Mechanics and technicians usually work full time on rotating eight-hour shifts. Overtime and weekend work often are required. Aircraft mechanics may receive paid vacations, holidays, and sick days; life and health insurance; and retirement benefits. These are usually paid by the employer. Aircraft mechanics may also receive free or reduced rates on flights and uniform cleaning allowances.

EMPLOYMENT AND OUTLOOK

Aircraft mechanics held about 149,500 jobs in 2016. Air traffic is expected to increase gradually over the coming decade, and will require additional aircraft maintenance, including that performed on new aircraft. Some airlines may outsource maintenance work to specialized maintenance and repair shops both domestically and abroad. This practice is expected to reduce employment growth opportunities in the air transportation industry over the next 10 years.

Percent change in employment, Projected 2016–26

Total, all occupations: 7%

Installation, maintenance, and repair occupations: 7%

Avionics technicians: 6%

Aircraft and avionics equipment mechanics and technicians: 5%

Aircraft mechanics and service technicians: 5%

Note: All Occupations includes all occupations in the U.S. Economy.
Source: U.S. Bureau of Labor Statistics, Occupational Employment Statistics

Because the airlines offer relatively high wages and attractive travel benefits, competition for these jobs is high. Job opportunities will be best with smaller airlines and in general aviation.

Experienced aircraft mechanics who keep up on technological advances in electronics and other areas and who are trained to work on complicated aircraft systems will be in the greatest demand.

Related Occupations
- Automotive Technician
- Diesel Service Technician
- Electrician
- Heavy Equipment Service Technician

Related Military Occupations
- Air Crew Member
- Aircraft Mechanic
- Flight Engineer
- Transportation Maintenance Manager

Conversation With...
SCOTT McNABB
Aircraft Maintenance Technician
Southwest Airlines, Dallas, TX
Aircraft Maintenance Technician, 18 years

1. What was your individual career path in terms of education/training, entry-level job, or other significant opportunity?

I come from a farming family, and my dad also built houses on the side. I didn't want to do either one of those things. I decided to join the military. I did well on testing, so I got to pick my specialty, which was the Air Force.

After basic training I went to Sheppard Air Force Base in Texas and trained to be a crew chief for the C130. It's a four-engine cargo plane. The military taught me the basics of aircraft maintenance. It had a very comprehensive on the job training program. When I was based in Germany, I also got a part-time job with a commercial air transport company, just to get more practical experience and check off the boxes I needed to get my airframe and powerplant mechanics license. The certifying license is issued by the Federal Aviation Administration. You also have to pass written, oral, and practical tests.

Besides going into the military, you can also prepare for the licensing exams by going to an aviation maintenance technical school approved by the FAA. The schools cost from $10,000 to $40,000. No matter how much the school charges, you come away with the same license.

You can also get experience on the job and study for the tests on your own, but that usually takes longer.

Airframe refers to the electrical systems and powerplant to the engine and related systems. You can be certified in just airframe or powerplant, but the bigger carriers where you make better money require both.

After 12 years in the Air Force I left the military and did contract work for a brief time before being hired by Southwest Airlines.

I worked in Chicago and Orlando. Now I am in a major overhaul facility in Dallas. We do major inspections of planes on a regular basis and conduct daily checks for everything from burnt out lightbulbs to broken seatbelts.

Aircraft Mechanics

Most recently, I also started working as an investigating team coordinator for the Aircraft Mechanics Fraternal Association. The union picks up the tab for any investigation work I do for the National Transportation Safety Board.

The NTSB wants to have mechanics handy to consult in case of an incident with any airline because mechanics are the ones who know the planes inside and out.

I don't fly planes, but I taxi them on the runway up to the flight line sometimes to test the engines. It's kind of fun.

2. What are the most important skills and qualities for someone in your profession?

You have to be mechanically inclined. You have to have a desire to learn. You have to be a self-motivator to further yourself in the career. I'm still learning.

Avionics is mostly what I do now. It's electronics. You're basically dealing with wires a lot—the radio system, the guidance system.

You have to be conscientious and enjoy problem solving. It all has to be done right. There's no room for error. Your brain is always on. Avionics isn't for everyone.

3. What do you wish you had known going into this profession?

You kind of have to pay your dues starting out. You have to work night shifts and you have odd days off.

4. Are there many job opportunities in your profession?

Yes. They are actually forecasting a shortage in the aviation mechanics career field. We're seeing schools not have the enrollment they used to have. It seems like more people want to work in front of computers. Being an aircraft mechanic is a good paying job, and it's very rewarding. Sometimes you work outdoors, other times in a hangar.

We travel for free. The airline you work for usually allows you and your family to fly standby. Plus there are jobs all over the world. If you want to work someplace else, just do it.

This career field is equally open to women. Women can do the job.

5. How do you see your profession changing in the next five years? How will technology impact that change and what skills will be required?

We're going to see aircraft design be a lot different. We're going to have more composite materials versus metals. Of course electronics are going to be more technologically advanced. That's happening now before our eyes. The highways in the skies are getting closer together. Avionics are going to have to be a lot more accurate, and people will have to be trained to work on those systems.

6. What do you enjoy most about your job? What do you like least about your job?

I like knowing my family and friends and flying customers are safe. It's a lot of responsibility, taking care of a plane that carries 175 passengers plus a crew. I like seeing it go over the fence and fly out of sight.

Everybody's least favorite thing is working on the lavatory and waste systems. Every now and again it's your turn.

7. Can you suggest a valuable "try this" for students considering a career in your profession?

Take some circuitry classes and see if you're mechanically inclined. Do you like to work on cars and car radios or boats and motorcycles? That interest can transfer over to a more complicated airplane. See if a local airline will provide a tour of an aircraft. You may walk on board and just be amazed. If you're amazed, it might just be the career for you.

MORE INFORMATION

**Aircraft Maintenance
Professionals Society (AMT)**
801 Cliff Road East, Suite 201
Burnsville, MN 55337
800.827.8009
www.amtsociety.org

**Association for Women in
Aviation Maintenance (AWAM)**
P.O. Box 1
Edgewater, FL 32132
386.416.0248
www.awam.org

**Aviation Technician Education
Council (ATEC)**
2090 Wexford Court
Harrisburg, PA 17112
717.540.7121
info@atec-amt.org
www.atec-amt.org

**Federal Aviation Administration
(FAA)**
800 Independence Avenue, SW
Washington, DC 20591
866.835.5322
www.faa.gov

**Professional Aviation
Maintenance Association (PAMA)**
717 Princess Street
Alexandria, VA 22314
703.778.4647
hq@pama.org
www.pama.org

Michael Auerbach/Editor

Airline and Commercial Pilots

Snapshot

Career Cluster(s): Transportation, Distribution & Logistics
Interests: Aviation, navigation, geography, engineering technology, physics, math, and geometry
Earnings (Median Pay): $115,670
Employment & Outlook: Slower Than Average Growth Expected

OVERVIEW

Sphere of Work

Pilots are professionals who use aircraft to transport people and freight, take photographs, launch weapons, dust crops, perform rescue missions, and other tasks. Most pilots are airline pilots and copilots, transporting passengers and cargo to and from their destinations. A small number of pilots are commercial pilots, and their duties can include spreading seeds for reforestation, conducting test flights, tracking military and criminal targets, monitoring traffic, and even fighting fires. The main vehicles used by pilots are large commercial airplanes, smaller fixed-wing aircraft and jets, military aircraft, and helicopters.

Airline and Commercial Pilots

Work Environment

Pilots work in a variety of environments. Most pilots work in the airline industry, flying regional, national, and international routes for major commercial airlines. Many pilots are in the military, using their aircraft for attacks and rescues, as well as surveillance and mapping purposes. Many pilots in the commercial industry got their start in the military, although this has declined in recent years.

In addition to commercial and military pilots, some pilots work in agriculture and forestry, flying over crops to dust with pesticides and to drop seeds in areas being reforested. Still other professional pilots work in the media industry, flying over traffic and incident scenes. In each of these environments, the work of a pilot is complex and potentially dangerous. Flying is also a demanding career choice, requiring that the pilot spend a great deal of time away from home.

Profile

Interests: Data, People, Things
Working Conditions: Work Inside
Physical Strength: Light Work
Education Needs: Junior/Technical/Community College, Bachelor's Degree
Licensure/Certification: Required
Physical Abilities Not Required: Not Climb, Not Kneel
Opportunities for Experience: Military Service
Holland Interest Score: IRE

* See Appendix A

Occupation Interest

Most people pursue their training as a pilot because of the excitement of such positions. Indeed, pilots sometimes travel all over the world using state of the art aviation equipment and technology. It is an exciting field, but comes with significant responsibility. As a rule, the pilot who has been designated pilot in command (PIC)—of any aircraft, small or large—has a legal obligation for and the final authority of that aircraft under Federal Aviation Administration (FAA) regulations. This means that the PIC is responsible for the safety of the aircraft, ultimately determines the aircraft's route, commands the flight crew, and holds the responsibility for the safe passage of any passengers. In the case of an emergency, the pilot is in command and has the authority to deviate from standard practice or make a decision that differs from the direction given by the control tower.

Pilots serve in the military, in commercial airline industry, can work for public or private entities fighting fires, transporting patients in crisis, or serving the agricultural sector. Pilots are essential to any industry or sector that needs safe and swift transport, or has needs best provided by air.

A Day in the Life—Duties and Responsibilities

The specific responsibilities of a pilot vary a great deal based on the industry in which he or she works. Overall, however, a pilot's primary responsibilities are to ensure the safety of the plane and its passengers and satisfy the requirements of his or her employers. To this end, pilots will conduct thorough safety and systems checks on a plane before departing, a process known as a "preflight," or a preflight inspection. During such reviews, the pilot will use a checklist to make sure all safety equipment, navigation technology, and other systems are operating normally. The pilot will check the plane's logs to review any issues the plane may have had in its previous flights and review weather reports and flight plans. A pilot oversees the plane's "pushback" and taxi from a gate or terminal before takeoff. During flight, the pilot will communicate with passengers, the flight crew, and air traffic control with any updates. When it is time to land, a pilot runs another series of checks, communicating with the tower of the receiving airport and re-checking landing gear and systems.

In addition to sharing many of the responsibilities described above, pilots who do not work for airlines have a number of other tasks. Helicopter pilots, for example, often photograph accident sites and conduct tours while flying their vehicles. Crop dusters and seeders must often load their payloads in addition to operating their airplanes. Many pilots who do not work for a major airline must also perform their own administrative tasks and business development activities in addition to flying.

Duties and Responsibilities

- Reviewing and examining papers to determine necessary flight data
- Performing preflight inspection of the aircraft and its cargo
- Contacting control tower by radio to receive instructions
- Controlling the airplane in flight
- Logging flight information

OCCUPATION SPECIALTIES

Navigators

Navigators establish the position of the plane and direct the course of airplanes on flights, using navigational instruments, atmospheric observations, or basic reasoning.

Agricultural Aircraft Pilots

Agricultural Aircraft Pilots fly airplanes or helicopters, at low altitudes, over agricultural fields in order to dust or spray them with seeds, fertilizers, or pesticides.

Commercial Airplane Pilots

Commercial Airplane Pilots fly passenger, mail, or freight planes.

Airplane-Patrol Pilots

Airplane-Patrol Pilots fly airplanes over pipelines, tracks, and communications systems to detect and radio the location and nature of the damage they are investigating.

Test Pilots

Test Pilots fly new or modified aircraft to evaluate the plane's airworthiness, performance, systems operation, and design.

Executive Pilots

Executive Pilots fly company-owned aircraft to transport company officials or customers. They file a flight plan with airport officials and obtain and interpret weather data based upon the flight plan.

Helicopter Pilots

Helicopter Pilots fly helicopters for purposes such as transporting passengers and cargo, search and rescue operations, fighting fires, and reporting on traffic and weather conditions.

WORK ENVIRONMENT

Immediate Physical Environment

A pilot primarily works at airports or similar aviation centers and landing sites. Military pilots may also be found on aircraft carriers and other naval ships. Each of these environments tend to be complex and extremely busy, with many working parts, including safety, luggage and cargo, air traffic control, fuel services, repair crews, and other elements all coming into contact with one another. Pilots for commercial airlines will often have layovers in distant cities where they must seek accommodation. The airline covers the cost of these overnight stays.

Human Environment

Pilots must work with a wide range of people on the ground and on board their planes. Such parties include maintenance crews, security personnel, flight attendants, air traffic controllers, luggage handlers and, of course, the passengers. Pilots must interact directly with many of these individuals, while communicating and coordinating with others on the ground while in flight. Pilots are sometimes responsible for unruly passengers. As part of the Homeland Security Act of 2002, some pilots have been deputized and are federal law enforcement officers, called Federal Flight Deck Officers.

Transferable Skills and Abilities

Communication Skills
- Speaking effectively
- Writing concisely

Organization & Management Skills
- Making decisions
- Meeting goals and deadlines
- Performing duties that change frequently
- Research and planning skills
- Using logical reasoning

Technical Skills
- Performing scientific, mathematical, and technical work
- Working with machines, tools, or other objects

Technological Environment

Pilots must work with what are often extremely complex pieces of engineering. As part of the preflight check, they must carefully examine each of these systems to ensure that they are running properly. During flight, they must be skilled with automatic pilot systems, weather gauges, communications equipment, and safety measures. Military pilots must also work with weapons systems. Helicopter and other pilots who work outside of the airline industry may also be expected to work with photographic equipment, payload release systems (such as crop dusters and firefighting helicopters and planes), and other systems.

EDUCATION, TRAINING, AND ADVANCEMENT

High School/Secondary

High school students interested in becoming pilots are encouraged to study such sciences as physics, math and geometry, and geography. Additionally, because communication with passengers, ground personnel, and passengers is critical to many pilots, aspiring pilots are encouraged to take courses that build verbal skills, such as English.

Suggested High School Subjects
- Algebra
- Applied Math
- Applied Physics
- Blueprint Reading
- College Preparatory
- English
- Geography
- Geometry
- Physics
- Trigonometry

Related Career Pathways/Majors

Transportation, Distribution & Logistics Cluster
- Transportation Operations Pathway

Famous First

The first pilot of an airplane to qualify as an astronaut by attaining a 50-mile altitude was Major Robert Michael White of the Air Force, who piloted his X-15 rocket airplane to an altitude of 314,750 feet on July 17, 1962. He was launched from a B-52 at Edwards Air Force Base, Muroc, CA, and landed on Rogers Dry Lake after a flight lasting about 11 minutes. He was awarded astronaut wings on July 18, 1962. White was the fifth to qualify as an astronaut, having been preceded by Alan B. Shepard, Jr., Virgil Grissom, John H. Glenn, and Scott Carpenter.

Source: "Transportation." *Famous First Facts*, Salem, 2016. *Salem Online*, https://online.salempress.com

Postsecondary

Many pilots receive postsecondary certification, such as an associate's degree, from a junior and/or community college. However, as the field of aviation is extremely competitive, pilots are encouraged to obtain at least a bachelor's degree in a related field and/or obtain direct pilot training through the military or civilian flight schools. In the past, many commercial pilots were ex-military. While no longer the trend, the military is a viable option for those seeking pilot training.

Related College Majors:
- Aircraft Piloting & Navigation (Professional)

Adult Job Seekers

Pilot jobs are very difficult to obtain due to the competitive nature of the industry. It is essential for pilots, particularly those aspiring to gain employment with a major airline, to log the most flight hours possible in order to have a chance at obtaining a better job. Many pilots begin their careers at small, regional carriers or gain their training through the military. For those pilots leaving the military, training in civilian regulations is necessary.

Professional Certification and Licensure

The central authority regulating pilots in the civilian arena is the Federal Aviation Administration (FAA). Pilots must receive their licenses from the FAA through a series of tests (including a written exam as well as a physical examination) and logged time in both flight simulators and in the air with qualified FAA officials. During the course of their careers, pilots should also receive separate licensure for flying through bad weather using instruments only. Airline pilots must also log 1,500 hours of FAA-approved flight time and certification in instrument and night flying. Physical exams and additional training are required on a yearly basis.

Additional Requirements

Pilots should demonstrate a strong attention to detail and be able to work long hours in stressful situations. They are expected to remain physically fit, with good hearing and eyesight. Furthermore, most airline pilots must undergo company orientation to assimilate the corporation's best practices and policies. When a pilot reaches 60 years of age, he or she usually must consider retirement.

Fast Fact

At any given time, there are about 61,000 people airborne over the United States.
Source: www.highflightacademy.com

EARNINGS AND ADVANCEMENT

Earnings depend on the employing airline; number of hours and miles flown; size, speed, and type of plane; the pilot's length of service and the type of flight (international or domestic). Extra pay may be provided for night and international flights. Pilots who fly jet aircraft usually earned higher salaries than nonjet pilots. Pilots working outside the airlines earned lower salaries.

Median annual earnings of airline pilots, copilots, and flight engineers were $140,340 in May 2018. The lowest 10 percent earned less than $65,690, and the highest 10 percent earned more than $208,000.

Median annual earnings of commercial pilots were $82,240 in May 2018. The lowest 10 percent earned less than $44,660, and the highest 10 percent earned more than $160,480

Median annual wages, May 2018

Airline pilots, copilots, and flight engineers: $140,340

Airline and commercial pilots: $115,670

Commercial pilots: $82,240

Air transportation workers: $74,530

Total, all occupations: $38,640

Note: All Occupations includes all occupations in the U.S. Economy.
Source: U.S. Bureau of Labor Statistics, Occupational Employment Statistics

Airline pilots usually begin their careers as first officers and receive wage increases as they accumulate experience and seniority.

In addition, airline pilots receive an expense allowance, or "per diem," for every hour they are away from home, and they may earn extra pay for international flights. Airline pilots and their immediate families usually are entitled to free or reduced-fare flights.

Federal regulations set the maximum work hours and minimum requirements for rest between flights for most pilots. Airline pilots fly an average of 75 hours per month and work an additional 50 hours per month performing other duties, such as checking weather conditions and preparing flight plans. Pilots have variable work schedules that may include several days of work followed by some days off.

Airline pilots may spend several nights a week away from home because flight assignments often involve overnight layovers. When pilots are away from home, the airlines typically provide hotel accommodations, transportation to the airport, and an allowance for meals and other expenses.

Commercial pilots also have irregular schedules. Although most commercial pilots remain near their home overnight, they may still work nonstandard hours.

Pilots may receive paid vacations, holidays, and sick days; life and health insurance; and retirement benefits. These are usually paid by the employer. Employers provide pilots with hotel accommodations during layovers, transportation between hotels and airports, and an expense account when they are away from home. Pilots employed by airlines may also receive free or reduced fare flights for themselves and family members.

EMPLOYMENT AND OUTLOOK

There were approximately 84,000 airline pilots, copilots, and flight engineers employed nationally in 2016. About 40,800 individuals were employed as commercial pilots. About two-thirds of all pilots worked for airlines. Many others worked as flight instructors at local airports or for large businesses that fly company cargo and executives in their own airplanes or helicopters. Some also worked for federal, state, and local governments.

Employment of pilots is expected to grow slower than average for all occupations through the year 2026, which means employment is projected to increase 4 percent for commercial pilots and 3 percent for airline pilots, copilots, and flight engineers.

Most job opportunities will arise from the need to replace pilots who leave the workforce. Over the next 10 years, many pilots are expected to retire as they reach the required retirement age of 65.

Job prospects may be best with regional airlines and nonscheduled aviation services because entry-level requirements are lower for regional and commercial jobs. There is typically less competition among applicants in these sectors than there is for major airlines.

Pilots attempting to get jobs at the major airlines will face strong competition, as those firms tend to attract many more applicants than they have jobs. Pilots who have logged the greatest number of flying hours in the more sophisticated equipment typically have the best prospects. For this reason, military pilots often have an advantage over other applicants.

Related Occupations
- Air Crew Member
- Airplane Navigator
- Airplane Pilot
- Helicopter Pilot
- Radar & Sonar Operator
- Space Operations Officer
- Special Operations Officer

Conversation With...
COSTAS SIVYLLIS

Pilot, Major US Airline
Pilot/First Officer, Boeing 757/767
Newark, NJ, Airline Pilot, 4½ years

1. What was your individual career path in terms of education/training, entry-level job, or other significant opportunity?

There was never a question: all I wanted to do was be an airline pilot. Growing up I flew frequently between Boston and Athens to see family and was inspired to pursue the profession.

I started to take flight lessons when I was 12 at Mansfield Municipal Airport in Massachusetts. I soloed on my 16th birthday, which was the minimum age you can do that and got my license at 17.

I went to college at Embry-Riddle Aeronautical University in Daytona Beach, FL, and graduated in 2012 with a bachelor's degree in aeronautical science and minor in business. I also completed my remaining flight ratings, including ratings for instrument, commercial, multiengine and flight instructor.

After college, I was a flight instructor at Embry-Riddle for two years. It's a really easy way to get your flight time. To get a job as an airline pilot you need between 750 to 1,500 hours of flight time depending on your flight training program—military, civilian or accredited aviation college.

Training to be a pilot works very much like major league baseball. You don't get drafted to the Red Sox right away. Usually you build your flight time then fly for a regional airline.

I was hired first as a first officer with a regional carrier once I met the requirements. I started flying 50- to 70-seat regional jets all around the eastern half of the United States, built experience and upgraded to a captain.

About five years ago I was hired by a major U.S. airline and now fly Boeing 757s and 767s. Most of my trips take me from New York to Europe.

I'm also chairman of national education for the Air Line Pilots Association. A big part of my role with ALPA is encouraging young people to go into the profession.

2. What are the most important skills and/or qualities for someone in your profession?

Being of a safety and security mind-set is the most important quality. Conscientiousness and attention to detail are critical.

Projecting a professional image is also important. Yes, we're in the cockpit, but we're also in the public eye. You need to instill confidence in the traveling public and act as a mentor to other pilots.

3. What do you wish you had known going into this profession?

The industry has changed a lot since I began my career nearly a decade ago. At that time, I barely earned enough money to make ends meet. ALPA has helped to improve pilots' pay, benefits, and quality of life and provide a path for career progression.

4. Are there many job opportunities in your profession? In what specific areas?

Opportunity is growing. All the airlines are going through a major shift. There used to be 10,000 applications for 20 pilot spots. Now each of the major airlines is hiring hundreds of pilots a year. A lot of those pilots hired during the 1980s and 1990s are hitting the mandatory retirement age of 65 and need to be replaced. When major airlines are hiring, it's a trickle-down effect. Vacancies are created at regional airlines.

After 9/11, the industry became stagnant for 10 years as airlines closed and the opportunity for pilots dried up. It was called the lost decade. That's all been flipped on its head. Pilots are in demand.

Airlines have restructured and developed a better business model. Combined with economic growth, which means more flights, the pilot ecosystem looks healthier than ever. Globalization also is affecting air travel. Twenty-five years ago, flying from New York to Europe was mainly for the elite and business travelers. Now it's more affordable than ever and it's safer than ever.

5. How do you see your profession changing in the next five years? How will technology impact that change, and what skills will be required?

It takes hard work and a huge financial commitment to become an airline pilot. The work doesn't stop when you get your first set of wings. We go through continuous training to keep our skies the safest in the world.

The recruiting system, however, is rapidly changing for the better. Airlines have anticipated the need for more pilots and partnered with aviation colleges to create defined career pathways.

6. **What do you enjoy most about your job? What do you like least about your job?**

   I love flying airplanes. My favorite part of my job is showing up for work and taking 250 people overseas and traveling. To have a job where I can experience the world is a huge gain.

   Unscheduled changes are the least fun thing about my job. You have to be flexible enough to roll with that.

7. **Can you suggest a valuable "try this" for students considering a career in your profession?**

   If you're interested in the profession, you should seek out a mentor. Go to the Air Line Pilots Association "Cleared to Dream" website at https://clearedtodream.org to read "day in the life" stories about real pilots. The site explains the different kinds of pilot jobs. Flying cargo is much different from flying passengers. You can also visit the site to request that an airline pilot visit your school.

   Go to your local airport and go on what is called a discovery flight to see if you like flying.

   Take part in a "Girls in Aviation Day" event, typically held in September.

   I hope you love it as much as I do.

MORE INFORMATION

Aircraft Owners and Pilots Association (AOPA)
421 Aviation Way
Frederick, MD 21701
301.695.2000
www.aopa.org

Air Line Pilots Association, International (ALPA)
1625 Massachusetts Avenue, NW
Washington, DC 20036
703.689.2270
www.alpa.org

Federal Aviation Administration (FAA)
800 Independence Avenue, SW
Washington, DC 20591
866.835.5322
www.faa.gov

International Society of Women Airline Pilots (ISWAP)
723 S. Casino Center Boulevard
2nd Floor
Las Vegas, NV 89101-6716
www.iswap.org

Michael Auerbach/Editor

Automotive Technician

Snapshot

Career Cluster(s): Manufacturing, Transportation, Distribution & Logistics

Interests: Automobiles, customer service, solving problems, working with machinery

Earnings (Yearly Average): $37,937

Employment & Outlook: Average Growth Expected

OVERVIEW

Sphere of Work

Automotive technicians maintain and repair cars and light trucks, using computers and other diagnostic tools to troubleshoot problems and a wide variety of hand and power tools to replace parts and make adjustments. They must be able to work with traditional tools and machinery while also keeping up with rapidly evolving technology, both in automobiles and in the diagnostic tools used to maintain and repair them.

Work Environment

Automotive technicians work in a variety of facilities, from single-bay garages attached to gas stations to large service bays at automobile dealerships. Some national automotive maintenance and repair chains offer consistent work environments, which tend to have standardized safety protocols and processes for carrying out routine work. Other facilities specialize in repairing one component of automobiles, such as brakes, mufflers, or transmissions. Repair shops can be very noisy, and technicians are frequently exposed to potentially hazardous substances such as grease, oil, and other system fluids. Because of the hazards inherent in the work, technicians must often wear safety equipment such as earplugs, safety glasses, and steel-reinforced boots.

Profile

Interests: Data, People, Things
Working Conditions: Work Inside
Physical Strength: Medium Work
Education Needs: On-the-Job Training, High School Diploma with Technical Education, Junior/Technical/Community College, Apprenticeship
Licensure/Certification: Required
Physical Abilities Not Required: Not Climb
Opportunities for Experience: Apprenticeship, Military Service, Part-Time Work
Holland Interest Score: RCI, RES, RIE, RSE

* See Appendix A

Occupation Interest

Individuals drawn to the profession of automotive technician tend to be independent workers who enjoy solving problems and working with automobiles. As automotive technicians must at times interact with customers, particularly at smaller shops, they must be capable of providing excellent customer service and explaining mechanical concepts in a clear, understandable manner. Automotive technicians must be quick learners able to keep up with rapidly evolving technology, and they should enjoy the challenge of working with complex machinery.

A Day in the Life—Duties and Responsibilities

The daily duties of an automotive technician vary widely according to the type of shop in which he or she is employed. An automotive technician who works on only one automotive system may spend days performing routine tasks such as oil changes or brake work. Since the structure and components of an automotive system vary with the make, model, and age of the vehicle, however, a high degree of skill is still necessary to perform even routine maintenance and repair.

Automotive technicians with a wider range of responsibilities must master all aspects of automobile repair and maintenance and engage in a much greater variety of activities. Typically, an automotive technician first assesses a vehicle in order to determine the source of the damage or malfunction, using traditional and technological diagnostic tools, and provides an estimate for repair to the customer. In some cases, the automotive technician may test-drive the vehicle to gain a better understanding of the problem.

Once the scope of the required repair is determined, the automotive technician will begin working on the vehicle. Automobile repair shops often use lifts or work pits to provide access to the undercarriage of vehicles, so automotive technicians must also manage these lift or jacking systems. They may employ a variety of gauges and testing equipment to determine compression, alignment, and pressure and may repair or replace parts depending on the extent of the damage. Automotive technicians may also complete routine inspections to test for common mechanical and safety issues. Once a repair is completed or routine maintenance work has been performed, the automotive technician will log the time and expense of the work. In many cases, he or she will interact directly with the customer to offer information about current and upcoming work.

Duties and Responsibilities

- **Examining vehicles and advising customers of their findings**
- **Planning work routines using charts and manuals**
- **Raising vehicles using a hydraulic jack or hoist**
- **Removing units such as engines and transmissions**
- **Rewiring ignition systems, lights, and instrument panels**
- **Relining and adjusting brakes**
- **Aligning front ends**

OCCUPATION SPECIALTIES

Air Conditioning Technicians

Air Conditioning Technicians install, repair, and service air conditioners in automobiles.

Auto Retrofitters

Auto Retrofitters make changes to existing vehicles to upgrade them to new environmental standards.

Brake Repairer Technicians

Brake Repairer Technicians repair automotive brake systems. They replace brake pads and linings, repair hydraulic cylinders, and turn discs and drums.

Front-End Technicians

Front-End Technicians repair steering mechanisms, suspension systems, and align and balance wheels.

Radiator Technicians

Radiator Technicians locate and repair radiator leaks and clean and install radiator systems.

Tune-Up Technicians

Tune-Up Technicians ensure efficient automotive engine performance using various testing machines to check overall performance capabilities.

WORK ENVIRONMENT

Transferable Skills and Abilities

Research & Planning Skills
- Analyzing information
- Identifying problems

Technical Skills
- Working with machines, tools, or other objects
- Working with your hands

Unclassified Skills
- Being physically active

Immediate Physical Environment

Automotive technicians work in a range of environments—from large repair facilities and dealerships with state-of-the-art equipment—to small garages. Service technicians stand for most of the day, and they typically work in well-ventilated and well-lit repair shops. Although technicians often identify and fix automotive problems with computers, they commonly work with greasy parts and tools, sometimes in uncomfortable positions.

These environments present a number of hazards, including significant noise and fumes from industrial fluids, so technicians must follow safety procedures at all times. All automotive technicians must also be able to lift and maneuver heavy parts and have excellent visual and manual acuity.

Human Environment

Automotive technicians often work alongside other technicians, but they may have limited opportunities for interaction while work is being performed. Periodic contact may be made with others to ask for advice or direction. Some automotive technicians have extensive contact with the public, so customer service and communication skills are needed.

Technological Environment

Automotive technicians work with a variety of testing and diagnostic equipment and should be familiar with project-management software. As automobile technology continues to develop, automotive technicians must keep abreast of the rapid advances in the field.

EDUCATION, TRAINING, AND ADVANCEMENT

High School/Secondary

Students interested in the field of automobile repair should take courses in mathematics and mechanics. Electronics or metal-shop classes, if offered, may also be beneficial. Many technical and vocational high schools offer courses in automobile repair, and students can gain additional experience through part-time work and personal automotive projects.

Suggested High School Subjects
- Applied Math
- Auto Collision Technology
- Auto Service Technology
- Blueprint Reading
- Electricity & Electronics
- English
- Machining Technology
- Metals Technology
- Shop Math
- Shop Mechanics
- Trade/Industrial Education
- Welding

Related Career Pathways/Majors

Manufacturing Cluster
- Maintenance, Installation & Repair Pathway

Transportation, Distribution & Logistics Cluster
- Facility & Mobile Equipment Maintenance Pathway

Famous First

The first windshield wiper was the invention of Mary Anderson of Birmingham, AL, who received a patent on November 10, 1903. Her device consisted of a rubber blade attached to a down-swinging arm that was manually operated from inside the vehicle.

Source: "Transportation." *Famous First Facts*, Salem, 2016. *Salem Online*, https://online.salempress.com

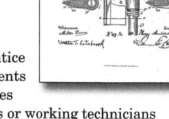

Postsecondary

Although postsecondary study is typically not required, some community and technical colleges offer courses in automobile technology as well as apprentice or work-study programs that allow students to gain hands-on experience. Such courses may be beneficial to aspiring technicians or working technicians seeking to gain additional skills.

Related College Majors:
- Auto/Automotive Mechanics.

Adult Job Seekers

Some experience in repairing automobiles or other machinery is typically required for those seeking to transition to the field of automobile repair, and adult job seekers hoping to advance to higher positions in the field may benefit from obtaining certification while on the job. Job seekers may obtain training in automobile repair through technical or vocational programs, military service, and in-house training programs and apprenticeships.

Professional Certification and Licensure

Though not required by law, certification is required by many employers. The National Institute for Automotive Service Excellence (ASE) is the primary certification body in the industry, certifying automotive technicians in such areas as collision repair, diesel engine diagnosis, and school bus repair. Each certification requires both a written test and work experience.

Additional Requirements

Automotive technicians often work 40 or more hours per week. Strength and stamina are crucial, as is a strong interest in mechanics and automobiles. Customer-service skills and attention to detail are also very important

Fast Fact

With automated cars on the horizon and companies like Uber and Lyft taking over for taxis, "disruption" is the word experts use to describe shifting transportation modes. It's happened before: New York City went from all horses to cars in only 13 years, between 1900–1913.

Source: sageautomation.com

EARNINGS AND ADVANCEMENT

Automotive technicians in repair shops are often paid a percentage of the labor charges for repairs they make. Skilled automotive technicians usually earn between two and three times as much as inexperienced apprentices who are paid an hourly rate until they are skilled enough to work on commission.

The median annual pay for automotive service technicians and mechanics was $40,710 in May 2018. The lowest 10 percent earned less than $23,420, and the highest 10 percent earned more than $66,950. Employers usually guarantee automotive technicians a minimum weekly salary.

Automotive technicians may receive paid vacations, holidays, and sick days; life and health insurance; and retirement benefits. These are usually paid by the employer. Some employers may provide uniforms and premium pay for overtime.

Median annual wages, May 2018

Vehicle and mobile equipment mechanics, installers, and repairers: $43,320

Automotive service technicians and mechanics: $40,710

Total, all occupations: $38,640

Note: All Occupations includes all occupations in the U.S. Economy.
Source: U.S. Bureau of Labor Statistics, Occupational Employment Statistics

EMPLOYMENT AND OUTLOOK

Automotive service technicians and mechanics held about 749,900 jobs in 2016. Employment of automotive service technicians and mechanics is projected to grow 6 percent from 2016 to 2026, about as fast as the average for all occupations. The largest employers of automotive service technicians and mechanics were as follows:

Automobile dealers	31%
Automotive mechanical and electrical repair and maintenance	27%
Self-employed workers	13%
Automotive parts, accessories, and tire stores	9%

The number of vehicles in use is expected to continue to rise. More entry-level service technicians will be needed to perform basic maintenance and repair, such as replacing brake pads and changing oil, on these vehicles. New technologies, however, such as electric vehicles, may limit future demand for automotive service technicians and mechanics because these vehicles will be more reliable and thus require less frequent maintenance and repair.

Job opportunities for qualified applicants should be very good, whether they obtained their knowledge through education or experience.

Many job openings will be in automobile dealerships and independent repair shops, where most service technicians currently work.

Percent change in employment, Projected 2016–26

Total, all occupations: 7%

Vehicle and mobile equipment mechanics, installers, and repairers: 7%

Automotive service technicians and mechanics: 6%

Note: All Occupations includes all occupations in the U.S. Economy.
Source: U.S. Bureau of Labor Statistics, Occupational Employment Statistics

Related Occupations
- Aircraft Mechanic
- Automotive Body Repairer
- Automotive Service Advisor
- Automotive Service Attendant
- Diesel Service Technician
- Farm Equipment Mechanic
- Heavy Equipment Service Technician
- Small Engine Mechanic

Related Military Occupations
- Automotive & Heavy Equipment Mechanic
- Heating & Cooling Mechanic

Conversation With... BOGI LATEINER

Auto Repair Shop Owner
180 Automotive Degrees, Phoenix, AZ
Auto Mechanic/Technician, 14 years

1. **What was your individual career path in terms of education/training, entry-level job, or other significant opportunity?**

   My path was a bit crooked. I had taken auto shop in high school in New Jersey, which was a tiny underfunded program. I was interested in auto shop specifically because I had a VW bug that I rebuilt from the ground up. I hated the way mechanics treated me as a woman.

   I went to Oberlin College in Ohio and studied pre-law and women's studies. When I graduated, I realized I didn't want to go into law.

   I moved to Arizona and enrolled in the Universal Technical Institute for automotive technology. From there, I had a very hard time getting a job. It's incredibly difficult to get that first job when you're young and inexperienced and female. Finally I got a job at an independent BMW shop. That introduced me to BMW and I did continuing education with them. Most of the manufacturers have dealership-level training and if you do that, you're pretty much guaranteed a job. I wanted to be taken seriously and to say I was a master BMW technician.

   Eventually, I got tired of dealership life. It just wasn't that satisfying. I was missing the bigger impact stuff. In academia, you're very much in your head. In college, I was a rape crisis counselor and domestic abuse counselor. That job is never done, whereas auto repair is tangible. A car is broken and you fix it. I liked that, but realized I was missing that other part. I decided to open my own shop. I have a five-bay shop with seven employees.

   Our entry-level job is pretty much reserved for a recent female graduate. I'm also on the show *All Girls Garage* on the Velocity channel. It's a lot of fun. I do customer service coaching and consulting through the Cecil Bullard Institute for Automotive Business Excellence and through WorldPac, a wholesale distributor of automotive equipment.

2. What are the most important skills and/or qualities for someone in your profession?

I think it's problem solving, the ability to follow processes and yet also think outside the box. For women in the industry, you have to have tenacity. It's still very much a man's world.

3. What do you wish you had known going into this profession?

I wish I had known how much personal investment you put into your tools. The average technician probably has a minimum of $50,000 worth of tools. I also wish I had less of a liberal arts background and more of a business background. You go into business for yourself because you love what you're doing, but once you do, you're not figuring out cars anymore or baking pies or whatever the case may be. You're building a business, and that looks very different.

4. Are there many job opportunities in your profession? In what specific areas?

Oh yes. There's a serious, serious lack of qualified automotive technicians. Once you get that first job and gain experience and show that you have good ethics and good skills, you will have no problem finding a job.

5. How do you see your profession changing in the next five years? What role will technology play in those changes, and what skills will be required?

Technology will continue to progress at a startling rate, affecting everything from a car's sound systems to its global position system (GPS). There will be automated parking and cars that drive themselves; and hybrid cars and cars that activate the brakes for you. It used to be that you learned to be a mechanic and you were done. More and more, automotive techs have to make a commitment to continuing education. There's a perception that smart kids go to college and dumb kids go to wood shop or the automotive track. That needs to shift. This is a highly skilled trade that requires a lot of intelligence and deserves respect.

6. What do you enjoy most about your job? What do you enjoy least about your job?

The thing I enjoy most is when you find that solution to a problem that was a mystery and you see the car leaving and you say, "I did that. I solved the unsolvable." I love helping customers understand their vehicle and take better care of it.

What I like least sometimes are the hours. And it's hard work. You're bending over, you're using your body. It can be physically exhausting. And there are the customers who don't trust you, who want to bring in their own parts, who buy into the stereotypes about mechanics.

7. Can you suggest a valuable "try this" for students considering a career in your profession?

Take a basic automotive class in your high school if you're still at the high school level. Going to trade school is great; getting an apprenticeship is great. Be willing to start at the bottom. You might work in a shop cleaning windows and filling coolant levels. Don't be afraid to tinker with your own car, play around and see how things work.

Note: This interview first appeared in *Careers in Technical Services & Repair* © 2015.

MORE INFORMATION

Automotive Aftermarket Industry Association (AAIA)
7101 Wisconsin Avenue, Suite 1300
Bethesda, MD 20814-3415
301.654.6664
aaia@aftermarket.org
www.aftermarket.org

Automotive Service Association (ASA)
8190 Precinct Line Road, Suite 100
Colleyville, TX 76034
800.272.7467
www.asashop.org

Automotive Youth Education Services (AYES)
101 Blue Seal Drive SE, Suite 101
Leesburg, VA 20175
703.669.6677
www.ayes.org

National Automotive Technicians Education Foundation (NATEF)
101 Blue Seal Drive, SE, Suite 101
Leesburg, VA 20175
703.669.6650
webmaster@natef.org
www.natef.org

National Institute for Automotive Service Excellence (ASE)
101 Blue Seal Drive, SE, Suite 101
Leesburg, VA 20175
703.669.6600
asehelp@ase.com
www.ase.com

Bethany Groff/Editor

Bus Drivers

Snapshot

Career Cluster(s): Hospitality & Tourism, Transportation, Distribution & Logistics
Interests: Driving, interacting with people, transportation
Earnings (Median Pay): $33,450
Employment & Outlook: Average Growth Expected

OVERVIEW

Sphere of Work

Bus drivers transport people between various places—including, work, school, and shopping centers—and across state and national borders. Some drive regular routes, and others transport passengers on chartered trips or sightseeing tours. They drive a range of vehicles, from 15-passenger buses to 60-foot articulated buses (with two connected sections) that can carry more than 100 passengers. Two major categorical designations exist among bus drivers: transit and intercity bus drivers, who transport passengers within a particular metropolitan area, between different cities or regions, or on chartered trips to specific destinations; and school bus drivers, who transport students to

and from school and school-related activities. Bus drivers usually follow precise time schedules and mapped routes. They are always responsible for transporting passengers to their destinations safely and on time.

Work Environment

Bus drivers spend the majority of their day seated behind the wheel and may be subject to long driving hours. They work in all weather conditions and often experience heavy traffic, unruly passengers, and unexpected delays and obstacles. School bus drivers work only during the school year and normally work split shifts—that is, in the morning and the afternoon, with time off in between—sometimes for less than 20 hours a week, though they may also transport students to school-related activities on evenings and weekends. Transit bus drivers generally work a 40-hour week throughout the year, including nights and weekends, and also often work split shifts. Intercity bus drivers may have more irregular schedules, and those who drive for larger companies usually average less than 40 hours per week. Most bus drivers work independently, without direct supervision.

Profile

Interests: Data, People
Things: Working Conditions, Work Inside
Physical Strength: Medium Work
Education Needs: No High School Diploma, On-the-Job Training
Licensure/Certification: Required
Physical Abilities Not Required: Not Climb, Not Kneel
Opportunities for Experience: Military Service, Part-Time Work
Holland Interest Score: RES

* See Appendix A

Occupation Interest

Individuals interested in becoming bus drivers should understand the rules of the road as well as the fundamentals of traffic rules and regulations. Bus drivers must always be pleasant, calm, and stoic, especially when dealing with unruly or volatile passengers. They should be organized, skilled at communicating and interacting with others, and able to juggle multiple tasks and shifting priorities. School bus drivers should find fulfillment in working with children and possess the patience necessary to adequately supervise them.

A Day in the Life—Duties and Responsibilities

Local transit and intercity bus drivers communicate with customers, collect tickets and cash fares, and answer questions regarding routes and schedules. They also help passengers needing special assistance, carry baggage, and make sure that passengers are properly seated. Occasionally, drivers handle onboard emergencies, fights, and other disruptions. Transit bus drivers usually travel the same route within one metropolitan area daily, making frequent stops throughout the day to pick up and drop off passengers, while intercity bus drivers may make very few stops along their route. Depending on the company they work for, transit and intercity bus drivers may be required to inspect their vehicles for any maintenance problems or equipment failures and check fuel, oil, and other fluid levels before departing from any location. In some cases, bus drivers must also handle minor repairs. Most drivers use logbooks to record trip information, report delays, and note any problems or difficulties that may have occurred.

School bus drivers follow a regular daily route, transporting students to and from school, to sporting events and field trips, and to other school-related activities. They follow strict safety and traffic regulations and do their best to ensure that students have a safe ride. They also prepare reports regarding passengers, fuel consumption, hours worked, and mileage. In addition to driving, school bus drivers must monitor students' behavior, maintain order, and address any emergency situations that arise. To that end, they should be familiar with first aid procedures.

Duties and Responsibilities

- **Complying with local traffic regulations**
- **Inspecting bus and checking gas, oil, tires, and water before departure**
- **Collecting and recording tickets or cash fares**
- **Loading and unloading baggage or express**
- **Regulating heating, lighting, and ventilating systems for passenger comfort**
- **Reporting delays or accidents**

The following are examples of types of bus drivers:

School bus drivers transport students to and from school and other activities. On school days, drivers pick up students in the morning and return them home in the afternoon. They also drive students to field trips, sporting events, and other activities. Between morning and afternoon trips, some drivers work at schools in other occupations, such as janitors, cafeteria workers, or mechanics. School bus drivers typically do the following:

- Ensure the safety of children getting on and off the bus
- Attend to the needs of children with disabilities
- Keep order and safety on the school bus
- Understand and enforce the school system's rules of conduct
- Report disciplinary problems to the school district or parents

Local transit bus drivers follow a daily schedule while transporting people on regular routes along city or suburban streets. They stop frequently, often every few blocks and when a passenger requests a stop. Local transit drivers typically do the following:

- Collect bus fares or manage fare box transactions
- Answer questions about schedules, routes, and transfer points
- Report accidents and other traffic disruptions to a central dispatcher

Intercity bus drivers transport passengers between cities or towns, sometimes crossing state lines. They usually pick up and drop off passengers at bus stations or curbside locations in downtown urban areas. Intercity drivers typically do the following:

- Ensure that all passengers have a valid ticket to ride the bus
- Sell tickets to passengers when there are unsold seats available, if necessary
- Keep track of when passengers get on or off the bus
- Help passengers load and unload baggage

Charter bus drivers, sometimes called motorcoach drivers, transport passengers on chartered trips or sightseeing tours. Trip planners generally arrange their schedules and routes based on the convenience of the passengers, who are often on vacation. Motorcoach drivers are sometimes away for long periods because they usually stay with the passengers for the length of the trip. Motorcoach drivers typically do the following:

- Regulate heating, air-conditioning, and lighting, for passenger comfort
- Ensure that the trip stays on schedule
- Help passengers load and unload baggage
- Account for all passengers before leaving a location
- Act as tour guides for passengers, if necessary

OCCUPATION SPECIALTIES

School Bus Drivers

School Bus Drivers transport students between pick-up points and school. They may drive a bus on special trips.

Motor-Coach Drivers

Motor-Coach Drivers drive diesel or electric powered transit buses to transport passengers over established city routes according to a set schedule.

Mobile-Lounge Drivers

Mobile-Lounge Drivers drive mobile lounges to transport aircraft passengers between airport terminal buildings and aircraft on the runways.

Day Haul or Farm Charter Bus Drivers

Day Haul or Farm Charter Bus Drivers drive buses to transport workers between a recruiting point and an agricultural work area. They find out from the employer the work to be done, the number of required workers and the field or area where the workers are required.

WORK ENVIRONMENT

Transferable Skills and Abilities

Communication Skills
- Speaking effectively
- Writing concisely

nterpersonal/Social Skills
- Being able to remain calm
- Cooperating with others
- Working as a member of a team

Organization & Management Skills
- Paying attention to and handling details
- Performing routine work

Work Environment Skills
- Driving a vehicle

Immediate Physical Environment

Bus drivers spend most of their time in their vehicles, which they must keep clean and well maintained for passengers. Drivers are also responsible for regulating the temperature levels and other environmental conditions inside the bus.

School bus drivers work only when school is in session. Some make multiple runs if schools in their district open and close at different times. Others make only two runs, one in the morning and one in the afternoon, so their work hours are limited.

Transit drivers may work weekends, late nights, and 3early mornings.

Motorcoach drivers travel with their passengers. The trip schedule dictates a driver's hours. Motorcoach drivers may work all hours of the day, as well as weekends and holidays. Intercity bus drivers can spend some nights away from home because of long-distance routes. Other intercity bus drivers make a round trip and go home at the end of each shift.

The Federal Motor Carrier Safety Administration (FMCSA) designates the hours-of-service regulations that all interstate bus drivers must follow. Bus drivers are allowed 10 hours of driving time and 15 hours of total on-duty time before they must rest for eight consecutive hours. Weekly maximum restrictions also apply, but can vary with the type of schedule that employers utilize.

Human Environment

Bus drivers interact with numerous individuals on a daily basis. They communicate with passengers of all ages and ethnicities, and often assist disabled or impaired individuals. Bus drivers do not normally work with other drivers, but may coordinate with them via phone or radio throughout the day. Though they work independently, bus drivers occasionally meet with supervisors to deal with administrative, training, or scheduling issues.

Technological Environment

Bus drivers must be familiar with a wide range of tools in order to operate their vehicles properly. They commonly utilize physical and electronic maps, two-way radios, and public address systems, and in some cases may also need to use first aid kits, emergency flares, fire extinguishers, tire pressure gauges, grease guns, snow chains, or wheelchair lifts and restraint systems.

EDUCATION, TRAINING, AND ADVANCEMENT

High School/Secondary

A high school diploma or its equivalent is sometimes required, though not always. High school students who are interested in becoming bus drivers will benefit from classes in communications, mathematics, and health, as well as courses that deal with automotive theories, business, and mechanics. When they reach the age of 16, students should obtain a driver's license and practice navigating local streets and following local bus routes. They should also travel locally by bus, paying close attention to the duties of the driver.

Suggested High School Subjects
- Auto Service Technology
- Child Care
- Diesel Maintenance Technology
- Driver Training
- English

- First Aid Training
- Mathematics

Related Career Pathways/Majors

Hospitality & Tourism Cluster
- Travel & Tourism Pathway

Transportation, Distribution & Logistics Cluster
- Transportation Operations Pathway

Famous First

The first trolley bus in a major American city began operation in Philadelphia in 1923. A trolleybus, also called a trackless trolley, is a bus powered by electricity from overhead wires, thus providing the advantages of an electric trolley system (silence, lack of emissions) without requiring that tracks be laid. Trolleybuses are still used in Philadelphia today, where they are operated by the Southeastern Pennsylvania Transportation Authority.

Source: "Transportation." *Famous First Facts*, Salem, 2016. *Salem Online*, https://online.salempress.com

Postsecondary

Bus drivers must have a commercial driver's license (CDL). This can sometimes be earned during on-the-job training. Bus drivers must have a driver's license and a clean driving record. Some employers require new bus drivers to pass a written test to demonstrate their understanding of complex bus schedules.

Most companies provide new drivers with two to eight weeks of instruction and training. Classroom instruction covers topics such as Department of Transportation rules, state and municipal driving regulations, schedule analysis, and record keeping; behind the wheel, drivers practice various maneuvers on set courses, in light traffic, and on crowded highways. After a period of time, they make mock trips along specified routes, without passengers, to simulate real driving. New bus drivers usually get help from an experienced driver who accompanies them along their routes, answering questions, giving advice, and noting their progress.

Related College Majors:
- Truck, Bus & Other Commercial Vehicle Operation.

Adult Job Seekers

Prospective bus drivers should contact local public and private schools, churches, or intercity and charter companies directly to inquire about openings. Bus driver unions and transportation authorities may also provide information about available jobs. Many new drivers start out by accepting part-time work and less desirable shifts and eventually work their way up to full-time employment.

Professional Certification and Licensure

Bus drivers are required to have a commercial driver's license (CDL) and can get endorsements for a CDL that reflect their ability to drive a special type of vehicle. All bus drivers must have a passenger (P) endorsement, and school bus drivers must also have a school bus (S) endorsement. Getting the P and S endorsements requires additional knowledge and driving tests administered by a certified examiner. CDL requirements vary by state, but normally include both knowledge and skills tests.

Bus drivers can contact the Federal Motor Carrier Safety Administration for more information on CDLs and endorsements.

Additional Requirements

Although some states allow bus drivers as young as 18 to operate within their borders, federal regulations require interstate drivers to be at least 21 years old, and many companies prefer their drivers be at least 24. Interstate bus drivers must also pass a physical examination every two years. Bus drivers should have good hearing and vision, normal blood pressure, and the ability to read and speak English. They must have no record of substance abuse and may be required to undergo periodic drug testing. Drivers may not be hired if ever convicted of a felony involving a motor vehicle or any such related crime. Some states require school bus drivers to pass a criminal and mental health background check.

Fast Fact

American school buses are yellow because you see yellow faster than any other color, 1.24 times faster than red in fact.

Source: https://encyclopaediaoftrivia.blogspot.com

EARNINGS AND ADVANCEMENT

Bus drivers are generally guaranteed a minimum number of miles or hours per pay period. Long distance bus drivers are usually paid on a mileage basis with the time required for the trip and the seniority of the driver as factors. Hourly wages for local transit bus drivers are usually highest in the larger cities. School bus drivers' wages vary with the individual driver's experience and the specific school system.

The median annual earnings of transit and intercity bus drivers were $42,080 in May 2018. The lowest 10 percent earned less than $25,550, and the highest 10 percent earned more than $69,070.

Median annual earnings of school bus drivers was $32,420 in May 2018. The lowest 10 percent earned less than $19,000, and the highest 10 percent earned more than $49,430:

Median annual wages, May 2018

Bus drivers, transit and intercity: $42,080

Total, all occupations: $38,640

Motor vehicle operators: $37,130

Bus drivers: $34,450

Bus drivers, school or special client: $32,420

Note: All Occupations includes all occupations in the U.S. Economy.
Source: U.S. Bureau of Labor Statistics, Occupational Employment Statistics

Bus drivers may receive paid vacations, holidays, and sick days; life and health insurance; and retirement benefits. These are usually paid by the employer. Some employers also provide uniforms.

EMPLOYMENT AND OUTLOOK

There were approximately 507,900 school or special client bus drivers employed nationally in 2016. Many of these positions were part time. About 40 percent worked for local school systems and 30 percent for companies that provide school bus services under contract.

Transit and intercity bus drivers held about 179,300 jobs in 2016. The largest employers of transit and intercity bus drivers is local governments (46 percent), following by urban transit systems (17 percent), charter bus companies (9 percent), and rural bus transportation (7 percent).

Growth will largely result from an increase in the number of school-age children. However, growth will most likely occur for contracting services that provide school bus transport as more school districts outsource their transportation needs. In addition, the demand for special-needs transportation will continue to increase because of the aging population.

Employment of transit and intercity drivers (including charter bus drivers) is projected to grow 9 percent from 2016 to 2026, about as fast as the average for all occupations. Some new Bus Rapid Transit (BRT) systems are opening throughout the country, which should create some employment opportunities. In addition, intercity bus travel that picks up passengers from curbside locations in urban downtowns should continue to grow. This form of travel is expected to remain popular due to the cheap fares and passenger conveniences, such as Wi-Fi.

Job opportunities for school bus drivers should be excellent as many drivers are expected to leave the occupation. Those willing to work part time or irregular shifts should have the best prospects.

Prospects for motorcoach and intercity drivers should also be very good as the industry struggles to attract and retain qualified drivers.

Related Occupations
- Taxi Driver & Chauffeur
- Truck Driver

Related Military Occupations
- Vehicle Driver
- Related Military Occupations
- Vehicle Driver

Conversation With...
ELI RANDOLPH

Streetcar/Transit Operator
Regional Transit Authority (RTA)
New Orleans, LA, Transit Operator, 10 years

1. What was your individual career path in terms of education/training, entry-level job, or other significant opportunity?

I used to drive 18-wheeler trucks. That's what got me into driving. But I've been interested in driving streetcars since I was a child. I used to ride the streetcar when I was in high school. That was my transportation back and forth.

I knew a few other operators at the RTA, and in 2003, I filled out an application and was called in for an interview. My first job for the RTA was driving buses. I was laid off in 2005 after Hurricane Katrina, but when the RTA was hiring again I got a job as a streetcar operator. My hire date was August 2009.

I went through two months of training. You start off with an instructor who teaches you how to start, stop, and switch. You learn to get the feel of the streetcar, which operates on 600 volts of electricity delivered by overhead cables. You learn to read traffic and expect the unexpected. The next step is the RTA sends you out with a platform instructor, under whose supervision you start picking up people and dealing with customers.

You must have a high school diploma to apply for a transit operator job. It helps to have some experience on commercial vehicles, but it's not necessary. I feel it's easier if you've driven something big in the past.

Transit operators must have a commercial driver's license and hold certifications in customer services and operating vehicles with air brakes.

2. What are the most important skills and/or qualities for someone in your profession?

You have to be a person that pays close attention and is able to multitask—someone who remains calm and doesn't panic. You have to be able to deal with the public. It's a job you get better at over the years. You learn how to read the tracks. You have to be very aware of your surroundings and watch out for cars driving onto the tracks. And you really have to be a good people person. That's an important part of the job.

3. What do you wish you had known going into this profession?

That it wasn't going to be easy. Once I got used to it, I liked it.

4. Are there many job opportunities in your profession? In what specific areas?

No, there are not many job opportunities in my profession. In New Orleans, it's unique and rare and there aren't that many positions available. There are only 66 streetcars and three 8-hour shifts per car. We have a limited number of streetcars and limited number of tracks. The opportunity for bus drivers is greater.

5. How do you see your profession changing in the next five years? How will technology impact that change and what skills will be required?

The profession will stay the same in the next five years. I would like to see more streetcar tracks and see the system expand. As far as technology, the Clever Device, a computer-aided dispatch/auto vehicle locator, changed the job somewhat. The device now calls out the stops for you. Out of habit, I still call them out too. I don't think there will be other technology changes. I operate the historic St. Charles Avenue Streetcar—the oldest continuously running streetcar in the world. It's 184 years old and still has wooden floors. It's part of history.

6. What do you enjoy most about your job? What do you like least about your job?

The people—that's what I enjoy most. I enjoy meeting people, helping the tourists get to where they need to go and suggesting good spots for them eat and listen to good music while they're in town. My run goes from Canal and Bourbon streets downtown through the Garden District out past the Audubon Zoo and Tulane University, all the way to uptown.

You also get a lot of residents using the streetcar every day for their local transportation back and forth to work, school kids on their way to school. The most exciting night was the time the Saints won the Super Bowl. It was like a party on every car.

I least like the inebriated folks at night. We have some characters that party a bit too much.

7. Can you suggest a valuable "try this" for students considering a career in your profession?

I would suggest students get permission to ride the streetcar alongside the driver. Let the driver explain all they see. They'll ask if you saw a car approaching and point out streetcar switches. There are still some manual switches that I have to get out and turn.

MORE INFORMATION

Amalgamated Transit Union (ATU)
5025 Wisconsin Avenue, NW
Washington, DC 20016
202.537.1645
www.atu.org

American Bus Association (ABA)
700 13th Street NW, Suite 575
Washington, DC 20005-5923
202.842.1645
abainfo@buses.org
www.buses.org

American Public Transportation Association (APTA)
1666 K Street NW, Suite 1100
Washington, DC 20006
202.496.4800
www.apta.com

Federal Motor Carrier Safety Administration (FMCSA)
1200 New Jersey Avenue, SE
Washington, DC 20590
800.832.5660
www.fmcsa.dot.gov

International Brotherhood of Teamsters (IBT)
25 Louisiana Avenue, NW
Washington, DC 20001
202.624.6800
www.teamster.org

National School Transportation Association (NSTA)
113 South West Street, 4th Floor
Alexandria, VA 22314
800.222.6782
info@yellowbuses.org
www.yellowbuses.org

United Motorcoach Association (UMA)
113 South West Street, 4th Floor
Alexandria, VA 22314
800.424.8262
www.uma.org

United Transportation Union (UTU)
24950 Country Club Boulevard
 Suite 340
North Olmsted, OH 44070-5333
216.228.9400
www.utu.org

Briana Nadeau/Editor

Cartographers and Photogrammetrists

Snapshot

Career Cluster(s): Agriculture, Food & Natural Resources, Architecture & Construction, Science, Technology, Engineering & Mathematics

Interests: Geography, maps and map-making, engineering, spatial data, demographics, mathematics

Earnings (Median Pay): $56,862

Employment & Outlook: Faster Than Average Growth Expected

OVERVIEW

Sphere of Work

Cartographers and photogrammetrists collect, measure, and interpret geographic information in order to create and update maps and charts for regional planning, education, and other purposes. Surveyors measure, record, and interpret features on and above the surface of the earth using specialized equipment. Cartographers are mapmakers: they use survey data, photographs, and satellite images to create digital or graphical maps and charts of geographical and demographic information. Government agencies, utility companies, architectural and

engineering firms, publishers, and other employers hire cartographers and photogrammetrists to provide information necessary to their business operations or sales. The work that cartographers and photogrammetrists produce leads to defining the earth's surface and position and to locating boundaries of countries, states, and properties.

Work Environment

Cartographers and photogrammetrists typically work 40 hours or more each week, both at the field sites and in the office. Cartographers tend to do more solitary, sedentary office work than fieldwork. Field measurements are often taken by groups working together to adjust and operate surveying equipment. Travel to remote field sites may be required. Fieldwork can be physically demanding, requiring long periods of standing, walking long distances, and climbing with heavy loads of survey instruments.

Profile

Interests: Data
Working Conditions: Work Outside, Work both Inside and Outside
Physical Strength: Medium Work
Education Needs: Bachelor's Degree
Licensure/Certification: Required
Physical Abilities Not Required: Not Climb, Not Kneel
Opportunities for Experience: Apprenticeship, Military Service Part-Time Work
Holland Interest Score: IER, IRE

* See Appendix A

Occupation Interest

Individuals interested in becoming cartographers and photogrammetrists are usually detail-oriented, fascinated by geography, and interested in maps and map-making. Prospective cartographers and photogrammetrists tend to be adept at understanding spatial information, demonstrate an ease with numbers and mathematical functions, and enjoy the outdoors. Cartographers and photogrammetrists have a great deal of responsibility as they provide critical geographical data for defense, first responders, and government agencies at all levels. They should be physically fit enough to meet the demands of fieldwork.

A Day in the Life—Duties and Responsibilities

Surveyors research land, air, and water features, primarily in the field but also in office settings. In the field, surveyors use a wide variety of tools to measure and record spatial information, such as latitude, longitude, elevation, position, and contour, among other physical characteristics. At the office, they analyze the collected data to write descriptions and reports and to create maps, charts, and other graphical representations. Since survey data is often used in legal documents and proceedings, surveyors or their work may occasionally be called upon in court. Surveyors may also research existing survey records, deeds, and boundaries to check their validity or gather information prior to conducting a new survey of an area. Experienced surveyors often focus on a single type of surveying, such as marine surveying or geodetic surveying, and supervise the work of technicians, apprentices, or assistants.

Cartographers typically do the following:

- Collect geographic data
- Create visual representations of data, such as annual precipitation patterns
- Examine and compile data from ground surveys, reports, aerial photographs, and satellite images
- Prepare maps in digital or graphic form for environmental and educational purposes
- Update and revise existing maps and charts

Photogrammetrists typically do the following:

- Plan aerial and satellite surveys to ensure complete coverage of the area in question
- Collect and analyze spatial data, such as elevation and distance
- Develop base maps that allow Geographic Information System (GIS) data to be layered on top

Cartographers are mapmakers who design user-friendly maps. Photogrammetrists are specialized mapmakers who use various technologies to build models of the Earth's surface and its features for the purpose of creating maps.

Cartographers and photogrammetrists use information from geodetic surveys (land surveys that account for the curvature of the Earth's surface) and remote-sensing systems, including aerial cameras and satellites. Some also use light-imaging detection and ranging (LIDAR) technology. LIDAR systems use lasers attached to planes or cars to digitally map the topography of the Earth. Because LIDAR is often more accurate than traditional surveying methods, it can also be used to collect other forms of data, such as the location and density of forests.

Cartographers and photogrammetrists often develop online and mobile maps. Interactive maps are popular, and cartographers and photogrammetrists collect data and design these maps for mobile phones and navigation systems.

Cartographers and photogrammetrists also create maps and perform aerial surveys for governments, to aid in urban and regional planning. Such maps may include information on population density and demographic characteristics. Some cartographers and photogrammetrists help build maps for government agencies for work involving national security and public safety. Accurate maps help emergency responders provide assistance as quickly as possible.

Cartographers and photogrammetrists who use GIS technology to create maps are often known as geographic information specialists. GIS technology is typically used to assemble, integrate, analyze, and present spatial information in a digital format. Maps created with GIS technology combine spatial graphic features with data. These maps are used to provide support for decisions involving environmental studies, geology, engineering, land-use planning, and business marketing.

OCCUPATION SPECIALTIES

Geodetic Surveyors

Geodetic Surveyors plan, direct, and conduct surveys of large areas of land such as states and counties.

Mine Surveyors

Mine Surveyors make surface and underground surveys for mine locations, tunnels, subways, and underground storage facilities.

Marine Surveyors

Marine Surveyors make surveys of harbors, rivers, and other bodies of water to determine shore lines, topography of bottom, or other features to determine navigable channels.

Land Surveyors

Land Surveyors establish official land and water boundaries; write descriptions of land for deeds, leases, and other legal documents; and measure construction and mineral sites.

Field-Map Editors

Field-Map Editors prepare maps using data provided by geodetic surveys, aerial photographs, and satellite data.

WORK ENVIRONMENT

Immediate Physical Environment

Although cartographers and photogrammetrists spend much of their time in offices, certain jobs require extensive fieldwork to collect data and verify results. For example, cartographers may travel to the physical locations they are mapping to better understand the topography of the region. Similarly, photogrammetrists may conduct fieldwork to plan for aerial surveys and to validate interpretations. Surveyors spend a great deal of time outdoors, in all types of weather conditions and across all kinds of terrain.

Human Environment

Surveyors must have strong communication skills as they often work in a team called a "survey party." Cartographers work with survey parties as well as independently. They may interact with survey technicians, assistants or apprentices, survey party chiefs, cartographic drafters, and supervisors.

Technological Environment

Cartographers and photogrammetrists use a vast range of equipment. They use global positioning system (GPS) instruments to locate various distance segments as well as total stations to measure and record angles and distances. Geographic information systems allow cartographers and photogrammetrists to collate, analyze, and store data in a digital platform. Light-imaging detection and ranging (LIDAR) helps them gather accurate spatial data, usually from aircraft. Cartographers also use CAD and imaging software, databases, film processors, copy cameras, and photographs.

EDUCATION, TRAINING, AND ADVANCEMENT

High School/Secondary

High school students interested in pursuing a career in surveying and cartography should prepare themselves by studying mathematics, technical drawing, computer science, and the sciences. Extracurricular activities that familiarize students with these subjects are also useful. While in high school, there may be opportunities to become an apprentice or assistant to a surveyor or cartographer to get work experience; however, postsecondary school training is usually required for surveyors and cartographers.

Suggested High School Subjects
- Algebra
- Applied Math
- Calculus
- College Preparatory
- English
- Geography
- Geometry
- Mechanical Drawing
- Physical Science
- Statistics
- Trigonometry

Related Career Pathways/Majors

Agriculture, Food & Natural Resources Cluster
- Environmental Service Systems Pathway
- Natural Resources Systems Pathway

Architecture & Construction Cluster
- Design/Pre-Construction Pathway

Science, Technology, Engineering & Mathematics Cluster
- Engineering & Technology Pathway
- Science & Mathematics Pathway

Famous First

The first radio navigation beacons were originally known as radio fog signals. The first successful radio beacons, which sent out signals by radio in all directions around the horizon, were established by the U.S. Lighthouse Service at three stations in the approaches to New York Harbor: the Ambrose Channel Lightship, the Fire Island Lightship, and the Sea Girt Lighthouse at Sea Girt, NJ. They were placed in regular operation on May 1, 1921. Tests of radio fog signal transmitting sets leading to the installation of these stations were begun in 1916–17 at Navesink Light Station, Atlantic Highlands, NJ, by the Lighthouse Service and the Bureau of Standards. The tests were interrupted when the United States entered World War I but were resumed in the fall of 1919 and lasted until September 1920.

Source: "Transportation." *Famous First Facts*, Salem, 2016. *Salem Online*, https://online.salempress.com

Postsecondary

To become a surveyor or cartographer, most states require a bachelor's degree cartography, geography, geomatics, or surveying. (Geomatics combines the science, engineering, math, and art of collecting and managing geographically referenced information.) Although it is not as common, some have a bachelor's degree in engineering, forestry, or computer science.

The growing use of GIS technology has resulted in cartographers and photogrammetrists requiring more courses in computer programming, engineering, math, GIS technology, surveying, and geography.

Cartographers must also be familiar with web-based mapping technologies, including newer modes of compiling data that incorporate the positioning capabilities of mobile phones and in-car navigation systems.

Photogrammetrists must be familiar with remote sensing, image processing, and LIDAR technology, and they must be knowledgeable about using the software that is necessary with these tools.

Many aspiring cartographers and photogrammetrists benefit from internships while in school.

Related College Majors:
- Geography
- Surveying

Adult Job Seekers

Adults seeking surveying and cartography jobs have generally earned a bachelor's degree. However, adults can join a survey crew or the armed forces and, with on-the-job training, work their way up. Many surveyors begin their careers as surveyor technicians or assistants. It may be useful to contact professional associations for networking, apprenticeships, continuing education opportunities, and licensing requirements.

Professional Certification and Licensure

Licensing requirements for cartographers and photogrammetrists vary by state. Some states require cartographers and photogrammetrists to be licensed as surveyors, and some states have specific licenses for photogrammetry and remote sensing. Although licensing requirements vary by state, candidates must meet educational requirements and pass a test.

Cartographers and photogrammetrists may also receive certification from the American Society for Photogrammetry and Remote Sensing (ASPRS). The United States Geospatial Intelligence Foundation offers certifications for GIS professionals. Candidates must meet experience and education requirements and must pass an exam. Although certifications are not required, they can demonstrate competence and may help candidates get a job.

All surveyors and some cartographers must obtain licensure from the National Council of Examiners for Engineering and Surveying (NCEES), which involves passing two written examinations taken four years apart. Between the two exams, candidates work under experienced surveyors. In addition, most states require surveyors to pass a state licensing board exam. Education prerequisites and continuing education requirements for renewal vary from state to state. The National Society of Professional Surveyors certifies surveyor technicians, which may be useful or necessary for promotions.

Additional Requirements

Visualization, accuracy, physical fitness and stamina, keen analytical abilities, and strong collaborative skills are essential qualities in surveyors and cartographers. Familiarity with computer technology and a college degree can provide a competitive edge in the field.

Fast Fact

North may be at the top of maps today, but that wasn't always the case. During the middle ages, most Western maps put east at the top instead. In Latin, the word for east is oriens, so to hold the map correctly, you had to "orient" it—that is, make sure East was on top. This is where we get the word "orientation" today.

Source: themaptoeverywhere.com

EARNINGS AND ADVANCEMENT

Earnings depend on the size and geographic location of the employer and the employee's education and experience. The median annual wage for cartographers and photogrammetrists was $64,430 in May 2018. The lowest 10 percent earned less than $40,960, and the highest 10 percent earned more than $101,400.

Cartographers and photogrammetrists may receive paid vacations, holidays, and sick days; life and health insurance; and retirement benefits. These are usually paid by the employer. Cartographers and photogrammetrists may also receive reimbursement for business-related travel expenses, but may be required to purchase their own uniforms and other work-related equipment.

Median annual wages, May 2018

Architects, surveyors, and cartographers: $73,210

Cartographers and photogrammetrists: $64,430

Total, all occupations: $38,640

Note: All Occupations includes all occupations in the U.S. Economy.
Source: U.S. Bureau of Labor Statistics, Occupational Employment Statistics

EMPLOYMENT AND OUTLOOK

There were approximately 12,600 cartographers and photogrammetrists employed nationally in 2016.

Employment of cartographers and photogrammetrists is projected to grow 19 percent from 2016 to 2026, much faster than the average for all occupations. However, because it is a small occupation, the fast growth will result in only about 2,400 new jobs over the 10-year period.

The management of forests, waterways, and other natural resources will continue to require constant updating of maps. Cartographers and photogrammetrists will be needed to operate GIS, which are increasingly being used to map and locate areas that are in need during natural disasters.

Consumer demand for accurate and reliable maps is expected to increase the need for more cartographers and photogrammetrists. The expanding use of maps for government planning should fuel employment growth. In addition, the growing number of mobile and web-based map products should result in new jobs for cartographers and photogrammetrists as they make the information usable by people who are not experts.

Federal, state, and local governments employed nearly one-half of all cartographers and photogrammetrists. Engineering and architectural firms employed about one-fourth of workers, while increasing demand for fast, accurate and complete geographic information will be the main source of growth for these occupations. Job openings will also result from the need to replace workers who transfer to other occupations or leave the labor force.

Percent change in employment, Projected 2016-26

Cartographers and photogrammetrists: 19%

Total, all occupations: 7%

Architects, surveyors, and cartographers: 7%

Note: All Occupations includes all occupations in the U.S. Economy.
Source: U.S. Bureau of Labor Statistics, Occupational Employment Statistics

Related Occupations
- Architect
- Civil Engineer
- Engineering Technician
- Geologist & Geophysicist
- Mathematician
- Mining & Geological Engineer

Related Military Occupations
- Surveying & Mapping Manager
- Surveying, Mapping & Drafting Technician

Conversation With...
CURT SUMNER, LS
Executive Director
National Society of Professional Surveyors,
Frederick, MD
Professional Surveyor, 35 years

1. What was your individual career path in terms of education/training, entry-level job, or other significant opportunity?

I began working as a survey technician for the Virginia Department of Transportation the day after I graduated from high school. I worked on projects such as the layout of I-77 where it passes through the mountains of Virginia into North Carolina, near where I grew up. I realized if I was going to do this for a living and be more than one of the guys on the crew, I'd have to get more education. I did that at community college and a university, although I didn't finish my bachelor's degree. I needed to work, and Virginia doesn't require a four-year degree for licensure—though some states do. I went to work for Anderson & Associates in Blacksburg, Virginia, and became a partner after I got my license.

In 1987, I decided to take a position near Washington, DC. At the same time, the Virginia Association of Surveyors chose me to represent them on the National Society of Professional Surveyors (NSPS) Board of Governors. I went on to chair its Board of Directors and to serve as President. In 1998, NSPS asked me to manage the national office for three months while they did an executive search. That three months has turned into a lot of years. I think what got me the job I have today is communication skills. I have been fortunate to meet surveyors all over the country and the world.

Although licensure as a professional surveyor is done on a state-by-state basis, and not all require a four-year degree, as far as I'm concerned, in today's environment an undergraduate degree is essential to prepare yourself for the technical and business aspects of the field.

2. What are the most important skills and/or qualities for someone in your profession?

You need good math and science skills, and for many jobs you must like being outside. But to be really successful, you must have a high level of interpersonal skills in order to communicate well and operate a business. I sometimes humorously say that professional surveyors must possess the skills of a detective, puzzle worker, and mind reader, due the job's equally important components of research, problem solving, and interaction with others. Surveyors interact with the public on a daily basis.

It's not a profession based on technology alone. It's based on evidence analysis, the history of a property, and how people have bought and used the land over time.

3. What do you wish you had known going into this profession?

This profession offers the opportunity to make a really good living. Most people think of surveyors as somebody who comes out and sets your property boundaries, but it can be much more than that. A surveyor is the only person involved in a project from beginning to end. At the beginning, they define boundaries. They go back and put down markers for construction of everything the project requires, down to the utilities. When it's finished, the surveyor returns and confirms it's been done the right way. This creates an opportunity to build relationships with an entire set of people: property owners, realtors, attorneys, contractors, and government officials.

4. Are there many job opportunities in your profession? In what specific areas?

One could perform boundary surveys in a small town or expand his/her business to incorporate every new technology that comes along related to measurement, spatial positioning, and data management. The average age of professional surveyors is approximately 58. The demand for surveyors is increasing, so job opportunities should remain high.

5. How do you see your profession changing in the next five years? What role will technology play in those changes, and what skills will be required?

Advancements will require both professional surveyors and surveying technicians to continually adapt to new technologies. Any new technology that has anything to do with data is going to impact surveying. The more rapidly, efficiently, and accurately you can gather and process data, the more effective you will be.

This is a job you'll be drawn to if you like technologies such as GPS, digital collection tools, drones, etc. You get many opportunities to play with really cool "toys."

6. Can you suggest a valuable "try this" for students considering a career in your profession?

Try pulling up a GIS map or parcel map from your local jurisdiction. Think about who provides the accurate positioning of the property lines, the alignment and grading instructions for roads, airport runways, walking trails, etc., and construction of shopping centers, houses, or office parks. You could try to find the historical documents for the property on which your house is located. It may have been owned at one time by someone famous or notorious!

MORE INFORMATION

American Society for Photogrammetry and Remote Sensing (ASPRS)
5410 Grosvenor Lane, Suite 210
Bethesda, MD 20814-2160
301.493.0290
asprs@asprs.org
www.asprs.org

National Council of Examiners for Engineering and Surveying (NCEES)
280 Seneca Creek Road
Seneca, SC 29678
800.250.3196
www.ncees.org

National Society of Professional Surveyors (NSPS)
6 Montgomery Village Avenue
Suite 403
Gaithersburg, MD 20879
240.632.9716
www.nspsmo.org

Susan Williams/Editor

Computer Programmers

Snapshot

Career Cluster(s): Architecture & Construction, Finance, Information Technology, Science, Technology, Engineering & Mathematics

Interests: Computer science, computer technology, solving problems, working alone, working with a team

Earnings (Median Pay): $75,663

Employment & Outlook: Average Growth Expected

OVERVIEW

Sphere of Work

Computer programmers write and test code that allows computer applications and software programs to function properly. They turn the program designs created by software developers and engineers into instructions that a computer can follow. In addition, programmers test newly created applications and programs to ensure that they produce the expected results. If they do not work correctly, computer programmers check the code for mistakes and fix them.

Computer programmers typically do the following:

- Write programs in a variety of computer languages, such as C++ and Java
- Update and expand existing programs
- Test programs for errors and fix the faulty lines of computer code
- Create and test code in an integrated development environment (IDE)
- Use code libraries, which are collections of independent lines of code, to simplify the writing

Programmers work closely with software developers, and in some businesses their duties overlap. When such overlap occurs, programmers can do work that is typical of developers, such as designing programs. Program design entails planning the software initially, creating models and flowcharts detailing how the code is to be written, writing and debugging code, and designing an application or systems interface.

A program's purpose determines the complexity of its computer code. For example, a weather application for a mobile device will require less programming than a social-networking application. Simpler programs can be written in less time. Complex programs, such as computer operating systems, can take a year or more to complete.

Work Environment

Computer programmers work in office environments and typically do most of their work at a desk in front of a computer terminal. Though many programmers work in company offices, some programmers may complete a portion of their work off-site and may work from home, depending on their access to appropriate equipment and networks. Many computer programmers work during regular business hours, though the nature of the work is such that programming may be completed at any time, and many programmers may choose to work irregular hours.

Though some computer programmers work independently, programmers often coordinate with other information technology (IT) professionals, including project managers, designers, and computer operators. Therefore, computer programmers benefit from skill in both customer service and interpersonal communication. Those who can work well as part of a team will have an advantage finding and maintaining employment in the field.

Computer programmers may work in a variety of organizations, from corporate offices to research facilities. Programmers who work as independent contractors may be hired by a variety of clients, from companies producing web content to film and production studios. Computer programming is at the forefront of technological development and has rapidly become an important facet of commerce, marketing, and communication for hundreds of modern industries.

Profile

Interests: Data
Working Conditions: Work Inside
Physical Strength: Light Work
Education Needs: Junior/Technical/Community College, Bachelor's Degree
Licensure/Certification: Recommended
Physical Abilities Not Required: Not Climb, Not Kneel, Not Hear and/or Talk
Opportunities for Experience: Internship, Military Service, Part-Time Work
Holland Interest Score: IRE

* See Appendix A

Occupation Interest

Those seeking a career in computer programming should be self-motivated and comfortable with tight schedules and deadlines. In addition, programmers must stay abreast of developments in the field and must be comfortable engaging in continuing education to stay informed about the latest evolutions in programming. Those seeking to work as independent contractors will also benefit from learning how to market their services to potential clients and must be motivated enough to pursue work and compete for projects.

A Day in the Life—Duties and Responsibilities

Most computer programmers spend their work hours in either home or work office environments and do most of their work at a desk in front of either a laptop or desktop computer terminal. While a specific project may have a strict deadline, programming work in general can be done at any time of day and can be broken up into numerous separate work periods.

During a typical day on the job, a programmer may write and test code for a certain application and may spend hours refining ongoing projects. In addition, programmers generally work alongside a number of other

IT professionals to complete certain projects. A certain amount of time must be dedicated to communicating with colleagues and customers. Part of a workday may also be spent in meetings with designers, project managers, or customers.

Computer programmers working in corporate environments may need to devote more of their time to working with members of a production team, while those working independently may be more able to organize their schedules according to personal preference. In addition, independent contractors must often spend time marketing their work and looking for new jobs. This process may involve sending out queries and applications as well as producing and maintaining a portfolio of work to show potential clients.

Duties and Responsibilities

- Studying problems and determining the steps necessary to solve them
- Documenting the steps involved to create the program
- Testing to make sure the instructions are correct and will produce the desired results
- Rewriting programs if desired results are not produced
- Modifying existing programs to meet new requirements
- Preparing an instruction sheet for use of the program

OCCUPATION SPECIALTIES

Engineering and Scientific Programmers

Engineering and Scientific Programmers write programs to solve engineering or scientific problems by applying a knowledge of advanced mathematics and an understanding of the computer.

WORK ENVIRONMENT

Immediate Physical Environment

Computer programmers tend to work in office environments, using a computer terminal to do their work. In large companies with multiple programmers, each programmer may occupy a cubicle, or they may work in shared or private offices, depending on the company. In many cases, programmers are able to complete work on variable schedules, and some may choose to work on certain projects outside of regular business hours. Independent contractors may work from home or from an independent office.

Transferable Skills and Abilities

Communication Skills
- Speaking effectively
- Writing concisely

Organization & Management Skills
- Following instructions
- Organizing information or materials
- Paying attention to and handling details
- Performing routine work

Research & Planning Skills
- Solving problems
- Using logical reasoning

Research & Planning Skills
- Solving problems
- Using logical reasoning

Human Environment

The human environment for a computer programmer can vary considerably according to the industry of employment and whether the individual works as an employee or an independent contractor. In corporate environments, programmers often work alongside designers, technicians, and project managers and function as part of an overall IT team that cooperates to complete projects. Independent contractors work alone most of the time and often work from home.

Whether working as an employee or an independent contractor, computer programmers benefit from strong interpersonal communication skills. Programmers often work to translate ideas produced by designers, project managers, and clients into functional programs. They benefit from strong communication skills and the ability to work with clients, customers, and colleagues.

Technological Environment

Computer programming is a rapidly developing field at the forefront of information technology, and programmers must be able to stay abreast of new developments. While the core languages used by programmers may change little from month to month, developers producing software and tools for programmers frequently introduce new products.

In addition, computer programmers must endeavor to remain at the forefront of hardware technology. Computer manufacturing companies frequently introduce new models and new components that provide advancements in speed and processing capability. Computer programmers also benefit from knowledge of computer maintenance and repair, which helps them to prevent hardware and equipment conflicts that can hinder their work.

EDUCATION, TRAINING, AND ADVANCEMENT

High School/Secondary

High school students can prepare for a career in computer programming by taking classes in basic computer science. Some high schools may offer more specific classes in subjects such as web navigation and design, graphic arts, and even basic programming. Students are advised to explore any computer classes offered in order to gain additional experience in basic computer literacy and operation.

Suggested High School Subjects
- Accounting
- Algebra
- Applied Communication
- Applied Math
- Bookkeeping
- Business & Computer Technology
- Business Data Processing
- Calculus
- College Preparatory

- Computer Programming
- Computer Science
- English
- Geometry
- Keyboarding
- Mathematics
- Statistics
- Trigonometry

Related Career Pathways/Majors

Architecture & Construction Cluster
- Design/Pre-Construction Pathway

Finance Cluster
- Banking & Related Services Pathway

Information Technology Cluster
- Programming & Software Development Pathway

Science, Technology, Engineering & Mathematics Cluster
- Science & Mathematics Pathway

Famous First

The first internet-based mapping was Xerox PARC Map Viewer, a static web-mapping site, developed in June 1993 by Steve Putz at Xerox Corporation's Palo Alto Research Center (PARC). Its initial purpose started as an experiment in providing interactive information retrieval, rather than access to only static files on the World Wide Web. Programmers used a customized CGI server module, that was written in Perl, to develop Map Viewer. Its images were generated in GIF format from a two-step process using two server side programs: The first, MAP-WRITER, was used to create the raster images from the geographic database. The second, RASTOGIF, converted the raster image into the GIF format. Xerox later discontinued the Map Viewer service.

Source: "Transportation." *Famous First Facts*, Salem, 2016. *Salem Online*, https://online.salempress.com

Postsecondary

Most colleges, universities, and technical schools now offer specialized degree and certificate programs in different areas of computer science. Many community colleges and four-year institutions offer classes in computer programming, which generally include one or more separate classes on each programming language.

Postsecondary students can pursue computer programming as a degree focus or as a secondary educational focus. In addition to undergraduate-level programs, several institutions offer graduate-level programs in computer programming for those holding degrees in computer science. Students pursuing degree or certification programs will typically complete assignments that can form the basis of their professional portfolios and can be shown to potential employers. Employers often evaluate potential employees based on the strength of their professional or personal portfolios.

Programmers who work in specific fields, such as transportation or logistics, may take classes in that field to supplement their degree in computer programming. In addition, employers value experience, which many students gain through internships.

Related College Majors:
- Computer Engineering
- Computer Maintenance Technology
- Computer Programming
- Computer Science
- Information Sciences & Systems
- Management Information Systems & Business Data Processing.

Adult Job Seekers

Adults seeking to enter the computer programming field are advised to seek out continuing education classes through a community college or technical school. Many institutions offer night and evening classes and online courses, which may or may not be part of a certification program. Adults can also audit classes at universities or community colleges to better assess whether computer programming is of interest as a career path.

Professional Certification and Licensure

Programmers can become certified in specific programming languages or for vendor-specific programming products. Some companies require their computer programmers to be certified in the products they use. Certification programs offer professional proof that a student has completed a certain number of hours working with a specific type of programming or programming language. Computer programmers should consult credible professional associations within the field and follow professional debate as to the relevance and value of any certification program.

Additional Requirements

Computer programmers must be highly self-motivated and detail oriented. Small errors in a program's code can lead to major problems in the final product, and programmers must therefore be capable of carefully checking and rechecking their work to ensure accuracy at every stage of the process.

Fast Fact

A driverless car first trekked cross-country in the spring of 2015, when Delphi Automotive's modified Audi Q4 SUV made it from San Francisco to New York in automated mode "99 percent of the drive." A human driver took over in particular circumstances, such as when police or construction blocked roads or caused serious congestion.

Source: nbcnews.com

EARNINGS AND ADVANCEMENT

The median annual wage for computer programmers was $84,280 in May 2018. The lowest 10 percent earned less than $48,790, and the highest 10 percent earned more than $134,630.

Median annual wages, May 2018

Computer occupations: $86,320

Computer programmers: $84,280

Total, all occupations: $38,640

Note: All Occupations includes all occupations in the U.S. Economy.
Source: U.S. Bureau of Labor Statistics, Occupational Employment Statistics

In May 2018, the median annual wages for computer programmers in the top industries in which they worked were as follows:

Software publishers	$103,530
Finance and insurance	$88,260
Computer systems design and related services	$83,230
Manufacturing	$82,710

Computer programmers may receive paid vacations, holidays, and sick days; life and health insurance; and retirement benefits. These are usually paid by the employer.

EMPLOYMENT AND OUTLOOK

Computer programmers held about 294,900 jobs in 2016. The largest employers of computer programmers were as follows:.

Computer systems design and related services	38%
Finance and insurance	7%
Software publishers	7%
Manufacturing	5%
Self-employed workers	5%

Employment of computer programmers is projected to decline 7 percent from 2016 to 2026. Computer programming can be done from anywhere in the world, so companies sometimes hire programmers in countries where wages are lower. This ongoing trend is projected to limit employment growth for computer programmers in the United States. However, the high costs associated with managing projects given to overseas programmers sometimes offsets the savings from the lower wages, causing some companies to bring back or keep programming jobs in the United States.

Job prospects will be best for programmers who have a bachelor's degree or higher and knowledge of a variety of programming languages. Keeping up to date with the newest programming tools will also improve job prospects.

Related Occupations
- Computer & Information Systems Manager
- Computer Engineer
- Computer Network Architect
- Computer Operator
- Computer Support Specialist
- Computer Systems Analyst
- Computer-Control Tool Programmer
- Database Administrator
- Information Security Analyst
- Mathematician

- Network & Computer Systems Administrator
- Operations Research Analyst
- Software Developer
- Web Administrator
- Web Developer

Related Military Occupations
- Computer Programmer
- Computer Systems Specialist

MORE INFORMATION

Association for Computing Machinery (ACM)
2 Penn Plaza, Suite 701
New York, NY 10121-0701
800.342.6626
acmhelp@acm.org
www.acm.org

Association of Information Technology Professionals (AITP)
401 N. Michigan Avenue, Suite 2400
Chicago, IL 60611-4267
800.224.9371
aitp_hq@aitp.org
www.aitp.org

IEEE Computer Society (IEEE)
2001 L Street NW, Suite 700
Washington, DC 20036-4928
202.371.0101
help@computer.org
www.computer.org

Institute for the Certification of Computer Professionals (ICCP)
2400 E. Devon Avenue, Suite 281
Des Plaines, IL 60018-4610
800.843.8227
office@iccp.org
www.iccp.org

National Association of Programmers (NAP)
P.O. Box 529
Prairieville, LA 70769
info@napusa.org
www.napusa.org

Micah Issitt/Editor

Computer Systems Analysts

Snapshot

Career Cluster(s): Business, Management & Administration, Finance, Information Technology, Science, Technology, Engineering & Mathematics

Interests: Computer science, solving problems, communicating with others

Earnings (Median Pay): $88,740

Employment & Outlook: As Fast as Average Growth Expected

OVERVIEW

Sphere of Work

Computer systems analysts, sometimes called systems architects, assist companies in improving their computer systems and processes by analyzing the technology currently in place and suggesting various improvements. They work with the information technology (IT) and business management departments so that both sides can collaborate more effectively and better understand one another's needs. Analysts put together detailed reports of the costs and the positive and negative aspects of a computer system so that management can decide what technologies and applications best suit the needs

of their business. Analysts also help design and secure new computer systems and train users.

Work Environment

Computer systems analysts work in a variety of different industries. They may be employed directly by the company they perform analysis for, or they may be contracted by various companies as consultants. Analysts who work as consultants may either be self-employed or work for an IT firm. Communications technologies such as video chat and web conferencing enable some analysts to work remotely, but the majority still travel to clients' locations to work. Office environments predominate.

Profile

Interests: Data, People
Working Conditions: Work Inside
Physical Strength: Light Work
Education Needs: Bachelor's Degree, Master's Degree
Licensure/Certification: Recommended
Physical Abilities Not Required: Not Climb, Not Kneel
Opportunities for Experience: Military Service, Part-Time Work
Holland Interest Score: IER

* See Appendix A

Occupation Interest

Computer systems analysis tends to attract individuals with a strong background in computer science. Analysts must possess excellent problem-solving skills in order to assess flaws and identify areas for improvement in a company's computer system. Communication is essential in order to understand the technological needs of the company and to instruct managers and other workers in how to best use the computer systems being implemented.

A Day in the Life—Duties and Responsibilities

Computer systems analysts spend the majority of their day working with computers. They also spend a great deal of time communicating with other IT employees and the managers of the company they are working for. Analysts use their education and skills to design computer systems, perform information engineering, and set up information systems that allow for greater efficiency and better communication. Analysts who work for a single company tend to specialize in the specific computer systems that company uses. For instance, if an analyst is employed by a financial company, then he or she will most likely specialize in financial computer systems. A contractor analyst is more likely to be experienced in a broad range of computer systems.

Depending on the issues computer systems analysts are called in to address, they may perform a wide variety of tasks. Typically, they begin by going over the existing computer system with IT workers and management. Analysts examine the needs of the company and the role that computer systems play in the business in order to determine the best possible system for the job. An analysis usually entails the preparation of a costs-and-benefits report that helps management decide whether they wish to implement a computer upgrade. Analysts also design and create new systems based on existing hardware and software and oversee the installation of these new systems.

Once the systems are installed, analysts typically run tests to make sure everything is running properly and the network is secure. Then they train employees and managers how to use the system through formal instruction and manuals as needed.

Computer systems analysts can work directly for an organization or as contractors, often working for an information technology firm. The projects that computer systems analysts work on usually require them to collaborate and coordinate with others.

Analysts who work on contracts in the computer systems design and related services industry may move from one project to the next as they complete work for clients.

Most systems analysts work full time. Some work more than 40 hours per week.

Duties and Responsibilities

- **Consulting with managers to determine the role of IT systems in an organization**
- **Researching emerging technologies to decide if installing them can increase the organization's efficiency and effectiveness**
- **Preparing an analysis of costs and benefits so that management can decide if IT systems and computing infrastructure upgrades are financially worthwhile**

Duties and Responsibilities

- Devising ways to add new functionality to existing computer systems
- Designing and implementing new systems by choosing and configuring hardware and software
- Overseeing the installation and configuration of new systems to customize them for the organization
- Conducting testing to ensure that the systems work as expected
- Training the systems' end users and writing instruction manuals

WORK ENVIRONMENT

Transferable Skills and Abilities

Communication Skills
- Speaking effectively
- Writing concisely

Organization & Management Skills
- Paying attention to and handling details
- Performing duties that change frequently

Research & Planning Skills
- Analyzing information
- Developing evaluation strategies
- Solving problems
- Using logical reasoning

Technical Skills
- Performing scientific, mathematical, and technical work
- Using technology to process information
- Working with machines, tools, or other objects

Immediate Physical Environment

Computer systems analysts spend a majority of their time in office environments. These environments vary from job to job. Travel to and from client locations is frequently required, so an analyst should expect to spend time in a car, plane, or other modes of transportation.

Human Environment

To accurately analyze a computer system, an analyst must collaborate closely with a company's IT department and management. He or she may also collaborate with other analysts if further help is needed with a computer system.

Technological Environment

Computer systems analysts work with a broad range of computer software and hardware. The software used varies depending on the type of computer system being analyzed; data-modeling systems are common. Sometimes analysts use communication technologies that allow them to telecommute.

EDUCATION, TRAINING, AND ADVANCEMENT

High School/Secondary

Computer systems analysts are usually required to have a high school diploma or an equivalent certificate. Useful high school courses include computer science, mathematics, and business-related classes. Any advanced computer-related courses will also be a great help.

Suggested High School Subjects
- Accounting
- Algebra
- Applied Communication
- Calculus
- Computer Programming
- Computer Science
- English
- Geometry
- Mathematics
- Statistics
- Trigonometry

Related Career Pathways/Majors

Business, Management & Administration Cluster
- Business Analysis Pathway

Business, Management & Administration Cluster
- Human Resources Pathway

Finance Cluster
- Banking & Related Services Pathway

Information Technology Cluster
- Information Support & Services Pathway

Information Technology Cluster
- Network Systems Pathway

Information Technology Cluster
- Programming & Software Development Pathway

Science, Technology, Engineering & Mathematics Cluster
- Engineering & Technology Pathway

Famous First

The first transatlantic flight by a robot airplane was done by the Skymaster, an Army C-54 four-engine military transport that took off from Stephensville, Newfoundland, Canada, on September 22, 1947, and arrived 10 hours and 15 minutes later at Brise Norton, England, near London, a distance of 2,400 miles. The robot piloting device was not touched after the throttles were opened to start the airplane. The plane carried 14 persons, including Colonel James Milligan Gillespie, the pilot and commander.

Source: "Transportation." *Famous First Facts*, Salem, 2016. *Salem Online*, https://online.salempress.com

Postsecondary

Employers typically require a computer systems analyst to have a bachelor's degree in a computer-related field. However, many analysts enter the field from a variety of different backgrounds, such as economics or business. Most companies prefer a systems analyst who holds a master's degree in information systems or computer science. An advanced degree is not commonly required for entry-level positions but is usually necessary for more advanced positions in the field.

Many technical schools offer computer-science training programs. These programs typically last six months to a year, and they provide students with both hands-on training and formal classroom instruction. These schools are a great place for students to network with others in the profession.

Because each company has special demands for their computer systems, analysts with specific educational backgrounds are needed. For example, an insurance company would need an analyst who has strong knowledge of the needs of that industry. Many analysts begin their careers working in an IT department and gain experience in computer-systems analysis over time.

Because computer technology is always changing, most analysts will continue their education throughout their career in order to stay competitive. An analyst who does not keep up with new and evolving technologies will find their methods quickly become obsolete.

Related College Majors:
- Computer Engineering
- Computer Engineering Technology
- Computer Maintenance Technology
- Computer Programming
- Computer Science
- Information Sciences & Systems

Adult Job Seekers

Computer systems analysis requires a deep knowledge of computer systems and their various applications, so interested individuals should be sure that they have the appropriate education and training. An individual with no experience in the field should enroll in a relevant program at a technical school or community college.

Professional Certification and Licensure

Although certification is not usually required by an employer, it is available from system manufacturers, schools, and professional certification organizations. Certificate programs in computer systems analysis are typically engineered for people who already have a strong knowledge of computer systems. Certification is offered for specific types of computer systems as well as for basic knowledge in a range of systems.

Certification is available in a variety of categories, including information systems development, information systems design, and business software development. These certificate programs usually cover fundamental strategies used by analysts.

Additional Requirements

Being a computer systems analyst means analyzing data from a variety of sources and then deciding the best way for a company to move forward. This requires strong analytical and problem-solving skills. An analyst also needs good communication and collaborative skills in order to work effectively with IT personnel and management.

Fast Fact

Space shuttles were not equipped with software that could handle a year change while in orbit so missions never took place between December and January.

Source: http://www.softschools.com

EARNINGS AND ADVANCEMENT

The median annual wage for computer systems analysts was $88,740 in May 2018. Computer systems analysts may increase their advancement opportunities by obtaining additional education. Earnings vary according to the geographic location of the employer, and the computer systems analyst's experience and education.

In May 2018, the median annual wages for computer systems analysts in the top industries in which they worked were as follows:

Computer systems design and related services	$91,520
Management of companies and enterprises	$91,220
Information	$90,740
Finance and insurance	$90,700
Government	$80,320

Median annual wages, May 2018

Computer systems analysts: $88,740

Computer occupations: $86,320

Total, all occupations: $38,640

Note: All Occupations includes all occupations in the U.S. Economy.
Source: U.S. Bureau of Labor Statistics, Occupational Employment Statistics

Computer systems analysts may receive paid vacations, holidays, and sick days; life and health insurance; and retirement benefits. These are usually paid by the employer.

EMPLOYMENT AND OUTLOOK

Computer systems analysts held about 600,500 jobs nationally in 2016. Although they are found in most industries, the greatest concentration of computer systems analysts is in the computer systems design and related services industry. A growing number are employed on a temporary or contract basis or as consultants.

The largest employers of computer systems analysts were as follows:

Computer systems design and related services	28%
Finance and insurance	13%
Management of companies and enterprises	9%
Information	8%
Government	6%

Employment of computer systems analysts is projected to grow 9 percent from 2016 to 2026, about as fast as the average for all occupations. This is a result of organizations continuing to adopt increasingly sophisticated technologies. The demand for "networking" to facilitate the sharing of information, the expansion of client/server environments, and the need for specialists to use their knowledge and skills in a problem-solving capacity will be major factors in the rising demand of computer systems analysts.

Percent change in employment, Projected 2016–26

Computer occupations: 13%

Computer systems analysts: 9%

Total, all occupations: 7%

Note: All Occupations includes all occupations in the U.S. Economy.
Source: U.S. Bureau of Labor Statistics, Occupational Employment Statistics

Related Occupations
- Computer & Information Systems Manager
- Computer Engineer
- Computer Network Architect
- Computer Programmer
- Computer Support Specialist
- Database Administrator
- Information Security Analyst
- Information Technology Project Manager
- Management Analyst & Consultant
- Mathematician
- Network & Computer Systems Administrator
- Operations Research Analyst
- Software Developer
- Web Administrator
- Web Developer

Related Military Occupations
- Computer Programmer
- Computer Systems Officer
- Computer Systems Specialist

MORE INFORMATION

Association for Computing Machinery (ACM)
2 Penn Plaza, Suite 701
New York, NY 10121-0701
800.342.6626
acmhelp@acm.org
www.acm.org

Association of Information Technology Professionals (AITP)
401 N. Michigan Avenue, Suite 2400
Chicago, IL 60611-4267
800.224.9371
aitp_hq@aitp.org
www.aitp.org

Computing Research Association (CRA)
1828 L Street NW, Suite 800
Washington, DC 20036
202.234.2111
info@cra.org
www.cra.org

Institute for the Certification of Computer Professionals (ICCP)
2400 E. Devon Avenue, Suite 281
Des Plaines, IL 60018-4610
800.843.8227
office@iccp.org
www.iccp.org

Institute of Electrical and Electronics Engineers Computer Society (IEEE)
2001 L Street NW, Suite 700
Washington, DC 20036-4928
202.371.0101
help@computer.org
www.computer.org

Patrick Cooper/Editor

Construction Equipment Operators

Snapshot

Career Cluster(s): Agriculture, Food & Natural Resources, Architecture & Construction

Interests: Managing heavy equipment, working outdoors, working as part of a team

Earnings (Median Pay): $46,990

Employment & Outlook: Faster Than Average Growth Expected

OVERVIEW

Sphere of Work

Construction equipment operators use one or several types of power construction equipment, such as motor graders, bulldozers, scrapers, compressors, pumps, derricks, shovels, tractors, or front-end loaders to excavate, move, and grade earth, erect structures, or pour concrete or other hard surface pavement. They may repair and maintain equipment in addition to other duties.

Work Environment

Construction equipment operators work in nearly all weather conditions. They often get dirty, greasy, muddy, or dusty. The majority of operators work full time, and some operators have irregular work schedules. Some construction projects, especially road building, are done at night. Construction equipment operators work in a large variety of outdoor environments, in all climates and weather conditions. They perform duties at commercial, industrial, residential, and roadside jobsites. When performing roadwork, a construction equipment operator may be required to work on the side of a highway. Construction equipment operators are typically exposed to a high level of noise from the machines themselves as well as the ongoing work and must take precautions to avoid hearing damage and ensure effective communication with other workers. Construction jobsites present a number of additional hazards, so safety measures must always be enforced.

Profile

Interests: Things
Working Conditions: Work Outside
Physical Strength: Heavy Work
Education Needs: On-the-Job Training, High School Diploma or GED, High School Diploma with Technical, Education, Apprenticeship
Licensure/Certification: Usually Not Required
Physical Abilities Not Required: N/A
Opportunities for Experience: Apprenticeship, Military Service
Holland Interest Score: REC

* See Appendix A

Occupation Interest

Work as a construction equipment operator encompasses many tasks, including hauling, leveling, and excavating. Those interested in this profession should be adaptable to the variety of challenging tasks and should enjoy working outdoors and with a team. They also must be able to focus consistently on the job, as bulldozers can be dangerous.

A Day in the Life—Duties and Responsibilities

Prior to beginning any construction or demolition work, a construction equipment operator must first inspect machinery to make sure all of the components are functioning properly. These components include levers, pedals, and the hydraulics that operate the blade. The blade, the large metal plate at the front of the bulldozer, is used to move, haul, or level materials. Depending on the job, a bulldozer may be equipped with a shovel or digging scoop rather than a blade. The bulldozer operator must next go over the day's tasks with the rest of the construction crew. Bulldozers move a large quantity of material and greatly alter the landscape, so significant coordination is required by the entire crew to ensure that nothing is done out of turn or incorrectly.

The bulldozer operator controls the movement of the machine using pedals similar to those of a car. The blade or scooper mechanism is controlled using a lever, also known as a joystick. If a bulldozer is being used to level a surface, the operator will lower the blade to the surface and slowly drive forward. This flattens the surface. For digging jobs, an operator will maneuver the blade or scooper mechanism to dig up and transport the materials to a designated spot. While carrying out these tasks, the operator must consistently meet safety standards.

Construction equipment operators use machinery to move construction materials, earth, and other heavy materials at construction sites and mines. They operate equipment that clears and grades land to prepare it for the construction of roads, bridges, and buildings, as well as runways, power generation facilities, dams, levees, and other structures.

The following are examples of types of construction equipment operators:

Bulldozer operators use levers, pedals, and the hydraulics to move the machinery and operate the blade. The blade, the large metal plate at the front of the bulldozer, is used to move, haul, or level materials. Depending on the job, a bulldozer may be equipped with a shovel or digging scoop rather than a blade. The bulldozer operator must next go over the day's tasks with the rest of the construction crew. Bulldozers move a large quantity of material and greatly alter the landscape, so significant coordination is required by the entire crew to ensure that nothing is done out of turn or incorrectly.

The bulldozer operator controls the movement of the machine using pedals similar to those of a car. The blade or scooper mechanism is controlled using a lever, also known as a joystick. If a bulldozer is being used to level a surface, the operator will lower the blade to the surface and slowly drive forward. This flattens the surface. For digging jobs, an operator will maneuver the blade or scooper mechanism to dig up and transport the materials to a designated spot. While carrying out these tasks, the operator must consistently meet safety standards.

Operating engineers and other construction equipment operators work with one or several types of power construction equipment. They may operate excavation and loading machines equipped with scoops, shovels, or buckets that dig sand, gravel, earth, or similar materials. In addition to operating bulldozers, they operate trench excavators, road graders, and similar equipment. Sometimes, they may drive and control industrial trucks or tractors equipped with forklifts or booms for lifting materials. They may also operate and maintain air compressors, pumps, and other power equipment at construction sites.

Paving and surfacing equipment operators control the machines that spread and level asphalt or spread and smooth concrete for roadways or other structures.

Asphalt spreader operators turn valves to regulate the temperature and flow of asphalt being applied to the roadbed. They must ensure a constant flow of asphalt into the hopper and that the machine distributes the paving material evenly.

Concrete paving machine operators control levers and turn handwheels to move attachments that spread, vibrate, and level wet concrete. They must watch the surface of the concrete carefully to identify low spots that need additional concrete.

Tamping equipment operators use machines that compact earth and other fill materials for roadbeds, railroads, or other construction sites. They also may operate machines with interchangeable hammers to cut or break up old pavement and drive guardrail posts into the ground.

Pile-driver operators use large machines mounted on skids, barges, or cranes to hammer piles into the ground. Piles are long, heavy beams of concrete, wood, or steel driven into the ground to support retaining walls, bridges, piers, or building foundations. Some pile-driver operators work on offshore oil rigs.

Duties and Responsibilities

- Moving levers and pushing pedals to move the tractor and manipulate the blade
- Reshaping and distributing earth to raise or lower the ground-to-grade specifications
- Estimating the depth of cuts by the feel of levers and the stalling action of the engine
- Repairing tractors and attachments

OCCUPATION SPECIALTIES

Scarifier Operators

Scarifier Operators strictly operate a bulldozer for the purpose of loosening soil.

Angledozer Operators

Angledozer Operators drive a bulldozer equipped with a special angled blade attached to the front.

Crawler-Tractor Operators

Crawler-Tractor Operators drive a tractor that is specially equipped to move over rough or muddy ground.

Fine-Grade-Bulldozer Operators

Fine-Grade-Bulldozer Operators grade land to close specification.

Scraper Operators

Scraper Operators operate bulldozers for the purpose of scraping surface clay to determine the existence and types of clay deposits or to gather clay into piles in preparation for its removal to brick-and-tile manufacturing plants.

WORK ENVIRONMENT

Transferable Skills and Abilities

Interpersonal/Social Skills
- Working as a member of a team

Technical Skills
- Working with machines, tools, or other objects

Unclassified Skills
- Using set methods and standards in your work

Work Environment Skills
- Working outdoors

Immediate Physical Environment

Construction equipment operators work in nearly every weather condition, although rain or extremely cold weather can stop some types of construction. Workers often get dirty, greasy, muddy, or dusty. Some operators work in remote locations on large construction projects, such as highways and dams, or in factories or mines. These sites are often very loud due to the heavy machinery being used and may present additional hazards based on the nature of the construction being carried out. Construction equipment operators risk injury from hazards such as slips, falls, and transportation incidents. Workers can generally avoid injury by observing proper operating procedures and safety practices. Bulldozers, scrapers, and pile-drivers are noisy and shake or jolt the operator, which may lead to repetitive stress injuries.

Human Environment

Because bulldozer operators must coordinate and collaborate with other workers on jobsites in order to complete their work successfully, strong communication skills are essential. Bulldozer operators are usually required to check in with site managers and contractors daily.

Technological Environment

In addition to bulldozers, a bulldozer operator may be required to operate other pieces of heavy machinery. This may include road graters and trench excavators. An operator will also handle light safety equipment such as reflector vests and hardhats.

Construction Equipment Operators

EDUCATION, TRAINING, AND ADVANCEMENT

High School/Secondary

Most employers require bulldozer operators to have completed high school or an equivalent degree program. Prospective bulldozer operators will benefit from high school courses in subjects such as geology and machine repair.

Suggested High School Subjects
- On-the-Job Training
- Apprenticeship
- High School Diploma or General Education Development (GED) certificate
- High School Diploma with Technical Education
- Junior/Technical/Community College

Related Career Pathways/Majors

Agriculture, Food & Natural Resources Cluster
- Natural Resources Systems Pathway

Architecture & Construction Cluster
- Construction Pathway
- Maintenance/Operations Pathway

Famous First

The first building in which wrought-iron beams were used was erected for Harper and Brothers in New York City in 1854. Wrought-iron beams were rolled for the first time in the United States in 1854 at the Trenton Iron Works, Trenton, NJ, of which Peter Cooper was the principal owner. These beams were intended for the Cooper Union building in New York City, but they were not ready in time, as it took two years to prepare them. They were seven inches deep, weighed 81 pounds per yard, and were of the type known as deck beams. Previously, cast-iron beams had been used in construction work.

Source: "Engineering." *Famous First Facts*, Salem, 2016. *Salem Online*, https://online.salempress.com

Postsecondary

A number of schools offer specialized vocational programs in the operation of construction equipment. These courses typically provide students with several weeks of hands-on training by qualified instructors. Students are also instructed in the basics of surveying, project layout, and safety and maintenance. Some of these courses allow students to earn operator credentials from the National Center for Construction Education and Research (NCCER).

Completion of an operation course at a vocational school may greatly increase an operator's ability to secure a job in the industry. An individual considering enrolling in such a course should research the school's reputation and credibility and consult established workers in the construction industry in regard to the relevance of any particular course.

Related College Majors:
- Construction Equipment Operation

Adult Job Seekers

An adult seeking to transition to a career as a bulldozer operator will benefit greatly from prior experience operating construction equipment or other heavy machinery. Adults with no background in the construction industry should consider applying for a specialized program at a vocational school. Such programs can properly train applicants and provide them with an easier transition into the industry.

Professional Certification and Licensure

Many workers learn their jobs by operating light equipment under the guidance of an experienced operator. Later, they may operate heavier equipment, such as bulldozers. Some construction equipment with computerized controls requires greater skill to operate. Operators of such equipment may need more training and some understanding of electronics.

Other workers learn their trade through a three- or four-year apprenticeship. For each year of the program, apprentices must have at least 144 hours of technical instruction and 2,000 hours of paid on-the-job training. On the job, apprentices learn to maintain equipment, operate machinery, and use technology, such as global positioning system (GPS) devices. In the classroom, apprentices learn operating procedures for equipment, safety practices, and first aid, as well as how to read grading plans.

A few groups, including unions and contractor associations, sponsor apprenticeship programs. The basic qualifications for entering an apprenticeship program are as follows:

- Minimum age of 18
- High school education or equivalent
- Physically able to do the work
- Valid driver's license

After completing an apprenticeship program, apprentices are considered journey workers and perform tasks with less guidance.

Once on the job, apprentices perform basic tasks and learn how to use and maintain construction equipment. As they progress, apprentices eventually become able to operate machinery with less supervision. Once the apprenticeship is complete, a bulldozer operator is considered a journeyman worker and may perform duties without any supervision.

Bulldozer operators may be required to hold a commercial driver's license (CDL) in order to transport a bulldozer to a jobsite.

Additional Requirements

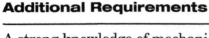

A strong knowledge of mechanics and an ability to handle physically demanding tasks are essential to a bulldozer operator. Problem-solving skills are especially important, as bulldozer operators must at times identify and repair mechanical malfunctions while on-site.

Construction equipment operators often need a CDL to haul their equipment to various jobsites. It allows an operator to drive a semitruck, a vehicle commonly used to haul construction equipment. Employers may be more likely to hire an operator who can transport as well as drive a bulldozer. The requirements for a CDL differ from state to state. In addition, some states have specific licenses for bulldozer operators. Few states have special licenses for operators of backhoes, loaders, and bulldozers.

Currently, 17 states require pile-driver operators to have a crane license because similar operational concerns apply to both pile-drivers and cranes. In addition, the cities of Chicago, Cincinnati, New Orleans, New York, Omaha, Philadelphia, and Washington, DC require special crane licensure.

Fast Fact

In Fayetteville, Georgia, some enterprising thieves somehow managed to steal a forklift and then used that stolen forklift to make off with an ATM machine. Security video reveals a forklift ramming into the 2,000-pound ATM machine and taking it out from its foundation.

Source: www.nfe-lifts.com

EARNINGS AND ADVANCEMENT

Earnings depend on the type of industry, location of the employer, and the type and size of equipment. Pay scales are generally higher in metropolitan areas. Earnings for the year can be lower than the weekly rates would indicate because work time may be limited by bad weather. In May 2018, bulldozer operators had median annual earnings of $46,990. The lowest 10 percent earned less than $30,660, and the highest 10 percent earned more than $83,190.

Median annual wages for construction equipment operators in May 2018 were as follows:

Pile-driver operators	$58,680
Operating engineers and other construction equipment operators	$47,810
Paving, surfacing, and tamping equipment operators	$39,780

In May 2018, the median annual wages for construction equipment operators in the top industries in which they worked were as follows:

Construction of buildings	$52,960
Heavy and civil engineering construction	$50,440
Specialty trade contractors	$47,160
Mining, quarrying, and oil and gas extraction	$45,750
Local government, excluding education and hospitals	$41,850

The starting pay for apprentices is usually between 60 percent and 70 percent of what fully trained operators make. They receive pay increases as they learn to operate more complex equipment.

Construction equipment operators may receive paid vacations, holidays, and sick days; life and health insurance; and retirement benefits. The employer and equipment operator may jointly contribute to union funds used to pay for these benefits.

EMPLOYMENT AND OUTLOOK

There were approximately 426,600 construction equipment operators employed nationally in 2016. Overall employment of construction equipment operators is projected to grow 12 percent from 2016 to 2026, faster than the average for all occupations. Employment growth is expected to vary across the construction equipment operator occupations.

Percent change in employment, Projected 2016–26

Construction equipment operators: 12%

Construction trades workers: 10%

Total, all occupations: 7%

Note: All Occupations includes all occupations in the U.S. Economy.
Source: U.S. Bureau of Labor Statistics, Occupational Employment Statistics

Spending on infrastructure is expected to increase, resulting in many new positions over the next 10 years. Across the country, many roads, bridges, and water and sewer systems are in need of repair. In addition, population growth will require new infrastructure projects, such as roads and sewer lines, which are also expected to generate jobs.

Workers with the ability to operate multiple types of equipment should have the best job opportunities. In addition, employment opportunities should be best in metropolitan areas, where most large commercial and residential buildings are constructed, and in states that undertake large transportation-related projects. Because apprentices learn to operate a wider variety of machines than do other beginners, they usually have better job opportunities.

As with many other types of construction worker jobs, employment of construction equipment operators is sensitive to fluctuations of the economy. On the one hand, workers may experience periods of unemployment when the overall level of construction falls. On the other hand, some areas may need additional workers during peak periods of building activity.

Related Occupations
- Construction Laborer
- Forklift Operator
- Freight, Stock & Material Mover
- Heavy Equipment Service Technician
- Highway Maintenance Worker
- Truck Driver

Related Military Occupations
- Combat Engineer
- Construction Equipment Operator

Conversation With...
CHRISTOPHER TREML
Director of Construction Training
International Union of Operating Engineers
Washington, DC
Heavy equipment operator, 28 years

1. What was your individual career path in terms of education/training, entry-level job, or other significant opportunity?

My father was training director for the apprentice program at Local 57 in Providence, Rhode Island, when I graduated from high school, so I applied to their three-year program. I trained in the classroom and had 6,000 on-the-job training hours because when you go through your apprenticeship program, you work for a contractor. I ended up working for that same contractor for almost twenty years. I ran all the equipment they had, such as bulldozers, cranes, backhoes, front-end loaders, bobcats, and asphalt paving equipment. I also repaired and maintained the equipment, which is part of an operating engineer's job.

During that time, I was hired by the union local to be a part-time instructor for their apprentice program, and then spent nine years as training director. Eventually I was offered a job at the international union in Washington, DC. I travel to different locals and supply them with curricula, training materials, and pieces of equipment. I provide the instructors with what they need to run their training programs smoothly. From time to time, I get on different pieces of equipment to demonstrate; there are more than thirty different machines we're responsible for operating and maintaining.

2. What are the most important skills and/or qualities for someone in your profession?

You have to love the outdoors and be willing to do physical labor because this is not just about sitting in machines and pulling levers. You may have your knuckles scratched on a job or be accidentally burned with a torch. You have to have mechanical ability, a willingness to work long hours, and be physically fit. You need to take care of your body—wear hearing and eye protection, don't jump off machines, and pay attention to your doctor's appointments to maintain your health as you get older.

You have to be a people person, because you're going to be working with a crew of people who come with a lot of different attitudes and at the end of the day, you have to get the job done.

3. What do you wish you had known going into this profession?

I knew what I was getting into because I followed my father into this profession. But one thing I see a lot today is that many young people need to learn how to manage their finances. Maybe 90 percent of operating engineers go from contractor to contractor, getting laid off from one job and moving on to another. The work is definitely seasonal; by Thanksgiving, guys may be laid off until spring. You need to manage your money through the slow times.

4. Are there many job opportunities in your profession? In what specific areas?

Yes, jobs are available because people are retiring. Equipment is computer-based now, so it's easier for young people to come in and troubleshoot because they are computer savvy.

5. How do you see your profession changing in the next five years? What role will technology play in those changes, and what skills will be required?

There will always be a need for operators because at the end of the day, you need someone in the machine to go through the normal paces because you can't have a machine in the middle of a city digging around gas and electrical lines. That said, computers are highly involved. For example, in excavation you have GPS pulling grades off satellites and dictating how much dirt to pull off or pull in. A computer tells you how much a load weighs so you can set up a crane.

6. What do you enjoy most about your job? What do you enjoy least about your job?

I enjoy all the people I've met throughout my career and I still enjoy making friends or picking up new ideas. The most difficult part of the job probably is getting on a new piece of equipment you're unfamiliar with. You can't be afraid to ask questions.

7. Can you suggest a valuable "try this" for students considering a career in your profession?

Different groups hold summer camps for young people so they can learn about the different trades. You should try to spend a day with each trade if you can. As an example of what might happen, you might get on a piece of equipment with us and help dig a hole. The University of Rhode Island holds a Construction Academy; maybe a guidance counselor can help you find one near your home.

Note: This interview first appeared in *Careers in Building Construction* © 2015.

MORE INFORMATION

Associated Builders and Contractors (ABC)
4250 N. Fairfax Drive, 9th Floor
Arlington, VA 22203
703.812.2000
gotquestions@abc.org
www.abc.org

Associated General Contractors of America (AGC)
Director, Construction Education Services
2300 Wilson Boulevard, Suite 400
Arlington, VA 22201
703.548.3118
info@agc.org
www.agc.org

Building Trades Association (BTA)
16th Street, NW
Washington, DC 20006
800.326.7800
info@buildingtrades.com
www.buildingtrades.com

Industrial Truck Association (ITA)
1750 K Street, NW, Suite 460
Washington, DC 20006
202.296.9880
www.indtrk.org

International Union of Operating Engineers (IUOP)
Director of Research and Education
1125 17th Street, NW
Washington, DC 20036
202.429.9100
www.iuoe.org

Laborers' International Union of North America (LIUNA)
905 16th Street, NW
Washington, DC 20006
212.737.8320
www.liuna.org

National Center for Construction Education and Research (NCCER)
13614 Progress Boulevard
Alachua, FL 32615
386.518.6500
www.nccer.org

United Construction Workers (UCW)
3109 Martin Luther King Jr. Avenue, SE
Washington, DC 20032
www.unitedconstructionworkers.com

Patrick Cooper/Editor

Delivery Truck Drivers and Driver/Sales Workers

Snapshot

Career Cluster(s): Manufacturing, Marketing, Sales & Service, Transportation, Distribution & Logistics

Interests: Working with your hands, working with a team

Earnings (Median Pay): $30,500 per year

Employment & Outlook: Slower Than Average Growth Expected

OVERVIEW

Sphere of Work

Delivery truck drivers and driver/sales workers pick up, transport, and drop off packages and small shipments within a local region or urban area. They drive trucks having a total weight of 26,000 pounds or less for vehicle, passengers, and cargo. Delivery truck drivers usually transport merchandise from a distribution center to businesses and households.

Delivery Truck Drivers and Driver/Sales Workers

Work Environment

Delivery truck drivers and driver/sales workers have a physically demanding job. Driving a truck for long periods can be tiring. When loading and unloading cargo, drivers do a lot of lifting, carrying, and walking.

Profile

Interests: Things
Working Conditions: Work Inside
Physical Strength: Medium Work
Education Needs: No High School Diploma, On-the-Job Training
Licensure/Certification: Usually Not Required
Physical Abilities Not Required: Not Climb, Not Kneel, Not Hear and/or Talk
Opportunities for Experience: Apprenticeship, Part-Time Work
Holland Interest Score: RCS; RES

* See Appendix A

Occupation Interest

Delivery truck drivers and driver/sales workers is an unskilled labor position that attracts employees from all realms of academic and professional experience. Training is conducted on the job. Some Delivery truck drivers and driver/sales workers undertake the position during the holiday season to earn extra income and to help retailers and manufacturers with overflow. Some are retirees who work part time for supplemental income, while others are high school or college students who take these positions temporarily or as transitional employment.

A Day in the Life—Duties and Responsibilities

Delivery truck drivers and driver/sales workers pick up, transport, and drop off packages and small shipments within a local region or urban area. They drive trucks having a total weight of 26,000 pounds or less for vehicle, passengers, and cargo. Delivery truck drivers usually transport merchandise from a distribution center to businesses and households. Most drivers generally receive instructions to go to a delivery location at a particular time, and it is up to them to determine the best route. Other drivers have a regular daily or weekly delivery schedule. All drivers must understand an area's street grid and know which roads allow trucks and which do not.

The following examples are types of delivery truck drivers and driver/sales workers:

Driver/sales workers are delivery drivers who also have sales responsibilities. They recommend new products to businesses and solicit new customers. These drivers may have a regular delivery route and be responsible for adding new clients located along their route. For example, they may make regular deliveries to a hardware store and encourage the store's manager to offer a new product.

Some driver/sales workers use their own vehicles to deliver goods to customers, such as takeout food, and accept payment for those goods. Freelance or independent driver/sales workers may use smartphone apps to find specific delivery jobs.

Light truck drivers, often called pickup and delivery or P&D drivers, are the most common type of delivery driver. They drive small trucks or vans from distribution centers to delivery locations. Drivers make deliveries based on a set schedule. Some drivers stop at the distribution center once only, in the morning, and make many stops throughout the day. Others make multiple trips between the distribution center and delivery locations. Some drivers make deliveries from a retail location to customers.

Duties and Responsibilities

- Loading and unloading their cargo
- Communicating with customers to determine pickup and delivery needs
- Reporting any incidents they encounter on the road to a dispatcher
- Following all applicable traffic laws
- Reporting serious mechanical problems to the appropriate personnel
- Keeping their truck and associated equipment clean and in good working order
- Accepting payments for the shipment
- Handling paperwork, such as receipts or delivery confirmation notices

WORK ENVIRONMENT

Immediate Physical Environment

Delivery truck drivers and driver/sales workers have a physically demanding job. Driving a truck for long periods can be tiring. When loading and unloading cargo, drivers do a lot of lifting, carrying, and walking.

Transferable Skills and Abilities

Organization & Management Skills
- Paying attention to and handling details
- Performing routine work

Technical Skills
- Working with machines, tools, or other objects
- Working with your hands

Human Environment

Delivery truck drivers and driver/sales workers must interact with fellow staff members on a routine basis to ensure the accuracy of orders and the protection of goods during shipping.

Technological Environment

Delivery truck drivers and driver/sales workers utilize a variety of hand tools, such as palette hand trucks, staple guns, tape guns, and packing equipment machines. Use of shipping software and industrial grade weights and measures may also be required.

EDUCATION, TRAINING, AND ADVANCEMENT

High School/Secondary

Delivery truck drivers and driver/sales workers typically enter their occupations with a high school diploma or equivalent. However, some opportunities exist for those without a high school diploma. Workers undergo one month or less of on-the-job training. They must have a driver's license from the state in which they work and have a clean driving record.

High school students can prepare for a career in the shipping industry with coursework in algebra, geometry, physics, and computer science. Drafting and industrial arts classes can serve as important precursors for future work in industrial and commercial settings.

Suggested High School Subjects
- English
- Industrial Arts
- Machining Technology
- Shop Math
- Shop Mechanics
- Woodshop

Related Career Pathways/Majors

Manufacturing Cluster
- Logistics & Inventory Control Pathway
- Production Pathway

Marketing, Sales & Service Cluster
- Distribution & Logistics Pathway

Transportation, Distribution & Logistics Cluster
- Warehousing & Distribution Center Operations Pathway

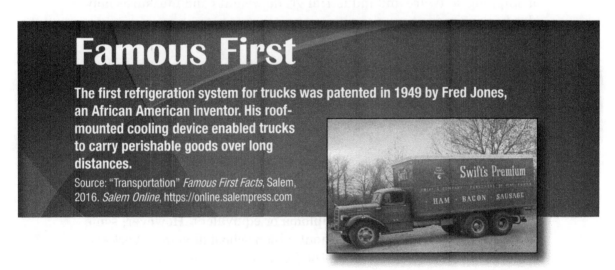

Famous First

The first refrigeration system for trucks was patented in 1949 by Fred Jones, an African American inventor. His roof-mounted cooling device enabled trucks to carry perishable goods over long distances.

Source: "Transportation" *Famous First Facts*, Salem, 2016. *Salem Online*, https://online.salempress.com

Postsecondary

Postsecondary education is not a prerequisite for employment as a delivery truck drivers and driver/sales workers.

Adult Job Seekers

Entry-level positions delivery truck drivers and driver/sales can offer opportunities for adult job seekers who are in between jobs, eager for employment, or looking for a job to take as a means of transition in their career path. Many companies hire delivery truck drivers and driver/sales workers through temporary staffing firms.

Professional Certification and Licensure

While no specific licensure is required, companies train new delivery truck drivers and driver/sales workers on the job. This may include training from a driver-mentor who rides along with a new employee to make sure that a new driver is able to operate a truck safely on crowded streets.

Driver/sales workers must learn detailed information about the products they offer. Their company also may teach them proper sales techniques, such as how to approach new customers.
All delivery drivers need a driver's license. Some delivery drivers begin as package loaders at warehouse facilities, especially if the driver works for a large company.

Additional Requirements

When completing deliveries, drivers often interact with customers and should make a good impression to ensure repeat business. Drivers need to observe their surroundings at all times while operating a vehicle. Because delivery truck drivers and driver/sales workers sometimes take payment, they must be able to count cash and make change quickly and accurately. When driving through heavy traffic congestion, delivery drivers must remain calm and composed. Driver/sales workers are expected to persuade customers to purchase new or different products. To have a driver's license, delivery truck drivers and driver/sales workers must be able to pass a state vision test.

Fast Fact

In 1889, King Umberto and Queen Margherita had the privilege of getting the first known pizza delivered by Raffaele Esposito, the most famous pizzaiolo (pizza chef) in Naples, Italy.

Source: 999thepoint.com

EARNINGS AND ADVANCEMENT

The median annual wage for driver/sales workers was $24,700 in May 2018. The lowest 10 percent earned less than $17,810, and the highest 10 percent earned more than $48,880.

The median annual wage for light truck or delivery services drivers was $32,810 in May 2018. The lowest 10 percent earned less than $20,260, and the highest 10 percent earned more than $62,690.

Some drivers/sales workers, such as pizza delivery workers, receive tips in addition to hourly wages. Sales workers can also receive commissions from the products they sell.

Most drivers work full time, and many work additional hours. Those who have regular routes sometimes must begin work very early in the morning or work late at night. For example, a driver who delivers bread to a deli every day must arrive before the deli opens. Drivers often work weekends and holidays.

Median annual wages, May 2018

Total, all occupations: $38,640

Motor vehicle operators: $37,130

Light truck or delivery services drivers: $32,810

Delivery truck drivers and driver/sales workers: $30,500

Driver/sales workers: $24,700

Note: All Occupations includes all occupations in the U.S. Economy.
Source: U.S. Bureau of Labor Statistics, Occupational Employment Statistics

EMPLOYMENT AND OUTLOOK

There were approximately 1,421,400 delivery truck drivers and driver/sales workers employed nationally in 2016. Employment is expected to grow slower than the average for all occupations through the year 2026, which means employment is projected to increase 3 percent to 4 percent. Many job openings will arise from the need to replace workers who transfer to other occupations, retire or leave the labor force for other reasons. Job openings should also occur as a result of the occupation being very large and turnover being very high.

Overall employment of delivery truck drivers and driver/sales workers is projected to grow 4 percent from 2016 to 2026, slower than the average for all occupations. Employment growth will vary by occupation.

Employment of light truck or delivery services drivers is projected to grow 7 percent from 2016 to 2026, about as fast as the average for all occupations.

Continued e-commerce growth should increase demand for package delivery services, especially for the large and regional shipping companies. More light truck and delivery drivers will be needed to fulfill the growing number of e-commerce transactions.

Employment of driver/sales workers is projected to show little or no change from 2016 to 2026. Self-employed or independent contractors, who sign up with smartphone-based food delivery companies, may be needed to deliver food from restaurants that previously only provided takeout services.

Job opportunities for delivery truck drivers and drivers/sales workers are expected to be good. Job applicants with experience and a clean driving record, or who work for a company in another occupation, should have the best job prospects.

Percent change in employment, Projected 2016–26

Total, all occupations: 7%

Light truck or delivery services drivers: 7%

Motor vehicle operators: 5%

Delivery truck drivers and driver/sales workers: 4%

Driver/sales workers: -1%

Note: All Occupations includes all occupations in the U.S. Economy.
Source: U.S. Bureau of Labor Statistics, Occupational Employment Statistics

Related Occupations
- Freight, Stock & Material Mover
- Stock Clerk

Conversation With...
DAN McMACKIN
Public Relations Manager/Former Driver
United Parcel Service (UPS)
Atlanta, GA
UPS/Transportation Industry, 41 years

1. What was your individual career path in terms of education/training, entry-level job, or other significant opportunity?

I started loading trucks at UPS when I was 17 in Wisconsin. The reason I wanted to work there is the hourly wage was really good, and I wanted to pay my own way through college. I started loading tractor-trailer units in the evenings.

I did that through two college degrees, my undergraduate in English literature from Marquette University, and a BS in business administration from the University of Wisconsin. I got the second bachelor's degree because I couldn't minor in business at Marquette.

At that point, I had a choice to make. I could leave UPS with my generalist educational background or I could become a driver. At that time, in the mid-80s, drivers were making $50,000 year plus pension and health care benefits. I also had built the seniority required to get into driving. I decided to stay with UPS.

When I was a driver, catalog deliveries filled our trucks, everything from clothing to food. During the holidays, 25 percent of what was in my truck would be Christmas-related. In Racine, WI, we delivered to a company called O and H Danish Bakery that made circular Danish called Kringle, and hundreds of thousands of those would be flowing through our system. You got to know your customers based on what they received. I had a guy who made fishing lures. He'd get blanks for the lures, and his deliveries and pickups would increase as the fishing season approached. I delivered to a woman who was a chocolatier and I would bring her raw goods and ship her finished goods. I'd deliver insulin to people—vital healthcare they needed to live.

It's a physical job. You need to be fit, and it keeps you fit. I think I was suited for the methodized regimen that UPS preaches. It's also a company known for hiring from within. After about two and a half years I let a few folks in the organization know I had an ability to write. I got an opportunity to write some stories and shoot photos for the company magazine. Then the company came knocking to see if I wanted a communications job.

Even though I've been in management for many years, I've continued to drive from time to time. Just about everyone in the company goes back out to help from late November through December.

Depending on their size and scope, transportation companies can have a tremendous variety of opportunities. I always have returned to roles in communications, but I've been an operations supervisor. I did a short stint in industrial engineering. I did health and safety and employment work for the human resources department. I've raised my hand for special assignments, such as the year I lived in a hotel and worked for UPS's airline and wrote for our newspaper targeted to pilots.

2. **What are the most important skills and/or qualities for someone in your profession?**

   Punctuality. When the company says 7 a.m., get there at 6:45, not 7:15. You need a work ethic. If somebody isn't giving you something to do, go and find it. What can you dig up? Can you find a solution to something?

3. **What do you wish you had known going into this profession?**

   As a green high school kid, I turned down a chance to go into management. I had no understanding of managerial roles at 18. I stayed in the hourly ranks for a long time and if I'd gone into supervision sooner, I would have received stock awards much sooner in my career. Sometimes, breaking up your comfort level is a good.

4. **Are there many job opportunities in your profession? In what specific areas?**

   There's a plethora of different opportunities. The transportation industry as a whole needs people who can drive safely, understand the need for punctuality, and work hard. You can be a driver for a company like UPS, but also look at the sharing economy such as Uber and Lyft. UPS is invested in something called Roadie, where people deliver things on their way to a place they're headed anyway. Within our organization, we need people to fill roles such as data analytics.

5. **How do you see your profession changing in the next five years? How will technology impact that change, and what skills will be required?**

   The transportation industry is undergoing nothing short of a revolution. UPS, for instance, is using drones to deliver medicine in Africa, and in medical testing units on campuses where it now takes three minutes to deliver supplies that used to take an hour because somebody had to drive around a campus. Understanding data analytics, we literally can tell when a truck is going to break down before it breaks down. Our advanced technology group is looking at everything from robotics to automation to data mining.

6. **6. What do you enjoy most about your job? What do you enjoy least about your job?**

   I love variety. It's very rare to ever have two days that are identical here. The other side of that is, it's not a 9 to 5 job. Some years ago, we had a plane crash and I worked 24/7.

7. **Can you suggest a valuable "try this" for students considering a career in your profession?**

   Start at a low-ranking position, something a college graduate wouldn't consider. Learning things from the bottom up prepares you for a better future, and lets you see how an operation works. If you go into a managerial position at a transportation company, you are going to cross paths with people on the front lines

MORE INFORMATION

Flexible Packaging Association (FPA)
971 Corporate Boulevard, Suite 403
Linthicum, MD 21090
410.694.0800
fpa@flexpack.org
www.flexpack.org

Institute of Packaging Professionals (IPP)
1833 Centre Point Circle, Suite 123
Naperville, IL 60563
630.544.5050
info@iopp.org
www.iopp.org

International Brotherhood of Teamsters (IBT)
25 Louisiana Avenue, NW
Washington, DC 20001
202.624.6800
www.teamster.org

Laborers' International Union of North America (LIUNA)
905 16th Street, NW
Washington, DC 20006
202.737.8320
www.liuna.org

Paperboard Packaging Council (PPC)
1350 Main Street, Suite 1508
Springfield, MA 01103-1670
413.686.9191
www.ppcnet.org

John Pritchard/Editor

Dispatchers

Snapshot

Career Cluster(s): Business, Management & Administration, Law, Public Safety & Security, Manufacturing, Transportation, Distribution & Logistics

Interests: Solving problems, organizing information, communicating with others

Earnings (Median Pay): $37,063

Employment & Outlook: Average Growth Expected

OVERVIEW

Sphere of Work

Dispatchers are communications professionals who receive and transmit information, traditionally via telephone or radio transceiver. Dispatchers are utilized across a variety of industries and organizations. Emergency dispatchers coordinate communications between the public and police, fire, and emergency medical personnel. Commercial dispatchers coordinate the delivery of goods across several areas of transport, including railways and trucking lines. Dispatchers are also utilized by taxi companies, bus companies, airlines, and the military. Public-utility

companies also use dispatchers extensively to coordinate maintenance crews and other staff in the field.

Work Environment

Dispatchers traditionally work out of organizational headquarters and communications hubs. Emergency dispatchers customarily work out of police, fire, and ambulance stations or in offices designated for emergency communication, such as 911 call centers and public-safety answering points. Commercial dispatchers normally work in major shipping centers that connect delivery routes across large regions of the country. Communication and public-utility dispatchers coordinate communications from major transportation and logistical hubs, including airports, power stations, train stations, and bus stations.

Profile

Interests: Data, People
Working Conditions: Work Inside
Physical Strength: Light Work
Education Needs: On-the-Job Training, High School Diploma or GED
Licensure/Certification: Required
Physical Abilities Not Required: Not Climb, Not Kneel
Opportunities for Experience: Part-Time Work
Holland Interest Score: CES, CSR, ECS, ERS, ESC, ESI, ESR, SEC

* See Appendix A

Occupation Interest

Professional communication dispatchers come from a variety of educational and experiential backgrounds. Dispatchers are multitasking problem solvers who are organized and enthusiastic about interacting with people. They should also be able to display patience and pragmatism in stressful situations and chaotic environments.

A Day in the Life—Duties and Responsibilities

Dispatchers are often assigned lengthy shifts that can range anywhere from eight to twenty-four hours in duration. Responsibilities of a dispatcher vary significantly depending on their particular area of employment.

Commercial dispatchers confirm delivery schedules with drivers, customers, and miscellaneous vendors. Their main goal is to synchronize logistics such as transport times, load specifications, and packing instructions to ensure that goods are delivered in an efficient and timely manner.

Similarly, dispatchers employed in the transportation industry communicate with drivers, engineers, and pilots to ensure that buses, trains, and planes complete their journeys in a timely manner, conveying information regarding weather conditions or delays at their intended destination. Dispatchers for taxi and bus companies, as well as those who work in emergency services, must be well versed in effective transportation routes and the overall geographic layout of the district in which they work.

The most specialized field of dispatching is police, fire, and ambulance dispatch. Emergency dispatchers determine the exact location of callers, confirm the nature and severity of emergencies, and are responsible for relaying that information to the appropriate officials in a quick and efficient manner. Emergency dispatchers must also provide 911 callers with medical and safety advice while emergency personnel are en route to their location, as well as strategies to get to a safer environment or mitigate further damage.

Duties and Responsibilities

- Handling customers' requests for pickup or delivery of freight
- Compiling lists of available vehicles
- Assigning drivers and vehicles
- Issuing keys, record sheets, equipment, and credentials to drivers
- Coordinating schedules
- Recording time of departure, destination, cargo, and expected time of return
- Maintaining records of mileage, fuel used, repairs made, and other expenses
- Computing pick-up and/or delivery costs
- Filing reports on shipping and receiving activities of company or agency

OCCUPATION SPECIALTIES

Taxicab Starters

Taxicab Starters use radios or telephones to dispatch taxicabs in response to requests by customers for transportation service.

Motor Vehicle Dispatchers

Motor Vehicle Dispatchers assign motor vehicles and drivers to move freight or passengers within or between cities.

Radio Dispatchers

Radio Dispatchers receive complaints and send messages concerning crimes, police activities and emergencies. In some locations they coordinate all police, fire, ambulance and other emergency requests, relaying instructions to the radio unit concerned.

WORK ENVIRONMENT

Immediate Physical Environment

Call centers vary in size depending on industry and service. Dispatchers in major urban areas tend to work in large call centers, while those in remote and rural locations may work out of traditional offices. Dispatchers can work in a variety of settings, including transportation hubs, corporate offices, hospitals, campuses, and warehouses.

Human Environment

Dispatching requires deft interpersonal communication skills and the ability to make decisions quickly under pressure. Individuals with an even temperament and a strong desire to help those in need make particularly good candidates for the role.

Transferable Skills and Abilities

Interpersonal/Social Skills
- Cooperating with others
- Working as a member of a team

Organization & Management Skills
- Coordinating tasks
- Managing people/groups
- Managing time
- Meeting goals and deadlines
- Organizing information or materials
- Performing duties that change frequently

Technical Skills
- Working with data or numbers
- Working with machines, tools, or other objects

Technological Environment

Dispatchers use a variety of communication technologies, ranging from telephone, email, and web conferencing to computerized inventory software and global positioning systems.

EDUCATION, TRAINING, AND ADVANCEMENT

High School/Secondary

Most dispatching positions require only a high school diploma or General Education Development (GED) certificate. Applicants who have completed secondary course work in the field are often given preference. High school students interested in a career as a dispatcher should take courses in English composition, keyboarding, and basic computer science to prepare for the technical aspects of the role. Immersion in foreign-language study is also advisable.

Suggested High School Subjects
- Business & Computer Technology
- Business English
- Business Math

Related Career Pathways/Majors

Business, Management & Administration Cluster
- Administrative & Information Support Pathway

Law, Public Safety & Security Cluster
- Emergency & Fire Management Services Pathway
- Law Enforcement Services Pathway

Manufacturing Cluster
- Logistics & Inventory Control Pathway

Transportation, Distribution & Logistics Cluster
- Transportation Operations Pathway

Famous First

The first ambulance service for hospitals was introduced by the Commercial Hospital (now the General Hospital), Cincinnati, OH, prior to 1865. The list of employees for the year ending February 28, 1866, names James A. Jackson, employee No. 27, as "driver of ambulance" at an annual salary of $360. A similar service was started in June 1869 by Bellevue Hospital, New York City.

Source: "Medicine and Health" *Famous First Facts*, Salem, 2016. *Salem Online*, https://online.salempress.com

Postsecondary

Certificate and associate-level educational programs in dispatching are offered nationwide. Those applying for dispatching jobs in the fields of emergency management or major transportation may be required to have an associate's or bachelor's degree in a related field, such as computer science, communications, or information technology. Certificate-level course work in dispatching familiarizes students with basic terminology utilized throughout the profession, such as citizen's band (CB) codes and drivers' slang, as well as the types of transportation technology dispatchers utilize on a day-to-day basis.

Related College Majors:
- Administrative Assistant/Secretarial Science, General
- General Retailing & Wholesaling Operations & Skills
- Receptionist Training.

Adult Job Seekers

Applicants with extensive professional experience, particularly in communications or information technology, can transition to the field with relative ease. Those who complete private certificate- or associate-level instruction in dispatching are normally given preference for vacancies. Familiarity with the region's transportation infrastructure and major roadways is also beneficial.

The lengthy work shifts and frequent stress inherent to the position may cause difficulty for professionals with families or young children. The indispensable nature of professional dispatchers, particularly those working in emergency services, requires them to work on several major holidays and weekends.

Professional Certification and Licensure

The certification requirements of dispatch professionals vary from state to state. Many states require a specified amount of supervised training time before a dispatcher is allowed to work on his or her own.

Additional Requirements

Dispatchers must possess excellent organizational skills and be able to maintain their patience and calm under pressure. Regardless of their particular area of industry, dispatchers are often required to solve complex problems, answer questions, and make important decisions on a moment's notice.

Fast Fact

A ten-year-old Brockton, Massachusetts boy called 911, then abruptly hung up. When the dispatcher called back, she discovered the problem: Much to the boy's annoyance, his mother was insisting that he go to bed.

Source: boston.com

EARNINGS AND ADVANCEMENT

Earnings of dispatchers depend on the geographic location and union affiliation of the employer. There can also be quite a difference in earnings depending on the type of industry which employs the dispatcher. For example, taxicab dispatchers typically earn less than bus and emergency vehicle road dispatchers, who in turn also earn less than police and ambulance vehicle dispatchers.

Median annual earnings of dispatchers, except police, fire, and ambulance, were $38,790 in May 2017. The lowest 10 percent earned less than $23,880, and the highest 10 percent earned more than $64,940.

Median annual earnings of police, fire, and ambulance dispatchers were $40,660 in May 2018. The lowest 10 percent earned less than $26,590, and the highest 10 percent earned more than $63,930.

Dispatchers may receive paid vacations, holidays, and sick days; life and health insurance; and retirement benefits. These are usually paid by the employer.

Median annual wages, May 2018

Police, fire, and ambulance dispatchers: $40,660

Total, all occupations: $38,640

Material recording, scheduling, dispatching, and distributing workers: $32,140

Note: All Occupations includes all occupations in the U.S. Economy.
Source: U.S. Bureau of Labor Statistics, Occupational Employment Statistics

In May 2018, the median annual wages for police, fire, and ambulance dispatchers in the top industries in which they worked were as follows:

State government, excluding education and hospitals	$47,650
Local government, excluding education and hospitals	$40,870
Colleges, universities, and professional schools; state, local, and private	$38,810
Hospitals; state, local, and private	$37,280
Ambulance services	$36,400

EMPLOYMENT AND OUTLOOK

Dispatchers held about 297,120 jobs in 2016. About one-third worked for police, fire, and ambulance services. Although dispatching jobs are found throughout the country, most work in urban areas, where large communications centers and businesses are located. Employment is expected to grow about as fast as the average for all occupations through the year 2026, which means employment is projected to increase 8 percent. Population growth and economic expansion are expected to spur employment growth for all types of dispatchers. The growing elderly population will increase demand for emergency services and stimulate employment growth of police, fire, and ambulance dispatchers.

Related Occupations
- Air Traffic Controller
- Production Coordinator
- Reservation & Ticket Agent

MORE INFORMATION

Airline Dispatchers Federation (ADF)
2020 Pennsylvania Avenue, NW #821
Washington, DC 20006
800.676.2685
www.dispatcher.org

Association of Public-Safety Communications Officials International (APSCOI)
351 N. Williamson Boulevard
Daytona Beach, FL 32114-1112
888.272.6911
apco@apcointl.org
www.apcointl.org

International Municipal Signal Association (IMSA)
P.O. Box 539
165 East Union Street
Newark, NY 14513-0539
800.723.4672
info@imsasafety.org
www.imsasafety.org

National Academies of Emergency Dispatch (NACD)
110 S. Regent Street, Suite 800
Salt Lake City, UT 84111
800.960.6236
www.emergencydispatch.com

Service Employees International Union (SEIU)
1313 L Street, NW
Washington, DC 20005
202.898.3200
www.seiu.org

John Pritchard/Editor

Flight Attendants

Snapshot

Career Cluster(s): Transportation, Distribution & Logistics
Interests: Aviation, travel, communicating with others, handling emergency situations
Earnings (Yearly Average): $56,000
Employment & Outlook: Faster Than Average Growth Expected

OVERVIEW

Sphere of Work

A flight attendant is an airline professional that ensures the overall security and safety of the airplane cabin, as well as the safety and comfort of its passengers. They will also attend to passenger's needs, and are responsible for serving food and beverages to the passengers and crew. A flight attendant guarantees successful compliance with standard aviation safety regulations and protocols, and must thoroughly understand the ways in which airplanes operate. Flight attendants report to a flight supervisor and also to the captain of the aircraft on which he or she is working.

Work Environment

Flight attendants spend most of their time aboard an aircraft, and are assigned a home base location from which they generally operate. Generally, they are away from their home base location for at least one-third of their working time, per month. Most flight attendants are expected to work nights, holidays, and weekends, in addition to regular hours during the week. They usually spend 65 to 85 hours per month in flight (with shifts lasting up to 14 hours), with the ability to request additional hours, and another 50 hours per month on the ground performing tasks such as flight and report preparation.

Profile

Interests: People, Things
Working Conditions: Work Inside, Work both Inside and Outside
Physical Strength: Light Work
Education Needs: High School Diploma or GED, Junior/Technical/Community College
Licensure/Certification: Required
Physical Abilities Not Required: Not Kneel
Opportunities for Experience: Military Service, Part-Time Work
Holland Interest Score: ESA

* See Appendix A

Occupation Interest

Potential flight attendants should be interested in learning about aviation, national and international travel, and safety and emergency regulations. They should also possess outstanding communication skills. Flight attendants must interact with diverse and, at times, difficult passengers, and must project a pleasant and personable attitude, regardless of the circumstances. Individuals interested in becoming flight attendants should possess poise as well as strength of character, as these qualities will help them remain calm and effective during crisis or emergency situations aboard an aircraft.

A Day in the Life—Duties and Responsibilities

When a flight attendant reports for duty, he or she will typically meet with the captain and other crew members one hour before takeoff to discuss evacuation procedures, airline crew coordination, flight duration, relevant passenger information (such as health or mobility issues), and anticipated weather conditions. Before passengers board the airplane, flight attendants take inventory of and prepare food and beverages and check first aid kits and emergency equipment. Once passengers begin boarding, flight attendants are responsible for greeting them, helping them find their seats, and assisting with the storage of carry-on luggage. Before takeoff, flight attendants check the aircraft for any dangerous materials and note any passengers exhibiting odd or potentially threatening behavior. They welcome passengers aboard the flight, and provide information regarding safety procedures and emergency escape routes.

A flight attendant ensures the safety and security of the passengers and attends to their comfort and satisfaction from the time they board the aircraft until they depart. This includes assisting sick or injured passengers, providing food and beverages, answering any questions passengers might have, and preparing the passengers and plane for a safe landing. To further ensure passenger satisfaction, a flight attendant might also calm the nerves of anxious passengers and supervise small children. Prior to departure, flight attendants also collect audio headsets and trash, as well as take inventory. Once the plane is on the ground, flight attendants assist passengers exiting the aircraft and report the condition of cabin equipment. The lead flight attendant supervises crewmembers aboard the airplane in addition to performing his or her own regular duties.

Duties and Responsibilities

- Attending a briefing session with crew members on weather conditions, number of passengers, and route
- Checking the cabin for supplies, emergency equipment, and food and beverages
- Greeting passengers and assisting them with coats and small baggage
- Verifying passengers' tickets
- Recording destinations
- Issuing a general welcome and explaining and demonstrating the use of emergency equipment
- Providing passengers with newspapers, magazines, pillows, and blankets
- Heating and serving cooked meals, sandwiches, or other light refreshments and beverages

WORK ENVIRONMENT

Immediate Physical Environment

The majority of a flight attendant's work takes place inside the cabin of a clean, well-ventilated airplane. He or she is required to wear a uniform representing the airline for which he or she works, and must stand for long periods of time. A flight attendant also spends time in or around airline terminals. Constant exposure to re-circulated air, repetitive lifting and pushing motions, and the lack of safety restraints as the airplane encounters turbulence all contribute to a higher than average rate of job-related illness and injury.

Transferable Skills and Abilities

Communication Skills
- Speaking effectively
- Writing concisely

Interpersonal/Social Skills
- Cooperating with others
- Working as a member of a team

Organization & Management Skills
- Demonstrating leadership
- Managing time
- Meeting goals and deadlines
- Performing duties that change frequently
- Performing routine work

Unclassified Skills
- Keeping a neat appearance

Work Environment Skills
- Traveling

Human Environment

Flight attendants work and deal with large groups of passengers, as well as other crewmembers. They report to flight supervisors and captains. Because they interact with so many people on a daily basis, flight attendants are susceptible to airborne illnesses and other sicknesses. In spite of work-related stressors, they must maintain a visibly positive attitude when in public situations, and must address passenger requests in a cordial yet authoritative manner.

Technological Environment

In addition to learning and understanding the basic functions of an airplane, flight attendants must use intercoms and public address systems, compact food and beverage carts, movie and music systems, first aid kits, microwave ovens, seating charts, and demonstration equipment, emergency survival equipment and systems, and other new technology as it becomes available.

EDUCATION, TRAINING, AND ADVANCEMENT

High School/Secondary

High school students who wish to become flight attendants can prepare by studying foreign languages, foods and nutrition, psychology, and public speaking. They should also take a basic first aid training and certification course. An understanding of the fundamentals of aviation, emergency procedures, and airplane operation and maintenance is useful. They should also participate in social clubs or volunteer groups that allow them to interact with peers and the public.

Suggested High School Subjects
- English
- First Aid Training
- Food Service & Management
- Foreign Languages
- Mathematics
- Psychology
- Speech

Related Career Pathways/Majors

Transportation, Distribution & Logistics Cluster
- Transportation Operations Pathway

Famous First

The first jumbo jet was the Boeing 747, introduced for flight service by the Boeing Company of Seattle, WA, in 1970. The wide-bodied, two-decked aircraft was taller than a six-story building and could carry up to 490 passengers, more than could easily be handled by the terminal facilities of the time. The first 747s went into transatlantic service for Pan American Airlines beginning on January 21, 1970.

Source: "Transportation." *Famous First Facts*, Salem, 2016. *Salem Online*, https://online.salempress.com

Postsecondary

Potential flight attendants are required to have earned a high school diploma or its equivalent. Certain schools and colleges also offer flight attendant training, but a postsecondary degree is generally not required; however, increasingly often, some airlines give preference to those candidates with a college degree or who have already completed some kind of related training. Flight attendants may find it helpful to study postsecondary subjects related to the hospitality industry, such as communications and travel and tourism. Flight attendants who wish to work for an international airline are usually proficient in at least one foreign language.

Related College Majors:
- Flight Attendant Training.

Adult Job Seekers

Potential flight attendants should have extensive experience working with the public and should demonstrate the ability to think on their feet and remain calm during a dispute or crisis. Most airlines require that flight attendants be at least 18 to 21 years of age, undergo thorough background checks, and pass stringent medical evaluations.

Professional Certification and Licensure

To become eligible to work aboard aircraft carriers, flight attendants must complete a training program, ranging from three to six weeks. The training usually takes place at the airline's flight training center and is required for Federal Aviation Admininstration (FAA) certification. Trainees learn emergency procedures such as evacuating aircraft, operating emergency equipment, and administering first aid. They also receive specific instruction on flight regulations, company operations, and job duties.

Toward the end of the training, students go on practice flights. They must complete the training to keep a job with the airline. Once they have passed initial training, new flight attendants receive the FAA Certificate of Demonstrated Proficiency and continue to receive additional on the job training as required by their employer.

Successful certification depends on a flight attendant's ability to fulfill specific training requirements, set forth by the FAA and the Transportation Security Administration (TSA), including safety procedures, evacuations, and medical emergencies. Flight attendants are certified for specific types of aircraft and must take new training for each type of aircraft on which they are to work. In addition, attendants receive recurrent training every year to maintain their certification.

Additional Requirements

Some flight attendants are constantly traveling to and from fun and exotic destinations; others may be just making a run between regional airports. Due to their schedule, flight attendants and other members of the aircrew are often away from home for long periods of time. Therefore, potential flight attendants should consider that they may never experience a "normal" schedule, and will have to leave family members and loved ones for extended periods.

Successful flight attendants possess an interest in working with people and a willingness to learn about other cultures. Flight attendants, above all else, must display calm under pressure and patience for difficult people and situations. Though air travel is not usually dangerous, some flights may be incredibly unpleasant because of turbulence, mechanical failure, or other mishaps. Because of this, flight attendants must handle themselves with poise and confidence under severe pressure or duress. Most airlines require that applicants be physically fit in proportion to their height, and stay within a certain weight range throughout their years of service. Most flight attendants pay union dues and belong to the Association of Flight Attendants (AFA), the Transport Workers Union of America (TWUA), or the International Brotherhood of Teamsters (IBT).

> **Fast Fact**
>
> In 1987 American Airlines saved $40,000 by removing one olive from each salad served in first class.
> Source: www.flightcentre.com.au

EARNINGS AND ADVANCEMENT

Earnings depend on the size of the airline company and the type of aircraft. Flight attendants are usually paid guaranteed monthly salaries based on a minimum number of flight hours—75 to 100 hours a month—and usually spend another 50 hours a month on the ground, preparing flights, writing reports, and waiting for planes to arrive. For time flown above the minimum guarantee or for night and international flights, they receive extra compensation.

Career advancement is based on seniority. On international flights, senior attendants frequently oversee the work of other attendants. Senior attendants may be promoted to management positions in which they are responsible for recruiting, instructing, and scheduling.

Median annual earnings of flight attendants was $56,000 in May 2018. The lowest 10 percent earned less than $28,950, and the highest 10 percent earned more than $80,870. Flight attendants also receive an allowance for meal expenses while on duty away from home.

Flight attendants may receive paid vacations, holidays, and sick days; life and health insurance; and retirement benefits. These are usually paid by the employer. Flight attendants may also receive free or reduced air fares for themselves and their families. Flight attendants are required to purchase uniforms and wear them while on duty. The airlines usually pay for uniform replacement items and may provide a small allowance to cover cleaning and upkeep of the uniforms.

Median annual wages, May 2018

Air transportation workers: $74,530

Flight attendants: $56,000

Total, all occupations: $38,640

Note: All Occupations includes all occupations in the U.S. Economy.
Source: U.S. Bureau of Labor Statistics, Occupational Employment Statistics

EMPLOYMENT AND OUTLOOK

Flight attendants held about 116,600 jobs nationally in 2016. Employment is expected to grow 10 percent from 2016 to 2026, faster than the average for all occupations. Population growth and an improving economy are expected to increase the number of airline passengers. As airlines enlarge their capacity to meet rising demand by increasing the number and size of planes in operation, more flight attendants will be needed.

Competition for jobs as flight attendants is expected to remain very strong because the number of applicants is expected to greatly exceed the number of job openings. As more career-minded people enter this occupation, job turnover will decline. Nevertheless, most job openings are expected from the need to replace flight attendants who stop working or transfer to other occupations. Employment of flight attendants is sensitive to cyclical swings in the economy

Percent change in employment, Projected 2016–26

Flight attendants: 10%

Total, all occupations: 7%

Air transportation workers: 7%

Note: All Occupations includes all occupations in the U.S. Economy.
Source: U.S. Bureau of Labor Statistics, Occupational Employment Statistics

Related Occupations
- Food & Beverage Service Worker
- Waiter/Waitress

Related Military Occupations
- Transportation Specialist

Conversation With . . .
PAULA McCAULEY

Flight Attendant
Major US Airline
Flight Attendant, 22 years

1. What was your individual career path in terms of education/training, entry-level job, or other significant opportunity?

When I graduated from college, a lot of my friends did the whole backpacking through Europe thing, but I never really traveled. I had a job at a software company for about a year. After church one Sunday, I saw an ad for what they called "a cattle call" back then. I was living in DC and drove to Baltimore. It was a whole day and there were hundreds of people, and you did interview after interview. I got hired on the spot. I never even thought about it until I saw the ad. I thought I would do it for a year. But my mom calls it "the golden handcuffs"—I'll never leave because there are so many perks!

2. What are the most important skills and/or qualities for someone in your profession?

You have to have patience. Just being patient and being kind goes a long way. And, honestly, you have to have some level of physical fitness. If you have an aborted landing, say, you have to open the door and the doors are heavy. That hardly ever happens, but it could.

My philosophy is being kind is not that hard. You have to be assertive and there are angry and drunk passengers. People get kicked off planes more often than you would think. Recently, we were flying to Madrid and had a woman, who was a New Yorker with an edge. She was forced to check her bag and took all kinds of stuff out of the bag and she had all these magazines on her lap. I went over and said, "What can I do to make your day better? Do you want me to store some of these magazines for you? You've had a rough time," and she said, "That's all I wanted. I just wanted to hear someone say that."

3. What do you wish you had known going into this profession?

What I didn't know at the beginning is that seniority is everything. The first couple of years you have to be on reserve. I had to carry a pager with me everywhere—this was before cell phones. It's almost like being a pledge in a sorority. You have to put in your time.

4. Are there many job opportunities in your profession? In what specific areas?

It's on and off. Right now we're not hiring flight attendants. But there's always somebody hiring, Jet Blue or Southwest. If you get on with the smaller companies like Express Jet and get experience, you'll get in with the bigger ones—American, Delta, United—eventually. The bigger the airlines, the more flight options. I have three kids, my husband, my parents—we all fly for free all over the world. It's standby. And we're paid better at the bigger airlines.

5. How do you see your profession changing in the next five years? What role will technology play in those changes, and what skills will be required?

I don't see it changing that much. People can be replaced by technology in some fields, but with flight attendants, we need to be there for security reasons. And it's all about the smiling flight attendant.

I'm not allowed to talk much about our training, but it has changed so much since 9/11. It used to focus on customer service. Now a large percentage of our training is about self-defense and how to spot certain things. I never thought I'd be learning tae kwon do as part of my training.

6. What do you enjoy most about your job? What do you enjoy least?

I love the flexibility. It is so unbelievably flexible for a mom. And I love being able to get away. Sunday I'm home and Monday I'm in a hotel in Miami. It's always great to be in the sun.

I love the travel and I love the people. I meet such fascinating people, crews included. Every day is different, and I don't take my work home with me.

Sometimes I think about the danger, just because I have three kids. In Billings, Montana, we had a flight attendant in critical condition; they hit a pocket of air and she hit the ceiling and broke her spine. But I try not to think about those things. Also, dealing with delays and irate passengers.

7. **Can you suggest a valuable "try this" for students considering a career in your profession?**

   Every time you fly, just pay attention and watch and learn. Customer service is what it is—whether you're waitressing, or bar tending, or working behind the counter at Macy's. Having any sort of customer service job will help you decide if this is right for you.

Note: This interview first appeared in *Careers in Hospitality & Tourism* © 2014.

MORE INFORMATION

Air Transport Association of America (ATAA)
Office of Communications
1301 Pennsylvania Avenue NW,
Suite 1100
Washington, DC 20004-1707
202.626.4000
ata@airlines.org
www.air-transport.org

Association of Flight Attendants (AFA)
501 3rd Street, NW
Washington, DC 20001
202.434.1300
info@afacwa.org
www.afanet.org

Transport Workers Union of America (TWUA)
501 3rd Street NW, 9th Floor
Washington, DC 20001
202.719.3900
www.twu.org

U.S. Department of Transportation
Federal Aviation Administration
800 Independence Avenue, SW
Washington, DC 20591
866.835.5322
www.faa.gov

Briana Nadeau/Editor

Hand Laborers and Material Movers

Snapshot

Career Cluster(s): Manufacturing, Marketing, Sales & Service, Transportation, Distribution & Logistics

Interests: Doing physical work, working with your hands, doing repetitive work

Earnings (Median Pay): $27,270

Employment & Outlook: Average Growth Expected

OVERVIEW

Sphere of Work

Hand laborers and material movers are general laborers who specialize in the transport and storage of material goods. Freight handlers and stock personnel work in a variety of industries, from transportation and commercial retailing to industrial supply, shipping, and manufacturing. While hand laborer and material-moving jobs are traditionally entry-level positions with little to no professional prerequisites, stock professionals must learn a wide variety of systems and technologies through on-the-job training in order to perform the job effectively.

Work Environment

Hand laborers and material movers work indoors and outdoors, in industrial warehouse settings and at airports, shipyards, and train depots. A vast majority of material movers work at major ports. Movement of freight and material requires a wide variety of interaction with other staff members to ensure the safety of both the material itself and the workers, who are transporting extremely heavy and potentially hazardous materials at a rapid pace.

Profile

Interests: Things
Working Conditions: Work both Inside and Outside
Physical Strength: Medium Work, Heavy Work
Education Needs: No High School Diploma, On-the-Job Training
Licensure/Certification: Usually Not Required
Physical Abilities Not Required: Not Hear and/or Talk
Opportunities for Experience: Part-Time Work
Holland Interest Score: RES

* See Appendix A

Occupation Interest

Hand laborers and material movers are traditionally young, unskilled workers seeking reliable employment with the opportunity for advancement. Freight movement typically attracts young workers due to the physical nature of the position, though management and supervisory staff may be senior professionals who have advanced from the ranks of general material handlers. Many freight handlers are temporary employees who are using the position as a source of transitional income.

A Day in the Life—Duties and Responsibilities

Hand laborers and material movers spend their days loading and unloading materials, preparing material for transport, and unpacking and disseminating received shipments. Some of these workers feed or remove material to or from machines, clean vehicles, pick up unwanted household goods, and pack materials for moving. The responsibilities of freight movers vary depending on their place of employment, time of shift, and specific industry.

Shipment preparation requires adherence to stock lists and logs, which indicate the contents of the shipments and their intended destinations. Material handlers are charged with properly identifying and demarcating containers with information relevant to their contents and intended recipients. Handlers are also required to label freight with information regarding its proper handling and storage and any potential hazards. This task is particularly crucial for material handlers working with perishable or hazardous materials.

Unloading shipments requires inspection of the contents of boxes, containers, and shipping crates to ensure that the quality and quantity of goods meets expectations. Material handlers are required to report any damage or loss of material that may have occurred during transport. Some are required to weigh incoming and outgoing shipments in order to guarantee that the exact amount of material arrives at its destination. Material handlers who work with liquefied or gaseous freight must be trained in the connection of transport machinery such as fuel tankers, hoses, and other specialized storage or transport devices. Material movers who handle food items, medical and scientific supplies, and other perishable or biohazardous materials may also require specialized training.

Duties and Responsibilities

- Reading work orders or following supervisors' directions
- Loading and unloading trucks, railroad cars, pallets, and conveyors
- Opening containers, using steel cutters or other hand tools
- Counting and weighing materials
- Recording information on the number of items shipped or the amount of material moved

The following are examples of types of hand laborers and material movers:

Cleaners of vehicles and equipment wash automobiles and other vehicles, as well as storage tanks, pipelines, and related machinery. They use cleaning products, vacuums, hoses, and brushes. Most of these workers clean cars at a carwash, an automobile dealership, or a rental agency. Some clean industrial equipment at manufacturing firms. Some—for example, those who work at a carwash, also known as carwash attendants—interact with customers.

Hand laborers and freight, stock, and material movers move materials to and from storage and production areas, loading docks, delivery trucks, ships, and containers. Although their specific duties may vary, most of these movers, often called pickers, work in warehouses. Some workers retrieve products from storage and move them to loading areas. Other workers load and unload cargo from a truck. When moving a package, pickers keep track of the package number, sometimes with a handheld scanner, to ensure proper delivery. Sometimes they open containers and sort the material.

Hand packers and packagers package a variety of materials by hand. They may label cartons, inspect items for defects, and keep records of items packed. Some of these workers pack materials for shipment and move them to a loading dock. Hand packers in grocery stores, also known as grocery baggers, bag groceries for customers at checkout.

Machine feeders and offbearers process materials by feeding them into equipment or by removing them from equipment. The equipment is generally operated by other workers, such as material-moving machine operators. Machine feeders and offbearers help the operator if the machine becomes jammed or needs minor repairs. Machine feeders also track the amount of material they process during a shift.

Refuse and recyclable material collectors gather garbage and recyclables from homes and businesses to transport to a dump, landfill, or recycling center. Many collectors lift garbage cans by hand and empty them into their truck. Some collectors drive the garbage or recycling truck along a scheduled route and may use a hydraulic lift to empty the contents of a dumpster into the truck.

WORK ENVIRONMENT

Transferable Skills and Abilities

Organization & Management Skills
- Following instructions
- Paying attention to and handling details
- Performing routine work

Technical Skills
- Working with machines, tools, or other objects

Immediate Physical Environment

Industrial and commercial settings predominate. Freight, stock, and material movers may be employed by warehouses, fuel companies, shipping companies, postal services, and industries such as agriculture, food processing, and transportation. Freight handlers work in transportation hubs, ports, factories, airports, and processing centers.

Human Environment

Freight handling traditionally requires strong collaboration skills. Material movers interact with fellow workers, vendors, and other professionals on a regular basis.

Technological Environment

Material movers use a variety of tools and other technologies related to shipping and materials management, from shipping software and material databases to hand tools such as box cutters, hand trucks, mechanical hoists, conveyors, and motorized vehicles such as forklifts and material transporters.

EDUCATION, TRAINING, AND ADVANCEMENT

High School/Secondary

High school students can prepare for a career in freight and material management with courses in math, physics, physical science, and computer science. Exposure to extracurricular activities and scholastic sports can help foster the ability to work in a team. Completion of course work related to machinery and industrial arts is also beneficial.

Suggested High School Subjects
- Business Math
- Driver Training
- English

Related Career Pathways/Majors

Manufacturing Cluster
- Logistics & Inventory Control Pathway

Marketing, Sales & Service Cluster
- Distribution & Logistics Pathway

Transportation, Distribution & Logistics Cluster
- Warehousing & Distribution Center Operations Pathway

Famous First

The first trading ship sent to China was the Empress of China, a 360-ton privateer commanded by Captain John Green. It left New York City on February 22, 1784, arrived in Canton, China, on August 28, left China on the return voyage on December 28, and returned to New York on May 11, 1785. Its owners made a profit of $30,727 on a $120,000 investment, which was financed by Robert Morris, Peter Whiteside, and William Whiteside.

Source: "Transportation." *Famous First Facts*, Salem, 2016. *Salem Online*, https://online.salempress.com

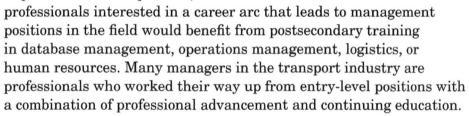

Postsecondary

Postsecondary education is not a requirement for the position, but professionals interested in a career arc that leads to management positions in the field would benefit from postsecondary training in database management, operations management, logistics, or human resources. Many managers in the transport industry are professionals who worked their way up from entry-level positions with a combination of professional advancement and continuing education.

Most positions for hand laborers and material movers require less than one month of on-the-job training. Some workers need only a few days of training, and most training is done by a supervisor or a more experienced worker who decides when trainees are ready to work on their own.

Workers learn safety rules as part of their training. Many of these rules are standardized through the Occupational Safety and Health Administration (OSHA).

Related College Majors:
- Truck, Bus & Other Commercial Vehicle Operation

Adult Job Seekers

Freight, stock, and material movers typically work long hours, including weekends. Unlike traditional industries, freight and material movement is a constant process, and workers may be required to perform shift work. The sporadic hours and numerous variables inherent to the role may make it difficult for professionals with young families or other responsibilities.

Professional Certification and Licensure

Refuse and recyclable material collectors who drive trucks that exceed a certain capacity—such as vehicles with the combined weight of the vehicle, passengers, and cargo exceeding 26,000 pounds—must have a commercial driver's license (CDL). Obtaining a CDL requires passing written, skill, and vision tests.

Additional Requirements

Freight, stock, and material movers must be organized, safety conscious, and able to complete numerous tasks simultaneously. Organization is perhaps the most important aspect of the role, particularly for stock movers employed in fast-paced environments in which workers deal with dozens if not hundreds of shipments of various materials on a daily basis. Also, material movers should be physically fit and strong enough to lift loads of one hundred pounds or more.

Fast Facts

Ancient Mesopotamians domesticated the horse for use in transportation about 4000 BCE. The Egyptians domesticated the donkey for the same reason at around the same time.

Source: gdintegrated.com

EARNINGS AND ADVANCEMENT

Earnings of hand laborers and material movers depend on the type of materials handled, the amount of equipment operation necessary, the extent of unionization and the type and size of the employer. The median annual wage for hand laborers and material movers was $27,270 in May 2018. The lowest 10 percent earned less than $20,000, and the highest 10 percent earned more than $44,670.

In May 2018, the median annual wages for hand laborers and material movers in the top industries in which they worked were as follows:

Wholesale trade	$29,570
Manufacturing	$29,390
Transportation and warehousing	$29,220
Administrative and support and waste management and remediation services	$25,080

Hand laborers and material movers may receive paid vacations, holidays, and sick days; life and health insurance; and retirement benefits. These are usually paid by the employer.

Median annual wages, May 2018

Total, all occupations: $38,640

Material-moving workers: $28,570

Hand laborers and material movers: $27,270

Note: All Occupations includes all occupations in the U.S. Economy.
Source: U.S. Bureau of Labor Statistics, Occupational Employment Statistics

EMPLOYMENT AND OUTLOOK

Employment of hand laborers and freight, stock, and material movers—about two-thirds of all the workers in this profile—is projected to grow 8 percent from 2016 to 2026, about as fast as the average for all occupations. Although some warehouses are installing equipment such as high-speed conveyors and sorting systems to increase efficiency, these workers will still be needed to move materials in nearly all sectors of the economy.

Employment of hand packers and packagers is projected to grow 2 percent from 2016 to 2026, slower than the average for all occupations. Grocery stores, which employ many hand packers and packagers, may employ fewer baggers as a growing number of stores also have self-checkouts where customers or existing cashiers bag groceries themselves. However, those employed in warehouses are expected to experience some employment gains as the industry grows.

Employment of refuse and recyclable material collectors is projected to grow 13 percent from 2016 to 2026, faster than the average for all occupations. Trash collection activity should be expected to increase as the population grows, and collectors will be needed to remove trash.

Employment of cleaners of vehicles and equipment is projected to grow 11 percent from 2016 to 2026, faster than the average for all occupations. Demand for automotive repair and maintenance services, as well as a growing automobile dealers industry, is expected to contribute to employment growth of cleaners of vehicles and equipment.

Employment of machine feeders and offbearers is projected to grow 2 percent from 2016 to 2026, slower than the average for all occupations. Many of these workers are employed in manufacturing industries, in which some functions are automated, so fewer of these workers will be required.

Percent change in employment, Projected 2016–26

Total, all occupations: 7%

Material-moving workers: 7%

Hand laborers and material movers: 7%

Note: All Occupations includes all occupations in the U.S. Economy.
Source: U.S. Bureau of Labor Statistics, Occupational Employment Statistics

Related Occupations
- Bulldozer Operator
- Construction Laborer
- Forklift Operator
- Lumber Production Worker
- Packer/Packager
- Rail Transportation Worker
- Refuse & Recyclable Material Collector
- Roustabout
- Ship Loader

MORE INFORMATION

International Brotherhood of Teamsters (IBT)
25 Louisiana Avenue, NW
Washington, DC 20001
202.624.6800
www.teamster.org

International Longshore and Warehouse Union (ILWU)
1188 Franklin Street, 4th Floor
San Francisco, CA 94109-6800
415.775.0533
www.ilwu.org

Laborers' International Union of North America (LIUNA)
905 16th Street, NW
Washington, DC 20006
202.737.8320
www.liuna.org

Transportation Communications International Union (TCIU)
3 Research Place
Rockville, MD 20850
301.948.4910
websteward@tcunion.org
www.tcunion.org

John Pritchard/Editor

Heavy and Tractor-Trailer Truck Drivers

Snapshot

Career Cluster(s): Transportation, Distribution & Logistics

Interests: Road travel, working alone, transportation, nonoffice work environment

Earnings (Median Pay): $43,680

Employment & Outlook: As Fast as Average Growth Expected

OVERVIEW

Sphere of Work

Heavy and tractor-trailer truck drivers transport goods from one location to another. Most tractor-trailer drivers are long-haul drivers and operate trucks with a total weight exceeding 26,000 pounds for the vehicle, passengers, and cargo. These drivers deliver goods over intercity routes that sometimes span several states.

Work Environment

Working as a long-haul truck driver is a lifestyle choice because these drivers can be away from home for days or weeks at a time. Truck drivers are typically on the road for 50 hours or more per week and do not follow a standard work schedule. They are often required to work at night, in early morning hours, during holidays, and on weekends. Long-distance drivers may work no more than 60 hours per week without taking 34 consecutive hours off, and they may not drive for more than 11 hours straight per day. Their work can be lonely (as they frequently travel alone), physically strenuous, boring, and exhausting. Many truck drivers are responsible for loading, lifting, carrying, and unloading cargo.

Profile

Interests: Things
Working Conditions: Work both Inside and Outside
Physical Strength: Medium Work
Education Needs: No High School Diploma, On-the-Job Training, High School Diploma or GED, High School Diploma with Technical Education
Licensure/Certification: Required
Physical Abilities Not Required: Not Climb
Opportunities for Experience: Apprenticeship, Military Service, Part-Time Work
Holland Interest Score: RIE, RSE

* See Appendix A

Occupation Interest

Individuals who are interested in pursuing a career in truck driving must be comfortable spending the majority of their week alone. Because a truck driver's schedule can often be irregular and he or she may be away from home for days at a time, becoming a truck driver is a major lifestyle decision. Prospective truck drivers should enjoy traveling on the open road and should be highly skilled in navigation, route calculation, and map reading. They must have high tolerance for tedium and possess physical strength and stamina.

A Day in the Life—Duties and Responsibilities

Most truck drivers begin by receiving work assignments from their dispatchers, who inform them of the details of their next pickup or delivery. They are then responsible for examining their trucks to make sure everything, including emergency equipment, is working properly. They load cargo from a warehouse or distribution center onto the truck, arranging it securely and fastening it properly. They may collect receipts and bills for delivered products, obtain payments, and return all documents and money collected to their employers.

On the road, long-haul truck drivers must fill out trip logs, listing the number of hours traveled and other details in accordance with regulations mandated by the Interstate Commerce Commission. They frequently stop to eat, rest, and refuel. Upon their return, truck drivers inspect their vehicles for any damage and report any mechanical failures they experienced.

Although the job requires truck drivers to be physically robust, technological advancements in the industry have allowed them to start using mechanical loading devices, such as forklifts and conveyor belts, to move and assemble freight as well as power-assisted steering, brakes, and gear shifting to improve safety. To monitor inventory, truck drivers use a radio- frequency identification (RFID) tracking system that helps ensure the correct products are delivered to the proper locations.

When traveling, truck drivers must follow Federal Motor Carrier Safety Administration rules (which relate to the delivery of freight between states), as well as those of the Federal Motor Carrier Safety Administration (which relate to the working hours of truck drivers).

Duties and Responsibilities

- Preparing and inspecting trucks to insure safe operation
- Checking the cargo to be sure it has been safely loaded
- Making assigned deliveries and pickups
- Obtaining customer signatures on receipts and freight bills
- Loading and unloading merchandise
- Turning in receipts, records, and money collected
- Completing trip logs and reports on the condition of the truck
- Representing the company in sales and customer service

OCCUPATION SPECIALTIES

Tank-Truck Drivers

Tank-Truck Drivers drive trucks to deliver gasoline, fuel oil, lubricating oil or any other bulk liquid, to customers.

Tractor-Trailer-Truck Drivers

Tractor-Trailer-Truck Drivers drive gasoline or diesel-powered tractor-trailer combinations, usually long distances, to deliver products to customers.

Garbage Collector Drivers

Garbage Collector Drivers drive packer-type trucks, dump trucks, or trucks equipped with hydraulic-lifting devices to collect garbage and trash and transport it to disposal areas.

Heavy Truck Drivers

Heavy Truck Drivers drive trucks with a capacity of more than three tons to and from specified locations.

WORK ENVIRONMENT

Immediate Physical Environment

Truck drivers spend most of their work hours behind the wheel of a large truck. They sit for extended periods and stop occasionally to stretch, rest, and eat. Long-haul truck drivers often sleep in the cab of their truck when traveling overnight. Road conditions can be treacherous, and they must often drive in unpleasant weather.

Transferable Skills and Abilities

Organization & Management Skills
- Following instructions
- Paying attention to and handling details
- Performing routine work

Human Environment

Truck drivers work alone or in pairs. Most report to dispatchers or private employers; some drivers are self-employed. When delivering or picking up materials, they communicate with distribution center or manufacturer workers, private clients, or vendors.

Technological Environment

In addition to learning to operate light trucks and/or tractor-trailer trucks, truck drivers may use two-way radios, maps, emergency road equipment, global positioning system (GPS) and route navigation systems, flashlights, and vehicle repair tools. They also regularly handle documents like travel orders, trip logs, accident and expense reports, and receipts and bills.

EDUCATION, TRAINING, AND ADVANCEMENT

High School/Secondary

High school students planning to begin a career in truck driving should prepare themselves by taking courses in communications, geography, technology, business, and mathematics, and by obtaining their standard driver's license (SDL) in a timely manner. In addition, students who are licensed to drive should practice navigating local roads and communities, using navigation software, and studying maps.

Suggested High School Subjects
- Applied Math
- Auto Service Technology
- Business Math
- Diesel Maintenance Technology
- Driver Training
- English

Related Career Pathways/Majors

Transportation, Distribution & Logistics Cluster
- Transportation Operations Pathway

Famous First

The first truck was designed and built in Pittsburgh, PA, in 1898–99 by Louis Semple Clarke and his associates. They were organized as the Pittsburgh Motor Vehicle Company and later incorporated as the Autocar Company. The first truck was pictured and described in Autocar's 1899 catalog as "a delivery wagon which can be made of any size or design, that will be fitted with five to eight horsepower motors. Complete with motors it will weigh from 900 to 1400 pounds—so simple in construction that any driver of ordinary intelligence can operate it with more safety than he could drive a horse."

Source: "Transportation." *Famous First Facts*, Salem, 2016. *Salem Online*, https://online.salempress.com

Postsecondary

Though it is not required for employment, most truck drivers receive a high school diploma or its equivalent. In order to operate trucks that weigh 26,001 pounds or more or that carry hazardous materials or oversized loads, truck drivers must obtain a commercial driver's license (CDL). Truck drivers who operate any other kind of truck need an SDL. After high school, prospective truck drivers usually enroll in a technical or vocational driver-training program to prepare for CDL testing. Courses in driver training teach students about highway driving, transportation regulations, airbrakes and transmissions, and truck and freight inspection. Select states and some private companies require truck driver candidates to pass a basic truck-driving course before receiving a CDL.

Related College Majors:
- Truck, Bus & Other Commercial Vehicle Operation

Adult Job Seekers

Prospective truck drivers can start as "extra drivers" for a company or firm, filling in for drivers who are out sick or on vacation. This allows candidates to gain practical experience and knowledge in the field so that they are ready for a regular assignment when one becomes available. They can also gain experience by working as a driver helper or warehouse worker or in a commercial driver training program. Membership in a professional association or union, such as the International Brotherhood of Teamsters (IBT), may provide access to lists of open truck driver jobs as well as job protection.

Professional Certification and Licensure

Truck drivers must obtain either a CDL or an SDL from the state in which they live and adhere to federal and state regulations regarding truck drivers. To receive a CDL, truck drivers must possess a clean driving record, pass a written test, and successfully complete a driving test. In order to transport hazardous materials, truck drivers must also obtain a special endorsement, which is contingent upon the results of a fingerprint analysis and a criminal background check administered by the Transportation Security Administration (TSA). Truck drivers whose routes cross state lines must be at least 21 years old. Truck drivers must also pass a physical examination every two years, which includes tests of hearing, vision, blood sugar levels, and blood pressure.

Additional Requirements

Truck drivers must remain alert, focus on safety, and practice defensive driving at all times while on the road. Because accidents can be highly dangerous or even fatal, federal regulations mandate that employers must test truck drivers regularly for alcohol and other controlled substances. In addition, truck drivers must have clean driving and criminal records; they will not be granted employment if they have ever been convicted of a felony involving a motor vehicle, have refused to submit to an alcohol test, or have been convicted of driving under the influence of drugs or alcohol. They must be proficient in English in order to communicate with customers, record information about deliveries and hours worked, and operate a vehicle safely.

Fast Facts

Only six percent of truck drivers are women. Lillie McGee Drennan was the first woman truck driver to earn a commercial driver's license, which she did in 1929.
Source: labelmaster.com

EARNINGS AND ADVANCEMENT

Earnings of truck drivers depend on the type and size of the truck they drive, the type of delivery and the geographic area in which they are located. Local truck drivers are usually paid by the hour and receive extra pay for working overtime. Long-distance drivers are generally paid by the mile, and their rate per mile can vary greatly from employer to employer. Their earnings increase with mileage driven and seniority.

The median annual wage for heavy and tractor-trailer truck drivers was $43,680 in May 2018. The lowest 10 percent earned less than $28,160, and the highest 10 percent earned more than $65,260.

Drivers of heavy trucks and tractor-trailers usually are paid by how many miles they have driven, plus bonuses. The per-mile rate varies from employer to employer and may depend on the type of cargo and the experience of the driver. Some long-distance drivers, especially owner-operators, are paid a share of the revenue from shipping.

Most heavy tractor-trailer drivers work full time. The Federal Motor Carrier Safety Administration regulates the hours that a long-haul truck driver may work. Drivers may not work more than 14 hours straight, comprising up to 11 hours driving and the remaining time doing other work, such as unloading cargo. Between working periods, drivers must have at least 10 hours off duty. Drivers also are limited to driving no more than 60 hours within seven days or 70 hours within eight days; then drivers must take 34 hours off before starting another seven- or eight-day run. Drivers must record their hours in a logbook. Truck drivers often work nights, weekends, and holidays.

Median annual wages, May 2018

Heavy and tractor-trailer truck drivers: $43,680

Total, all occupations: $38,640

Motor vehicle operators: $37,130

Note: All Occupations includes all occupations in the U.S. Economy.
Source: U.S. Bureau of Labor Statistics, Occupational Employment Statistics

EMPLOYMENT AND OUTLOOK

There were approximately 1.9 million truck drivers employed nationally in 2016. Employment of heavy and tractor-trailer truck drivers is projected to grow 6 percent from 2016 to 2026, about as fast as the average for all occupations. As the demand for goods increases, more truck drivers will be needed to keep supply chains moving.

The economy depends on truck drivers to transport freight and keep supply chains moving. As the demand for goods increases, more truck drivers will be needed. Trucks transport most of the freight in the United States, so, as households and businesses increase their spending, the trucking industry should grow.

Technological advancements should result in trucks that are more fuel efficient and easier to drive. For example, automatic transmissions, blindspot monitoring, braking assistance, and variable cruise control are all recently developed features that may become more standard throughout the trucking industries within the next decade. In addition, technological advances may lead to further developments in platooning, which is a method of transport where several trucks form a line and automatically mimic the speed, braking, and steering behaviors of the lead truck. These technologies can help ease driver burden and create a safer driving environment for all vehicles.

Job prospects are projected to be very good for heavy and tractor-trailer truck drivers with the proper training and a clean driving record. Because of truck drivers' difficult lifestyle and time spent away from home, many companies have trouble finding and retaining qualified long-haul drivers. In addition, many truck drivers are expected to retire in the coming years, creating even more job opportunities.

Percent change in employment, Projected 2016–26

Total, all occupations: 7%

Heavy and tractor-trailer truck drivers: 6%

Motor vehicle operators: 5%

Note: All Occupations includes all occupations in the U.S. Economy.
Source: U.S. Bureau of Labor Statistics, Occupational Employment Statistics

Related Occupations
- Bulldozer Operator
- Bus Driver
- Taxi Driver and Chauffeur

Related Military Occupations
- Transportation Specialist
- Vehicle Driver

Conversation With . . .
KELSEY M. DELOOF
Solo Company Driver
Albertville, MN
Long-Haul Trucking, 3 years

1. What was your individual career path in terms of education/training, entry-level job, or other significant opportunity?

Originally, I wanted to be a nurse and took classes in high school and community college. During that time, I also took care of my father, who was sick. I realized nursing wasn't for me.

I knew about truck driving because my mother was a driver before I was born. Because of my father's illness, we moved from California to Texas and I ended up working as a nanny for a truck driver. I thought it was really cool when he would leave, or talk about being in California for a few days. Traveling really excites me, and traveling and getting paid for it is really awesome.

Then a friend went to training for his commercial drivers' license training and it snowballed. Driving is an option because once you get that CDL, doors open.

I went through three weeks of CDL training. The first week you learn the laws and regulations, take tests, and basically get a learner's permit. Then you go behind the wheel to learn how to operate on the road—how to maneuver, adjust for the space you need to make a turn, back up, and things like that.

I got my license and went to work for a megacarrier for three years, mostly hauling dry van trailers which are the everyday box trailers you see on the road. When you reach your destination, you basically are dropping a trailer. There's not a lot of activity. I wanted to do something more physically demanding that paid more.

Now I drive a flat bed. I chain and strap every load and haul things like aluminum coils used to make automobiles, granite counter tops, or even the cars for a roller coaster that was being built. I haul to all lower 48 states, live in Texas, and work for a company in Minnesota. That's another nice thing about driving: Often, you don't have to live in the same place as your company.

I drive a sleeper truck. The front of the cab is the driving part. It has a curtain, and behind it there's a bed, fridge, tabletop, and shelves so you can basically live there. I'm usually gone about a month at a time.

I'm not a paranoid kind of person. In terms of safety, I go with my gut and make sure my doors are locked, and park under lights in an area with traffic—not out in the middle of somewhere by myself. I pay attention to my surroundings. Anything that involves going back and forth to the truck stop, I do during daylight.

I do some review searches in an app that lets you do a Google-type search of truck stops. I'm also cautious of what I tell people—man or woman—because you don't know people's intentions. You don't tell them what you're hauling, and you don't tell them where you're going.

2. **What are the most important skills and/or qualities for someone in your profession?**

Patience, because we need to be very responsible because of what we're hauling and how much damage it can do with other people's safety. These can be deadly machines. You also need a willingness to learn because you can be out here 20-plus years and still be learning every day. For example, I've learned to pay attention to surroundings including mile markers and exit numbers. You can see key indicators of something that might go wrong so you can adjust in case of emergency.

3. **What do you wish you had known going into this profession?**

How little people actually respect you while you're driving. I also wish I'd known how much responsibility comes with this job. I learned early on, but when I first decided to get my license, I didn't realize what all went with it—good and bad.

4. **Are there many job opportunities in your profession? In what specific areas?**

Once you get your license, opportunities are endless. Some jobs mean you can be home every day, some just on weekends. Some are all over the country, some go into other countries.

5. **How do you see your profession changing in the next five years? How will technology impact that change, and what skills will be required?**

I see self-driving vehicles come into play more. Personally, I think it's our responsibility as drivers not to forget the old-school ways of life. GPS is great, but they're at fault sometimes. If you don't know how to work without them, you're going to put yourself in a situation that doesn't end well. Trucks have gotten stuck somewhere off the road and been damaged. It's great to keep up with apps but it's also good to know how to read a map or call ahead to get directions.

6. **What do you enjoy most about your job? What do you enjoy least about your job?**

   The best part is getting paid to travel and wake up someplace different every morning. That's the best thing ever. I get to interact with people from other walks of life, get to respect people who have completely different points of view, and learn new things. Also, I'm a photographer so I get to go to the coolest places and take pictures.

   I least enjoy being away from family. I miss a lot of family functions, concerts, hanging out with my dog. A cousin is pregnant right now and I can't enjoy the daily aspect of spending time with her. Everything has to be planned ahead.

7. **Can you suggest a valuable "try this" for students considering a career in your profession?**

   The easiest thing to do is find a truck show. There are dozens all over the country and you'll be surrounded by truck drivers who do all kinds of things within the industry. See the trucks, how big they are, and talk to the people who own them. The trucking companies are also there.

MORE INFORMATION

American Trucking Associations (ATA)
950 N. Glebe Road, Suite 210
Alexandria, VA 22203-4181
703.838.1700
media@trucking.org
www.truckline.com

Federal Motor Carrier Safety Administration (FMCSA)
U.S. Department of Transportation
1200 New Jersey Avenue, SE
Washington, DC 20590
800.832.5660
www.fmcsa.dot.gov

International Brotherhood of Teamsters (IBT)
25 Louisiana Avenue, NW
Washington, DC 20001
202.624.6800
www.teamster.org

Mid-Atlantic Professional Truck Drivers Association (MAPTDA)
P.O. Box 501
Fishersville, VA 22939
info@maptda.org
www.maptda.org

Professional Truck Driver Institute (PTDI)
555 E. Braddock Road
Alexandria, VA 22314
703.647.7015
ptdi@truckload.org
www.ptdi.org

Transportation Security Administration (TSA)
601 S. 12th Street
Arlington, VA 20598
866.289.9673
www.tsa.gov

Briana Nadeau/Editor

Industrial Designers

Snapshot

Career Cluster(s): Arts, Audio/Visual Technology & Communications

Interests: Design, consumer culture, technological trends, solving problems, being creative

Earnings (Median Pay): $66,590

Employment & Outlook: Slower Than Average Growth Expected

OVERVIEW

Sphere of Work

Industrial designers, also known as commercial designers or product designers, plan and create new products that are both functional and stylish. They improve older products by enhancing certain features or by making them safer or more user-friendly. They usually specialize in certain consumer goods, such as cars, toys, housewares, or personal grooming accessories. In addition to designing products, some industrial designers also design packaging for the products or displays for trade shows and may even put their creative skills to work on corporate branding campaigns.

Transportation design is a specialized offshoot of industrial or product design. Although often thought of as simply car design, this area of study now is broadening to include other forms of transportation such as motorcycles, buses, recreational vehicles, and even bicycles. It combines some mechanical and practical knowledge with artistic three-dimensional (3D) abilities. The work is most often with corporations, either as a staff designer or as a consultant to those corporations.

Work Environment

Industrial designers are employed by specialized design firms as well as larger companies and manufacturers. Some are self-employed. They spend much of their time in offices or studios where they design products and in conference rooms with members of product development teams, typically comprised of engineers, strategic planners, financial managers, advertising and marketing specialists, and other creative consultants. They may need to spend some time working in factories and/or testing facilities. Most work a 40-hour week, with additional evening and weekend hours as needed to meet deadlines.

Profile

Interests: Data, People, Things
Working Conditions: Work Inside
Physical Strength: Light Work
Education Needs: Bachelor's Degree, Master's Degree
Licensure/Certification: Usually Not Required
Physical Abilities Not Required: Not Climb, Not Kneel
Opportunities for Experience: Internship
Holland Interest Score: AES

* See Appendix A

Occupation Interest

Industrial design attracts artistic people who look upon consumer products as potential canvases for their creativity. They take satisfaction in products that look good while also being functional and user-friendly. Industrial designers keep up with the latest trends and stay engaged with contemporary consumer culture, design, and technological trends. They must be technically savvy, with strong spatial, communication, and problem-solving skills. The ability to work under deadlines is important.

A Day in the Life—Duties and Responsibilities

The work performed by an industrial designer depends on the size and type of his or her employer and the particular types of products that employer manufactures or builds. Although many industrial designers work for product manufacturers, others work for specialized businesses like architectural firms and medical companies, and still others are self-employed. The work done by industrial designers is increasingly more commercial as companies focus more closely on consumer trends and market research.

Industrial designers are included early on in the corporate product development phase. They may be asked to sketch products that have already been identified or specific details or components for products that need to be upgraded. In some cases, an industrial designer sees a need for a product and recommends the idea to a research and development team for consideration. During the early stages, the designer may research other products, sometimes attending a trade show to view the competition, or survey potential users for desired features.

Once a product has been conceptualized, the industrial designer sketches out designs, either by hand or with design software. The designs might show a smaller model, a product that is easier to hold or more ergonomic, or some other type of innovation. The designer might also create a model from clay or foam board, often first rendering it in 3D software. The designer suggests specific colors, materials, and manufacturing processes that are within the limitations of the budget. Those who work for manufacturers might render drawings in computer-aided industrial design (CAID) programs that can direct machines to build the products automatically. Industrial designers also communicate their designs and ideas in writing and give presentations to clients or managers.

Before a product is released for the market, the industrial designer might oversee or participate in its testing, at which time he or she may need to make refinements to the design to correct unforeseen issues or improve the quality of the product.

Some industrial designers focus on a particular product category. For example, they may design medical equipment or work on consumer electronics products, such as computers and smartphones. Other designers develop ideas for products such as new bicycles, furniture, housewares, and snowboards.

Other designers, sometimes called user interface designers or interaction designers, focus on the usability of a product, such as an electronic device, and ensure that the product is both simple and enjoyable to use.

Industrial designers imagine how consumers might use a product and test different designs with consumers to see how each design looks and works. Industrial designers often work with engineers, production experts, and market research analysts to find out if their designs are feasible. They apply the input from their colleagues' professional expertise to further develop their designs. For example, industrial designers may work with market research analysts to develop plans to market new product designs to consumers.

Computers are a major tool for industrial designers. Industrial designers use two-dimensional computer-aided design and drafting (CADD) software to sketch ideas, because computers make it easy to make changes and show alternatives. Three-dimensional computer-aided design (CAD) software is increasingly being used by industrial designers as a tool to transform their two-dimensional designs into models with the help of three-dimensional printers. If they work for manufacturers, they also may use CAID software to create specific machine-readable instructions that tell other machines exactly how to build the product

Duties and Responsibilities

- Consulting with clients to determine requirements for designs
- Researching the various ways a particular product might be used, and who will use it
- Sketching ideas or creating renderings, which are images on paper or on a computer that provide a visual of design ideas
- Using computer software to develop virtual models of different designs
- Creating physical prototypes of their designs
- Examining materials and manufacturing requirements to determine production costs
- Working with other specialists, such as mechanical engineers and manufacturers, to evaluate whether their design concepts will fill needs at a reasonable cost
- Evaluating product safety, appearance, and function to determine if a design is practical
- Presenting designs and demonstrating prototypes to clients for approval

WORK ENVIRONMENT

Immediate Physical Environment

Industrial designers usually work in comfortable offices or studios. Those who regularly oversee product manufacturing might be at some risk for health issues related to their factory environments. Work spaces for industrial designers often include work tables for sketching designs, meeting rooms with whiteboards for brainstorming with colleagues, and computers and other office equipment for preparing designs and communicating with clients. Although industrial designers work primarily in offices, they may travel to testing facilities, design centers, clients' exhibit sites, users' homes or workplaces, and places where the product is manufactured.

Transferable Skills and Abilities

Communication Skills
- Expressing thoughts and ideas
- Speaking effectively

Creative/Artistic Skills
- Being skilled in art, music, or dance

Interpersonal/Social Skills
- Cooperating with others
- Working as a member of a team

Organization & Management Skills
- Making decisions
- Paying attention to and handling details
- Performing routine work

Research & Planning Skills
- Creating ideas
- Setting goals and deadlines
- Using logical reasoning

Technical Skills
- Performing scientific, mathematical, and technical work
- Working with data or numbers

Human Environment

Industrial designers usually report to the creative director of the design firm or manager of a department, and they may oversee an intern or assistant as he or she gains experience. Interaction with clients and other members of a product development team may include lively brainstorming sessions as well as harsh criticism about ideas and designs. Self-employed industrial designers interact with others less often as they usually work from home offices.

Technological Environment

Industrial designers use a variety of art tools and supplies to build models and sketch designs, but much of their work is also performed using CAD software, CAID software, and modeling, animation, and design software.

EDUCATION, TRAINING, AND ADVANCEMENT

High School/Secondary

Students should take a college-preparatory program that includes courses in English, math, and science, including physics and trigonometry. Electives should include drafting, drawing, and other art courses (sculpture, painting, ceramics, and photography) and/

or industrial arts (woodworking and metalworking). Other useful courses include psychology, engineering, and business. Students need to prepare a portfolio for admission to postsecondary art and design programs. Because this is a hands-on field, students should put together models, visit art museums, and engage in other cultural and educational activities that encourage critical and creative thinking skills.

Suggested High School Subjects
- Algebra
- Applied Communication
- Applied Math
- Applied Physics
- Arts
- Blueprint Reading
- College Preparatory
- Drafting
- English
- Geometry
- Industrial Arts
- Mechanical Drawing
- Photography
- Pottery
- Trigonometry
- Woodshop

Related Career Pathways/Majors

Arts, A/V Technology & Communications Cluster
- Audio & Video Technologies Pathway
- s

Famous First

The first locomotive cowcatcher was invented by Isaac Dripps and used in 1833 on the Camden and Amboy Railroad between Bordentown and Hightstown, NJ. It consisted originally of a small attachment on two wheels with projecting points, but since the prongs impaled animals, it was replaced by a heavy bar set at right angles to the rails.

Source: "Transportation." *Famous First Facts*, Salem, 2016. *Salem Online*, https://online.salempress.com

Postsecondary

A bachelor's degree in industrial design or engineering, ideally with a minor in art or design, is the standard minimum requirement for most entry-level jobs in this field; some employers prefer to hire those with a master's degree. Students must acquire skills in drawing, CAD and design software, and building 3D models by hand, as well as knowledge about industrial materials and manufacturing processes. Courses that build understanding of humans and society, such as psychology, anthropology, human ecology, and philosophy, are also important. Business skills are required for some jobs. Students should plan to apply for an internship and prepare a portfolio of their best work.

Related College Majors:
- Industrial Design
- Industrial/Manufacturing Technology

Adult Job Seekers

Industrial design draws on many different abilities, skills, and knowledge. Adults with a close familiarity with industry-specific products, such as medical equipment or sporting goods, could build upon that experience by taking industrial design classes. Adults with a background in art might simply need to add engineering and/or CAD training to their current skill set. Interested adults should discuss options with college admissions counselors.

Most industrial designers begin their careers as interns. They are given assignments of increasing responsibility and prestige as they become more experienced and prove their abilities. In time, an industrial designer may be able to advance to a supervisory position or establish his or her own design firm. Teaching at the college level, writing books, and consulting are other options for those with adequate experience and education.

Professional Certification and Licensure

No professional license or certification is required. Certificates are sometimes awarded upon completion of associate's degree programs.

Additional Requirements

Designers must have good eyesight, including the ability to see different colors. Problem-solving skills, creativity, self-discipline, awareness of cultural trends, and open-mindedness are all desirable. Industrial designers should develop a strong portfolio of their work, as this is often the deciding factor in the hiring process.

Fast Fact

Artists, craftsmen, and architects were the original "industrial designers" of the ancient world. These people designed and created products, with varying levels of beauty and functionality, to be consumed by their respective consumers. When the industrial revolution came, engineers quickly became the primary designers of products.

Source: http://www.beratekindustries.com

EARNINGS AND ADVANCEMENT

Earnings of industrial designers depend on the individual's education and experience and the type, size, and geographic location of the employer. Industrial designers who have their own consulting firms may have fluctuating incomes, depending on their business for the year. Some industrial designers may work on retainers, which means they may receive flat fees for given periods of time. During any given period, industrial designers can work on retainers for many different companies.

Experienced designers in large firms may advance to chief designer, design department head, or other supervisory positions. Some designers become teachers in design schools or in colleges and universities. Many teachers continue to consult privately or operate small design studios in addition to teaching. Some experienced designers open their own design firms.

Median annual earnings of industrial designers was $66,590 in May 2018. The lowest 10 percent earned less than $38,630, and the highest 10 percent earned more than $108,040.

Industrial designers may receive paid vacations, holidays, and sick days; life and health insurance; and retirement benefits. These are usually paid by the employer.

Median annual wages, May 2018

Commercial and industrial designers: $66,590

Art and design workers: $46,660

Total, all occupations: $38,640

Note: All Occupations includes all occupations in the U.S. Economy.
Source: U.S. Bureau of Labor Statistics, Occupational Employment Statistics

EMPLOYMENT AND OUTLOOK

Industrial designers held about 39,700 jobs in 2016. Employment is expected to grow 4 percent from 2016 to 2026, slower than the average for all occupations. Demand for industrial designers will stem from continued emphasis on product quality and safety, design of new products that are easy and comfortable to use and high technology products in medicine, transportation and other fields.

Prospects should be best for job applicants who have a strong background in 2D- and 3D-computer-aided design and drafting (CADD) and CAID. The increasing trend toward the use of sustainable resources is likely to improve prospects for applicants who know how to work with sustainable resources.

In addition, as more products become digitized and internet-capable, applicants with experience in user interface (UI), user experience (UX), and interactive design (IxD) may have better job prospects.

Percent change in employment, Projected 2016–26

Total, all occupations: 7%

Commercial and industrial designers: 4%

Art and design workers: 4%

Note: All Occupations includes all occupations in the U.S. Economy.
Source: U.S. Bureau of Labor Statistics, Occupational Employment Statistics

Related Occupations
- Designer
- Graphic Designer
- Merchandise Displayer
- Multimedia Artist & Animator

Conversation With... ANDY SCHAUDT

Project Director
Virginia Tech Transportation Institute (VTTI)
Center for Automated Vehicle Systems (CAVS)
Blacksburg, VA
Human Factors Field, 18 years

1. **What was your individual career path in terms of education/training, entry-level job, or other significant opportunity?**

   In high school, I was very focused and thought I'd get a biology degree and go into a medical-related field. My first semester biology class at the University of Idaho was designed to weed people out and it was not enjoyable. I did like psychology, so I switched. I enjoyed studying human behavior and the human brain.

   As part of my university's psychology programs, we could participate in studies and do research. Sophomore year, my professor invited me to check out his lab. He did human factors work, which focuses on how people work around technology and how you can design for that. Next door was a flight simulator lab, and that really connected. I joined both labs.

   I entered graduate school to study human factors psychology tailored toward surface transportation because there were more jobs. I also had internships that influenced me to shift from the sky to the ground.

   After earning my MS from the University of Idaho, I came to Virginia Tech as research faculty at VTTI and earned an MBA in Business Administration and Management from the university's Pamplin College of Business, where I still teach. I've consulted on a number of human factors projects and worked for organizations such as MedStar Health in Washington, DC, where I advised on human factors aimed at reducing medical errors and improving patient experiences.

   I returned to VTTI to co-lead CAVS. We are a group of people with different skill sets, and our research is automated vehicle systems such as adaptive cruise control. We already have automated systems in our cars, and the end goal is to remove the human from the loop.

   My main focus is leading and motivating our team. Recently I hired 12 undergraduate and graduate students for the summer across every discipline I could find. So we have industrial design students, finance students....people who, when they get into the transportation area, maybe bring more and new thoughts into the space.

We work on two dozen projects a year across a lot of different areas. It's really fun to see cars come here cloaked in camouflage because the car companies don't want anyone to see them. We just finished a study for the National Highway Safety Administration looking at how somebody's expectations going into an automated vehicle for the first time influence how much they trust it. It's really a delicate balance to design technology for fickle people like humans.

2. **What are the most important skills and/or qualities for someone in your profession?**

   You have to have a healthy work ethic, whether you're working for a car company or doing research or transportation policy. Right now, transportation is in disruption and you need to be disciplined. This is also a culture of not just focusing on the car—the shiny object—but the person behind the wheel. You need to understand physics, and you need the technical skills such as programming, data visualization and other things associated with big data because we have more data coming out of our cars than our military's fighter jets.

3. **What do you wish you had known going into this profession?**

   I found my niche, which is more a leadership than technical role. I could probably be better at technical skills like programming. I wish I'd known cars would turn into computers.

4. **Are there many job opportunities in your profession? In what specific areas?**

   Part of the industry's current disruption is the entry of companies like Tesla and Google trying to play in the space. They like to go much faster than car companies, which typically take five to seven years to develop a car. So, the car companies are trying to catch up. Right now, there are many job opportunities, not just for human factors researchers, but in applications of transportation. There's a new field, micro-mobility—such as electric scooters—so there are startup companies like dockless moped companies trying to come out in New York. New applications people haven't thought of before are coming into play to try to bridge gaps. It's an opportunity to connect all moving things together so we work more smartly together.

5. **How do you see your profession changing in the next five years? How will technology impact that change, and what skills will be required?**

   We're coming to the top of the hype cycle about new technology—self-driving cars and the like—and people are realizing how hard it is. Everybody is going to be working to make these new things work. So I don't see that change in the next five years, but ten years out you're going to see increased aptitude of computers with driving. Electric vehicles are going to be big. Micro-mobility, such as automated taxis and shuttles in an urban environment, will be in view. After that, a shakeup of all of this will be applied to rural areas. It's more of an evolution than a revolution.

6. **What do you enjoy most about your job? What do you enjoy least about your job?**

   I most enjoy the opportunity to save lives. In the US we have 37,000 to 40,000 auto-related deaths a year. It's awful, but an opportunity for improvement. Automated systems will remove humans from the loop where it makes sense. It's really heroic and gets us out of bed every day.

   I don't really know if there's anything I don't like my job. We collect millions of miles of data, and that can be hard. Sometimes it takes a lot of work to make a change in this field.

7. **Can you suggest a valuable "try this" for students considering a career in your profession?**

   Depending on where you live, there can be a lot of opportunity to participate in transportation research with companies or universities. Focus on a category of transportation that interests you. Go shadow what they do and learn. Maybe you're interested in helping blind people get around. I have a bunch of students who are passionate about scooters. You will meet people, and the more people you meet, the more opportunity you will find.

MORE INFORMATION

Association of Women Industrial Designers (AWID)
P.O. Box 468, Old Chelsea Station
New York, NY 10011
info@awidweb.com
www.awidweb.com

Core77
561 Broadway, 6th Floor
New York, NY 10012
212.965.1998
mail@core77.com
www.core77.com

Industrial Designers Society of America (IDSA)
45195 Business Court, Suite 250
Dulles, VA 20166-6717
703.707.6000
idsa@idsa.org
www.idsa.org

Sponsors undergraduate and graduate scholarships:
www.idsa.org/idsa-gianninoto-graduate-scholarship

Sponsors Student Merit Awards:
www.idsa.org/education

Sponsors student IDEA awards:
www.idsa.org/content/content1/student-idea-award-winners

Organization of Black Designers (OBD)
300 M Street SW, Suite N110
Washington, DC 20024-4019
202.659.3918
OBDesign@aol.com
www.core77.com/OBD/welcome.html

University & College Designers Association (UCDA)
199 W. Enon Springs Road, Suite 300
Smyrna, TN 37167
615.459.4559
info@ucda.com
www.ucda.com

Sally Driscoll/Editor

Industrial Engineers

Snapshot

Career Cluster(s): Agriculture, Food & Natural Resources, Manufacturing, Science, Technology, Engineering & Mathematics, Transportation, Distribution & Logistics

Interests: Science, engineering, mathematics, developing solutions

Earnings (Median Pay): $87,040

Employment & Outlook: Faster Than Average Growth Expected

OVERVIEW

Sphere of Work

Industrial engineering is essential to the successful performance of manufacturing processes and services. Industrial engineers design and refine manufacturing systems to improve their efficiency in order to reduce waste and achieve the desired product within budgetary constraints. They are often responsible for reviewing and streamlining work flows and other manufacturing procedures in order to expedite production processes. Some industrial engineers may specialize in one technological component or aspect of production systems.

Transportation engineering or transport engineering is the application of technology and scientific principles to the planning, functional design, operation and management of facilities for any mode of transportation in order to provide for the safe, efficient, rapid, comfortable, convenient, economical, and environmentally compatible movement of people and goods transport.

Some industrial engineers work as consultants or hold nonmanufacturing positions in the communications or medical industries. These engineers are frequently responsible for projects associated with health and safety engineering.

Work Environment

Industrial engineers typically work in office settings as well as in factories or manufacturing plants where they may observe the machinery and procedures implemented in order to determine how effectively their solutions function and identify elements for further improvement. As industrial engineers collaborate with professionals from a variety of disciplines, they must have a knowledge of terminology relevant to related fields and be capable of communicating engineering concepts effectively.

Profile

Interests: Data, Things
Working Conditions: Work Inside
Physical Strength: Light Work
Education Needs: Bachelor's Degree, Master's Degree, Doctoral Degree
Licensure/Certification: Required
Physical Abilities Not Required: Not Climb, Not Kneel
Opportunities for Experience: Internship, Apprenticeship, Military Service, Part-Time Work
Holland Interest Score: EIR

* See Appendix A

Occupation Interest

Industrial engineering encompasses a variety of technical, scientific, and managerial tasks. Most industrial engineers enjoy addressing the complex issues associated with their projects and developing solutions to achieve efficiency while maintaining overall quality. People who are detail oriented, creative, and capable of thinking creatively to develop alternative solutions are particularly well suited to a career in industrial engineering.

A Day in the Life—Duties and Responsibilities

Industrial engineers often begin the day with meetings, discussing production and financial parameters in groups consisting of other engineers, scientists, manufacturers, business advisers, and managers, with whom they consult as needed while carrying out projects. These meetings help industrial engineers determine how best to allocate their time between offices, laboratories, factories, and testing sites. Industrial engineers aspire to achieve optimal manufacturing efficiency and quality and consistency in the production and distribution of products. They analyze the best methods for preventing waste during various stages of production, from the extraction of raw resources through the distribution of the completed products. Other engineers may work to improve services, simplifying processes such as the hospitalization of patients or the processing of bank transactions.

Industrial engineers work to minimize energy usage and toxic emissions, promoting sustainable practices. Some industrial engineers are supervisors or obtain managerial positions based on their qualifications. Industrial engineers are responsible for suggesting improvements to engineering standards and for establishing safety procedures. They may also serve as investigators when accidents occur in industrial settings, recording what happened and assessing whether regulations were violated before preparing statements for the management and authorities.

In academia, industrial engineers teach, advise students, and guide research projects. Inventive industrial engineers may need to protect their unique designs and methods with patents or seek out entrepreneurs interested in purchasing the rights to use their technologies and processes in other factories and businesses. Occasionally, industrial engineers serve as consultants for governmental groups, offering their expertise to aid politicians in developing policies and legislation relevant to the fields of engineering and technology.

Some industrial engineers, called manufacturing engineers, focus entirely on the automated aspects of manufacturing processes. They design manufacturing systems to optimize the use of computer networks, robots, and materials.

Industrial engineers focus on how to get the work done most efficiently, balancing many factors, such as time, number of workers needed, available technology, actions workers need to take, achieving the end product with no errors, workers' safety, environmental concerns, and cost.

The versatility of industrial engineers allows them to engage in activities that are useful to a variety of businesses, governments, and nonprofits. For example, industrial engineers engage in supply chain management to help businesses minimize inventory costs, conduct quality assurance activities to help businesses keep their customer bases satisfied, and work in the growing field of project management as industries across the economy seek to control costs and maximize efficiencies.

Duties and Responsibilities

- **Reviewing production schedules, engineering specifications, process flows, and other information to understand methods that are applied and activities that take place in manufacturing and services**
- **Figuring out how to manufacture parts or products, or deliver services, with maximum efficiency**
- **Developing management control systems to make financial planning and cost analysis more efficient**
- **Enacting quality control procedures to resolve production problems or minimize costs**
- **Designing control systems to coordinate activities and production planning in order to ensure that products meet quality standards**
- **Conferring with clients about product specifications, vendors about purchases, management personnel about manufacturing capabilities, and staff about the status of projects**

Industrial engineers apply their skills to many different situations, from manufacturing to healthcare systems to business administration. For example, they design systems for
- moving heavy parts within manufacturing plants
- delivering goods from a company to customers, including finding the most profitable places to locate manufacturing or processing plants

OCCUPATION SPECIALTIES

Time-Study Engineers

Time-Study Engineers develop work measurement procedures and direct time-and-motion and incentive studies to promote the efficient use of employees and facilities.

Safety Engineers

Safety Engineers develop and implement safety programs to prevent or correct unsafe environmental working conditions, utilizing knowledge of industrial processes, mechanics, chemistry, psychology, and industrial health and safety laws.

Manufacturing Engineers

Manufacturing Engineers plan, direct, and coordinate manufacturing processes in industrial plants.

Quality-Control Engineers

Quality-Control Engineers plan and direct the development, application and maintenance of quality standards for processing materials into partially finished or finished products.

WORK ENVIRONMENT

Immediate Physical Environment

Most industrial engineers alternate between working in office settings and traveling to laboratories, industrial sites, and test facilities, where they analyze the implementation and operation of manufacturing systems and services.

Plant Environment

Industrial engineers often travel to plants, testing sites, and factories. As they may encounter dangerous machinery and risk exposure to toxic substances used in manufacturing processes when visiting these locations, engineers must adhere to all safety procedures.

Human Environment

Industrial engineers collaborate with a diverse array of workers from a variety of disciplines. They must be able to interact effectively with other engineers and scientists, managers, business advisers, technical assistants, and consumers. Industrial engineers benefit from having clear communication skills, which will help them to understand the needs of their clients and implement their feedback.

Technological Environment

Industrial engineers rely on a variety of simple and complex technologies to perform their work, including advanced computer software and hardware used to model prototypes.

Transferable Skills and Abilities

Communication Skills
- Speaking effectively
- Writing concisely

Interpersonal/Social Skills
- Cooperating with others
- Working as a member of a team

Organization & Management Skills
- Coordinating tasks
- Managing people/groups
- Paying attention to and handling details
- Performing duties that change frequently

Research & Planning Skills
- Creating ideas
- Using logical reasoning

Technical Skills
- Performing scientific, mathematical, and technical work
- Working with machines, tools, or other objects

EDUCATION, TRAINING, AND ADVANCEMENT

High School/Secondary

High school students who are intrigued by industrial engineering should take courses in mathematics, physics, chemistry, biology, and computer science. Economics, political science, business, sociology, and English courses also help to provide students with the well-rounded education essential to success in the field. When available, students should take advanced-placement (AP) classes, especially mathematics, science, and business courses.

Workshops and camps hosted by universities and professional industrial engineering groups provide opportunities for students to explore the engineering profession. Students may also benefit from preparing projects for science and engineering contests and participating in mathematics, science, and technical clubs as well as Junior Achievement and Future Business Leaders of America programs. High school students are sometimes eligible for internships that will help them to meet and work with industrial engineers and experience the demands and opportunities associated with the field.

Suggested High School Subjects
- Algebra
- Applied Communication
- Applied Math
- Applied Physics
- Blueprint Reading
- Calculus
- Chemistry
- College Preparatory
- Composition
- Computer Science
- Drafting
- English
- Geometry
- Humanities
- Machining Technology
- Mathematics

- Mechanical Drawing
- Physical Science
- Physics
- Science
- Shop Mechanics
- Statistics
- Trigonometry

Related Career Pathways/Majors

Agriculture, Food & Natural Resources Cluster
- Food Products & Processing Systems Pathway

Manufacturing Cluster
- Health, Safety & Environmental Assurance Pathway
- Manufacturing Production Process Development Pathway

Science, Technology, Engineering & Mathematics Cluster
- Engineering & Technology Pathway

Transportation, Distribution & Logistics Cluster
- Warehousing & Distribution Center Operations Pathway

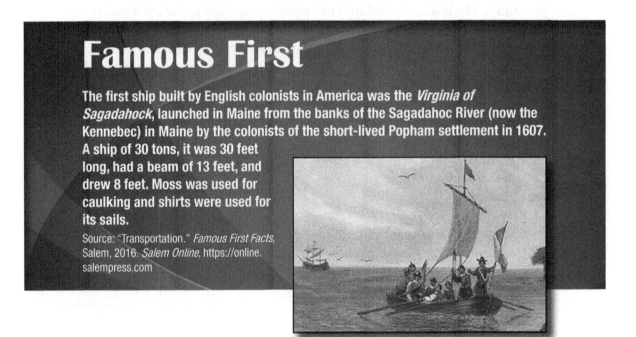

Famous First

The first ship built by English colonists in America was the *Virginia of Sagadahock*, launched in Maine from the banks of the Sagadahoc River (now the Kennebec) in Maine by the colonists of the short-lived Popham settlement in 1607. A ship of 30 tons, it was 30 feet long, had a beam of 13 feet, and drew 8 feet. Moss was used for caulking and shirts were used for its sails.

Source: "Transportation." *Famous First Facts*, Salem, 2016. *Salem Online*, https://online.salempress.com

Postsecondary

A number of accredited colleges and universities offer bachelor's degree programs in industrial engineering that provide students with the knowledge necessary to work in the field. Graduates of related engineering, science, or business programs may also pursue industrial engineering careers. Undergraduate industrial engineering students complete classes that emphasize engineering foundations, with courses focusing on information technology, manufacturing processes, quality control, and ergonomics. Students may also complete minors in management, economics, or systems theory to supplement their engineering knowledge and thereby increase their value to potential employers.

Graduate degrees enable industrial engineers to concentrate on specialized fields of study or related disciplines, such as marketing or finance, in order to extend their comprehension of various industrial engineering applications. Managerial positions in the field of industrial engineering often require candidates to hold advanced degrees.

Schools with accredited engineering programs and professional organizations such as the Institute of Industrial Engineers (IIE) often offer internships or other networking opportunities for students. In addition to attending academic courses, many students take cooperative education jobs, which enable them to gain work experience, income, and contacts that will help them secure jobs after graduation.

Related College Majors:
- Engineering, General
- Engineering/Industrial Management
- Industrial/Manufacturing Engineering

Adult Job Seekers

Industrial engineers seeking to reenter the field can educate themselves about recent industrial engineering developments by taking courses at local community colleges, participating in training workshops, attending conferences, and consulting professional materials available from the IIE and other technical groups. Some industrial engineers take classes in allied fields to expand their expertise and employability.

Professional organizations and alumni groups provide returning industrial engineers with opportunities to network with people in their field and potential employers. Industrial engineers can benefit by accepting short-term research projects in order to acquire skills they can add to their resumes.

Professional Certification and Licensure

Most industrial engineers, particularly those working for businesses with government contracts, become licensed engineers in order to comply with professional standards. To become licensed engineers, individuals must pass the Fundamentals of Engineering exam, which assesses their comprehension of engineering knowledge, and be certified as engineers in training. After acquiring work experience under the supervision of licensed engineers, the engineers in training may take the Principles and Practice of Engineering exam, successful completion of which will certify them as professional engineers. Several states require industrial engineers to take continuing education courses to retain their licenses.

Additional Requirements

Competent industrial engineers benefit from continual professional development in order to stay abreast of new information, technologies, and methods. As such, aspiring industrial engineers should be willing to devote themselves to lifelong learning.

Fast Fact

The first Ferris Wheel was created by Pittsburgh, Pennsylvania engineer, George W. Ferris, in 1893. The wheel is supported by two 140-foot steel towers and connected by a 45-foot axle—the largest single piece of forged steel ever made at that time.

Source: www.nspe.org

EARNINGS AND ADVANCEMENT

Earnings depend on the employer and the employee's experience and education.

The median annual earnings of industrial engineers was $87,040 in May 2018. The lowest 10 percent earned less than $56,470, and the highest 10 percent earned more than $132,340.

Industrial engineers may receive paid vacations, holidays, and sick days; life and health insurance; and retirement benefits. These are usually paid by the employer.

Median annual wages, May 2018

Engineers: $93,080

Industrial engineers: $87,040

Total, all occupations: $38,640

Note: All Occupations includes all occupations in the U.S. Economy.
Source: U.S. Bureau of Labor Statistics, Occupational Employment Statistics

EMPLOYMENT AND OUTLOOK

There were about 257,900 industrial engineers employed nationally in 2016. Employment is expected to grow faster than the average for all occupations through the year 2026, which means employment is projected to increase 10 percent. Jobs will be created as companies look to industrial engineers to develop efficient processes in an effort to reduce costs, delays, and waste and increase productivity.

The largest employers of industrial engineers were as follows:

Transportation equipment manufacturing	18%
Professional, scientific, and technical services	13%
Computer and electronic product manufacturing	13%
Machinery manufacturing	8%
Fabricated metal product manufacturing	6%

Percent change in employment, Projected 2016–26

Industrial engineers: 10%

Engineers: 8%

Total, all occupations: 7%

Note: All Occupations includes all occupations in the U.S. Economy.
Source: U.S. Bureau of Labor Statistics, Occupational Employment Statistics

Related Occupations
- Cost Estimator
- Energy Conservation & Use Technician
-
- Marine Engineer & Naval Architect
- Mechanical Engineer
- Operations Research Analyst

Related Military Occupations
- Environmental Health & Safety Officer
- Industrial Engineer

Conversation With...
HESHAM A. RAKHA
Samuel Reynolds Pritchard Professor of Engineering
Virginia Tech Transportation Institute
Director, Center for Sustainable Mobility
Blacksburg, VA
Transportation Research Field, 16 years

1. What was your individual career path in terms of education/training, entry-level job, or other significant opportunity?

My mother is English and my dad, Egyptian. I was born in Scotland and lived in the UK, Egypt, Zambia and Pakistan growing up. In grade 11, in Pakistan, the education system required me to decide whether I was going the medical route or the engineering route, science or math. Math was my passion. When I finished grade 12, I wanted to do engineering, but the question was, what kind? A family friend was an architect. He told me transportation was really emerging as a field, and to consider going into civil engineering. I took his advice.

I earned a BSc in Civil Engineering from Cairo University, then applied to universities in Canada, Australia, the UK and the United States for my Master's. I received very good offers, but decided to go for Queen's University in Kingston, Ontario. I felt there would be more opportunity in Canada once I finished. I was very fortunate that my advisor was a young faculty member named Mike, who became my friend and mentor. I earned an MSc in Civil Engineering, then stayed and did my PhD in Civil Engineering with the same advisor despite a scholarship I received from the University of California at Irvine. At the time, my father recently had passed and my brother had an offer from Queen's.

My father, a veterinarian, held a PhD. It was second nature for me to want to do a PhD. He was my role model.

After earning that degree, I worked for my adviser's consulting firm. My wife was Canadian (she passed away in 2013), and we wanted to stay. However, Mike went on to become a faculty member at Virginia Tech and offered me a research scientist position at the Virginia Tech Transportation Institute. I loved working for him, but I started applying for faculty positions because people were criticizing me for being a clone of Mike. I had two offers, one at Rutgers University and one at Virginia Tech. I took the job at Virginia Tech. Unfortunately, Mike died during this time at the age of 39.

He had been director of VTTI's Center for Sustainable Mobility. After he passed, given our close working relationship, I was the best person to lead the center.

We do research in ways to reduce traffic congestion and at the same time reduce the carbon footprint of transportation systems.

What I do is like a chess game. When we change a network, travelers change their travel behavior. If, for example, we add a shoulder lane for peak traffic hours, more vehicles are going to travel that lane. That's why congestion never goes away.

I don't think we'll ever solve the problem but at least we can reduce the effects of congestion. There are two approaches to reduce it: one is on the demand side and one is on the supply side.

The demand side entails reducing the number of vehicles traveling on the network through public transportation or ride-sharing. U.S. cities are typically sprawled and thus not efficient for public transportation. Take Washington, DC. Certain subway lines get you most of your way, but how do you get that so-called last mile, from the subway system to your destination? Options like bikeshares, scooters, or Uber and Lyft, might work. The supply side means adding extra lanes, such as using the shoulder during peak hours, or using emerging technology such as automated vehicles. We've been able to achieve considerable benefits using these methods.

The center works with different organizations including federal agencies and the Virginia Dept. of Transportation, and we consult with companies such as Toyota and Ford.

2. **What are the most important skills and/or qualities for someone in your profession?**

Persistence. There are going to be failures. You need to believe and keep plugging away and be flexible and willing to change course.

In my work, I also need to be able to communicate, both to my students and to the people I want to fund my research. You also need to be able to write and be creative to conduct research.

3. **What do you wish you had known going into this profession?**

I think electrical engineering's skill set is better equipped for transportation than civil engineering's skill set. Had I known I would have studied electrical engineering.

4. **Are there many job opportunities in your profession? In what specific areas?**

There are tons of jobs given the evolving transportation modes such as Uber or Lyft, vehicle technology, and urban congestion. All my students get multiple offers.

5. **How do you see your profession changing in the next five years? How will technology impact that change, and what skills will be required?**

   There's going to be automation. The driver will be in the car, but automation will make the task easier, less tedious, and more efficient. There will be connectivity, communicating via our phones or cars to the cloud, with other vehicles, or with traffic signals, for example. I also see interchangeability of modes of transportation coming into play. We will be using public transportation in addition to bike shares, scooters, and electric vehicles.

6. **What do you enjoy most about your job? What do you enjoy least about your job?**

   I most enjoy the research and teaching. Research means I'm doing new things every day and never know the outcome. Teaching, I'm changing lives. It's satisfying, to see a changed person at the end of the semester. I'm also impacting the lives of people on the roadways. For example, we recommended truck driving lanes on I-81, and every time I drive that stretch of road, I think, "I had a say." I least enjoy the administrative paperwork that comes as you climb higher in your organization.

7. **Can you suggest a valuable "try this" for students considering a career in your field?**

   The unique thing about our profession is that everyone thinks they're an expert. We all experience traffic congestion. I don't think we all understand the complexity of the problem, because we're dealing with the psyche of human beings. Find someone in this field and shadow them. VTTI has a school day, for instance, and we give tours.

   Also: travel. Go see the world. In the Netherlands, people ride bikes. Meet different people. You never learn as much as when you travel.

MORE INFORMATION

American Society for Engineering Management (ASEM)
MST-223 Engineering Management Building
600 W. 14th Street
Rolla, MO 65409
573.341.6228
www.asem.org

American Society for Quality (ASQ)
P.O. Box 3005
Milwaukee, WI 53201-3005
800.248.1946
help@asq.org
www.asq.org

American Society of Safety Engineers (ASSE)
Educational Department
1800 E. Oakton Street
Des Plaines, IL 60018
847.699.2929
info@asse.org
www.asse.org

Association for the Advancement of Cost Engineering International (AACEI)
1265 Suncrest Towne Centre Drive
Morgantown, WV 26505-1876
304.296.8444
www.aacei.org

Association of Technology, Management, and Applied Engineering (ATMAE)
1390 Eisenhower Place
Ann Arbor, MI 48108
734.677.0720
www.atmae.org

Human Factors and Ergonomics Society (HFES)
P.O. Box 1369
Santa Monica, CA 90406-1369
310.394.1811
www.hfes.org

The Institute for Operations Research and the Management Sciences (INFORMS)
7240 Parkway Drive, Suite 300
Hanover, MD 21076
443.757.3500
www.informs.org

Institute of Industrial Engineers (IIE)
3577 Parkway Lane, Suite 200
Norcross, GA 30092
800.494.0460
cs@iienet.org
www.iienet.org

National Action Council for Minorities in Engineering (NACME)
440 Hamilton Avenue, Suite 302
White Plains, NY 10601-1813
914.539.4010
info@nacme.org
www.nacme.org

National Society of Black Engineers (NSBE)
205 Daingerfield Road
Alexandria, VA 22314
703.549.2207
info@nsbe.org
www.nsbe.org

Society of Hispanic Professional Engineers (SHPE)
13181 Crossroads Parkway N
Suite 450
City of Industry, CA 91746-3497
323.725.3970
shpenational@shpe.org
www.shpe.org

Society of Women Engineers (SWE)
203 N. La Salle Street, Suite 1675
Chicago, IL 60601
877.793.4636
hq@swe.org
www.swe.org

Technology Student Association (TSA)
1914 Association Drive
Reston, VA 20191-1540
703.860.9000
general@tsaweb.org
www.tsaweb.org

Elizabeth D. Schafer/Editor

Information Technology Project Managers

Snapshot

Career Cluster(s): Business, Management & Administration, Information Technology, Science, Technology, Engineering & Mathematics

Interests: Science, technology, mathematics, computer science, multitasking, communicating with others

Earnings (Median Pay): $98,125

Employment & Outlook: Average Growth Expected

OVERVIEW

Sphere of Work

Information technology project managers, often abbreviated as IT project managers, oversee the design and implementation of information technology systems and related infrastructure. The proliferation of computer systems throughout the world has made IT project managers relevant in nearly every type of business and industry. IT project managers work closely with other managers in their organization to understand the company's IT needs. They then direct and supervise the technical staff in implementing the necessary hardware or

software to address those needs, be they data storage, network security, or inventory management. IT project managers are also responsible for ensuring that all IT projects are completed within budget and on schedule.

Work Environment

IT project management professionals work primarily in administrative and office settings, though their exact locations may vary depending on their area of expertise and the type of company that employs them. The work of IT project managers requires extensive interaction with coworkers, outside vendors, and technical staff members. IT project managers must be able to draw out and interpret the specific IT needs of a department or organization and utilize that feedback to develop customized systems. Project managers are also supervisors charged with ensuring that their staff of IT professionals is continually contributing to project advancement in a timely and organized manner.

Profile

Interests: Data, People
Working Conditions: Work Inside
Physical Strength: Light Work
Education Needs: Bachelor's Degree, Master's Degree
Licensure/Certification: Recommended
Physical Abilities Not Required: Not Climb, Not Kneel
Opportunities for Experience: Internship, Military Service, Volunteer Work, Part-Time Work
Holland Interest Score: ECI

* See Appendix A

Occupation Interest

IT project managers are results-oriented multitaskers who thrive in environments where numerous tasks and objectives are active simultaneously. IT project management covers a diverse array of scientific, technical, and managerial knowledge and skills. The majority of IT project management professionals are graduates and professionals who have a strong foundation in mathematics, computer engineering, programming, or computer science. Many IT professionals also possess an academic or professional background in software development, database management, or IT project administration.

Many universities now offer specific undergraduate and postgraduate programs in information technology and project management, but many professionals enter the field with professional and academic backgrounds that span a wide variety of computer-science disciplines.

IT project managers must have strong communication and interpersonal skills as well as excellent management skills.

A Day in the Life—Duties and Responsibilities

A day in the life of an IT project manager involves planning future projects, monitoring the progress of projects that are currently active, and overseeing system maintenance, upkeep, and security tasks. These numerous responsibilities require IT managers to work in close concert with their staff, which can vary in size and scope depending on their organization of employment and particular realm of industry.

In addition to monitoring the progress of active projects, IT project managers also spend a considerable amount of time developing project plans for new initiatives in collaboration with other departmental and organizational staff members. Before work begins on new IT projects, the entire scope of each initiative must be outlined, with specific focus on the systems, schedules, funding, and required staff for each project.

IT project managers hold frequent meetings with subordinates to gauge the progress of active projects. In addition to providing technological and strategic input to resolve project delays or other concerns, IT project managers must also be able to prevent future problems through forethought and a reliance on previous project experience.

IT project managers are often responsible for reporting to executive management in order to outline the successes of previously implemented projects and to address any IT-related concerns relevant to a company or organization as a whole.

Duties and Responsibilities

- Analyzing their organization's computer needs and recommending possible upgrades for top executives to consider
- Planning and directing the installation and maintenance of computer hardware and software
- Ensuring the security of an organization's network and electronic documents
- Assessing the costs and benefits of new projects and justifying funding on projects to top executives
- Learning about new technology and looking for ways to upgrade their organization's computer systems
- Determining short- and long-term personnel needs for their department
- Planning and directing the work of other IT professionals, including computer systems analysts, software developers, information security analysts, and computer support specialists
- Negotiating with vendors to get the highest level of service for the organization's technology

OCCUPATION SPECIALTIES

The following are examples of types of computer and information systems managers:

Chief information officers (CIOs)

Chief information officers (CIOs) determine the technology or information goals of an organization and then oversee implementation of technology to meet those goals.

CIOs may focus on a specific area, such as electronic data processing or information systems, but CIOs tend to focus more on long-term or big picture issues. At small organizations a CIO has more direct control over the IT department, and at larger organizations other managers under the CIO may handle the day-to-day activities of the IT department.

CIOs who do not have technical expertise and who focus solely on a company's business aspects are included in top executives.

Chief technology officers (CTOs)

Chief technology officers (CTOs) evaluate new technology and determine how it can help their organization. When both CIOs and CTOs are present, the CTO usually has more technical expertise.

The CTO usually reports directly to the CIO and is responsible for designing and recommending the appropriate technology solutions to support the CIO's policies and directives. CTOs also work with different departments to implement the organization's technology plans.

When a company does not have a CIO, the CTO determines the overall technology strategy for the firm and presents it to top executives.

IT directors

IT directors, including management information systems (MIS) directors, are in charge of their organizations' information technology (IT) departments, and they directly supervise other employees. IT directors help to determine the business requirements for IT systems, and they implement the policies that have been chosen by top executives. IT directors often have a direct role in hiring members of the IT department. It is their job to ensure the availability of data and network services by coordinating IT activities. IT directors also oversee the financial aspects of their department, such as budgeting.

IT security managers

IT security managers oversee their organizations' network and data security. They work with top executives to plan security policies and promote a culture of information security throughout the organization. They develop programs to keep employees aware of security threats. These managers must keep up to date on IT security measures. They also supervise investigations if there is a security violation.

WORK ENVIRONMENT

Transferable Skills and Abilities

Communication Skills
- Speaking effectively
- Writing concisely
- Listening attentively
- Reading well

Interpersonal/Social Skills
- Motivating others
- Cooperating with others
- Asserting oneself
- Being able to work independently

Organization & Management Skills
- Paying attention to and handling details
- Performing duties that change frequently
- Managing people/groups
- Managing time
- Managing equipment/materials
- Demonstrating leadership
- Making decisions
- Meeting goals and deadlines
- Working quickly when necessary

Research & Planning Skills
- Analyzing information
- Developing evaluation strategies
- Using logical reasoning
- Setting goals and deadlines
- Defining needs
- Identifying problems
- Solving problems

Immediate Physical Environment

IT project managers work in a variety of settings across all types of business and industry, including corporate offices, schools, government offices, transportation centers, and industrial or medical settings.

Human Environment

IT project managers must be savvy communicators who can successfully supervise, manage, and coordinate a variety of professionals on a daily basis.

Technological Environment

IT project managers utilize a broad range of technologies, including collaborative operational software, application servers, networking servers, web-development software, and programming languages.

Technical Skills
- Performing scientific, mathematical, and technical work
- Using technology to process information
- Understanding which technology is appropriate for a task
- Applying the technology to a task

EDUCATION, TRAINING, AND ADVANCEMENT

High School/Secondary

High school students can prepare for a career in IT project management by completing course work in algebra, calculus, geometry, trigonometry, computer programming, and computer science. Advanced placement (AP) classes in computer-related subjects are especially recommended.

Participation in volunteer work, charities, or team sports can help foster the leadership and managerial skills necessary for large-scale project management. Many IT professionals gain additional experience through summer jobs or internships with computer-related organizations. Supplemental information technology courses offered by universities and community colleges are also helpful.

Suggested High School Subjects
- Accounting
- Algebra
- Applied Communication
- Applied Math
- Business & Computer Technology
- Business Data Processing
- Calculus
- College Preparatory
- Computer Programming

- Computer Science
- English
- Geometry
- Keyboarding
- Mathematics
- Statistics
- Trigonometry

Related Career Pathways/Majors

Business, Management & Administration Cluster
- Management Pathway

Information Technology Cluster
- Programming & Software Development Pathway

Science, Technology, Engineering & Mathematics Cluster
- Engineering & Technology Pathway

Famous First

The first winner of the Grand Challenge robotic vehicle race was a modified Volkswagen Touareg nicknamed "Stanley," customized by researchers from Stanford University under team leader Sebastian Thrun. The competition was held on October 8, 2005, along a rugged 131.6-mile desert course north of Primm, CA. It was sponsored by the federal Defense Advanced Research Projects Agency, which offered a $2 million purse, and was meant to spur development of unmanned robot transports for military use. The robots had to navigate the course unaided, without human intervention or remote control, in less than 10 hours. Of the 23 vehicles that qualified for the race, only five reached the finish line. This was the second Grand Challenge held; no vehicle was able to complete the course in the first competition.

Source: "Science and Technology." *Famous First Facts*, Salem, 2016. *Salem Online*, https://online.salempress.com

Postsecondary

Undergraduate programs related to IT include core course work in UNIX system administration software and programming languages such as Java and C+. In addition to a survey of wireless-network technology and database-management techniques, undergraduate IT students also study business models, network security systems, and infrastructure, as well as information-security management.

Postgraduate and doctoral-level programs in information technology are traditionally dedicated to the exploration and discovery of new strategies and technologies, grounded in a strong foundational knowledge of the history of the field. Graduate students are required to complete a thesis or capstone project related to an emerging trend in information technology; this is often highly specialized work that can be an important precursor for their professional growth and eventual career path.

Related College Majors:
- Computer Programming
- Computer Science
- Information Sciences & Systems
- Management Information Systems & Business Data Processing

Adult Job Seekers

Like many supervisory and management professionals, IT project managers work extensive hours. The role often requires evening and weekend work. Due to the vast amount of academic and professional experience required, IT project management is not a traditional choice for those seeking to begin a new career path. The long hours required of the position, particularly in large organizations and corporations, may also pose difficulty for adult professionals eager to achieve a harmonious work-life balance.

Professional Certification and Licensure

Specific certification and licensure is not required for a career as an IT project manager, though numerous national and international professional organizations exist. Voluntarily completing a certification program will give professionals in the field a competitive advantage.

Additional Requirements

IT project managers are talented multitaskers who can simultaneously execute a wide variety of managerial responsibilities. In addition to being able to monitor all active projects, IT project management professionals must also possess the professional and academic experience necessary to predict and eliminate potential pitfalls before they occur in order to ensure that the systems and infrastructure continue to operate effectively and efficiently.

Fast Facts

Hewlett Packard, Microsoft, as well as Apple have one not so obvious thing in common—they were all started in a garage.
Source: websitemagazine.com

The word "logistics" comes from a 19th-century French word, *logistique*. This French word was originally exclusively associated with the transportation of soldiers and military supplies until it was later adopted for civilian applications.
Source: www.auptix.com

EARNINGS AND ADVANCEMENT

According to the Robert Half Technology 2012 Salary Guide, median annual earnings of information technology project managers were $98,125 in 2012. The lowest 10 percent earned less than $79,000, and the highest 10 percent earned more than $117,250.

Information technology managers may receive paid vacations, holidays and sick days; life and health insurance; and retirement benefits. These are usually paid by the employer.

Most jobs for computer and information systems managers require several years of experience in a related IT job. Lower-level management positions may require only a few years of experience. Directors are more likely to need 5 to 10 years of related work experience. A chief technology officer (CTO), who oversees the technology plan for a large organization, may need more than 15 years of experience in the IT field before being considered for a job.

The number of years of experience required varies with the organization. Generally, smaller or newer companies do not require as much experience as larger or more established ones.

Computer systems are used throughout the economy, and IT employees may gain experience in a variety of industries. However, an applicant's work experience should be in the same industry they are applying to work in. For example, an IT security manager should have previously worked in information security. A hospital IT director should have experience in the healthcare field.

Most computer and information systems managers start out as lower-level managers and advance to higher positions within the IT department. IT directors or project managers can advance to become CTOs. A CTO or other manager who is especially business-minded can advance to become a chief information officer (CIO), the person in charge of all IT-related decisions in an organization. CIOs can advance to become top executives in an organization.

Median annual wages, May 2018

Computer and information systems managers: $142,530

Operations specialties managers: $118,580

Total, all occupations: $38,640

Note: All Occupations includes all occupations in the U.S. Economy.
Source: U.S. Bureau of Labor Statistics, Occupational Employment Statistics

EMPLOYMENT AND OUTLOOK

Computer and information systems managers, of which information technology project managers are a part, held about 367,600 jobs nationally in 2016. Employment of information technology project managers is expected to grow 12 percent from 2016 to 2026, faster than the average for all occupations.

Percent change in employment, Projected 2016–26

Computer and information systems managers: 12%

Operations specialties managers: 12%

Total, all occupations: 7%

Note: All Occupations includes all occupations in the U.S. Economy.
Source: U.S. Bureau of Labor Statistics, Occupational Employment Statistics

Demand for computer and information systems managers will grow as firms increasingly expand their operations to digital platforms. Computer and information systems managers will be responsible for implementing these goals.

Employment growth will result from the need to bolster cybersecurity in computer and information systems used by businesses. Industries such as retail trade will need to implement more robust security policies as cyber threats increase.

An increase in the popularity of cloud computing may result in firms outsourcing services from in-house IT departments to cloud-computing companies. This will shift IT services from IT departments in noncomputer industries, such as financial firms or schools, to firms engaged in computer systems design and related services and those in data processing, hosting, and related services.

In addition, as organizations rely more and more on technology to grow their revenue, information technology projects managers who have strong communication skills and a good understanding of business practices will have excellent opportunities.

Related Occupations
- Computer & Information Systems Manager
- Computer Engineer
- Computer Network Architect
- Computer Support Specialist
- Computer Systems Analyst
- Database Administrator
- General Manager & Top Executive
- Information Security Analyst
- Medical Records Administrator
- Network & Computer Systems Administrator
- Operations Research Analyst
- Software Developer
- Web Administrator
- Web Developer

Related Military Occupations
- Computer Programmer
- Computer Systems Officer

Conversation With...
CHRIS CASEY
Project Leader
Penske Logistics
Columbus, OH
Logistics Field, 5 years

1. What was your individual career path in terms of education/training, entry-level job, or other significant opportunity?

I wanted to go into IT when I went to college, but I switched to logistics due to a professor whose classes and teaching style I enjoyed. A lot of business students wanted to get into finance and sales, but I realized that logistics and manufacturing professionals are the ones who deliver the promise of what a salesperson would provide.

I got an IT internship at a manufacturing company and later transitioned into their internal logistics department. For me, a lightbulb had gone off. Companies like Amazon and Uber are opening minds as to how transportation and delivery of a product is really important and has an effect on the bottom line. I earned my BS/BA in logistics and management from John Carroll University.

Today, I manage cost savings projects for a customer's outbound finished goods network. I'm able to look at data in different ways and put it in charts so it is visible, and others can understand trends. You can see how the economy and other industries are impacting trends which, in the transportation industry, fuels employment. If you don't have enough drivers to move freight, that increases costs.

I also am working on an MBA with a focus on Supply Chain Management Sustainability at Fisher School of Business, The Ohio State University.

2. What are the most important skills and/or qualities for someone in your profession?

Being able to interpret data. That involves a lot of analytical and creative thinking. You also need to be able to work well with others in a teamwork situation. As a project leader, I need the ability to motivate people and get them aligned on the same goal. Public speaking skills help internally, as well as with customers.

3. **What do you wish you had known going into this profession?**

   I told my favorite college professor that I didn't think trust is an important part of business. You have a contract, so the requirements are in black and white. I couldn't have been more wrong. I have to trust people here to get their jobs done. I have to trust the carriers and clients to complete their part of the job. You have to trust people to work on projects to have the same motivation you do. Trust is a valuable part of any relationship.

4. **Are there many job opportunities in your profession? In what specific areas?**

   There's a talent shortage in the supply chain field, which has a lot of job security right now. You can move into an analytics position very quickly and become desirable to other companies. Science, technology, engineering, and mathematics (STEM) jobs will be huge. Management and engineering jobs are available. As we bring in more and more clients who want to save money, many jobs are open for engineers and creative thinkers who can solve problems and create efficiency. Healthcare distribution is an area where the cost and the promptness and service are most important.

5. **How do you see your profession changing in the next five years? How will technology impact that change, and what skills will be required?**

   We are seeing more transportation-specific tech companies. New electronic logging devices mean our understanding of the trucking industry is increasing. My focus is sustainability. Trucks might not be full. So, we are looking at freight-matching, which is pairing up with another company to fill up the truck coming and going. That requires good systems, and collaboration between companies in separate industries who aren't directly competitive but share cost savings benefits.

6. **What do you like most about your job? What do you like least about your job?**

   I enjoy working directly with customers. My phone is always on and I answer it before two rings. The more service I can provide, the more I'm relied on for bigger and better things.

   I least like working with "the way we've always done it." Technology is forcing the hand of companies and increased transportation costs will continue to force our customers to ask for more savings.

7. **Can you suggest a valuable "try this" for students considering a career in your profession?**

One summer in high school, I helped my grandmother sell her antiques by opening her eBay store and got a firsthand look at the supply chain. That would be an easy experiment anyone could do. I had to deliver to the customer, who literally rated my service on the site. I understood that it was going to cost more for me to send an item farther, faster, safer. Also, keep your eyes open when traveling. I recently found myself standing on Puget Sound and realized I could see four different transportation modes: a railroad, planes leaving Sea-Tac Airport, the ocean cargo port, and trucks moving by. It is one big orchestra of logistics, moving valuable goods from one place to another. Finally, organizations such as the Council of Supply Chain Management Professionals (cscmp.org) have roundtables, routinely tour facilities, and hold educational seminars and networking events where you can meet your next boss, just like I did.

MORE INFORMATION

Association of Information Technology Professionals (AITP)
330 N. Wabash Avenue, Suite 2000
Chicago, IL 60611
800.224.9371
aitp_hq@aitp.org
www.aitp.org

Network Professional Association (NPA)
1401 Hermes Lane
San Diego, CA 92154
888.672.6720
www.npa.org

John Pritchard/Editor

Logisticians

Snapshot

Career Cluster(s): Agriculture, Food & Natural Resources Business, Management & Administration, Manufacturing, Marketing, Sales & Service, Transportation, Distribution & Logistics

Interests: Logistics, supply chain management, warehousing and distribution, international business, customer service, and satisfaction

Earnings (Median Pay): $102,850

Employment & Outlook: Average Growth Expected

OVERVIEW

Sphere of Work

Logisticians analyze and coordinate an organization's supply chain—the system that moves a product from supplier to consumer. They manage the entire life cycle of a product, which includes how a product is acquired, allocated, and delivered.

Work Environment

Transportation managers work primarily in office settings, though their work may frequently take them to manufacturing facilities, distribution centers, or warehouses operated by their employing organizations.

Transportation managers are in frequent communication with their fleet, so much of their work is done out of a singular location where telephone, internet, and radio communications systems are on hand.

Profile

Interests: Data, People
Working Conditions: Work Inside
Physical Strength: Light Work
Education Needs: Junior/Technical/Community College, Bachelor's Degree
Licensure/Certification: Usually Not Required
Physical Abilities Not Required: Not Climb, Not Kneel
Opportunities for Experience: Military Service, Part-Time Work
Holland Interest Score: ESR

* See Appendix A

Occupation Interest

The field of transportation management traditionally attracts those who are interested in logistics and customer satisfaction. Like all managers, transportation management professionals must also possess leadership qualities that can motivate others.

A Day in the Life—Duties and Responsibilities

The main duties and responsibilities of transportation managers surround the supervision of shipments. In addition to planning, organizing, and managing shipping logistics, transportation managers must also direct warehouse and distributions staffs to ensure that orders of lading are properly fulfilled, safely packed, and sent to their intended destination.

Worker safety is an additional responsibility of transportation managers, who must ensure that goods are transported in accordance to state and federal laws protecting employee safety. Employees must also be briefed periodically on safety procedures in organizational meetings often directed by transportation managers. Documentation and legalities related to international shipping, including tariffs and security documentation also falls to transportation managers.

Transportation managers negotiate contracts with shipping and logistics firms based on their particular company's bulk shipping needs. They are also the point person for complaints related to merchandise received in poor condition or in incomplete or damaged supply. Lastly, transportation managers must coordinate with product designers and marketers to ensure that shipping containers and product packaging is shipped in the most economically viable manner possible, to maximize the efficiency of the shipping process and to keep costs reasonable.

Duties and Responsibilities

- Managing a product's life cycle from design to disposal
- Directing the allocation of materials, supplies, and products
- Developing business relationships with suppliers and clients
- Understanding clients' needs and how to meet them
- Reviewing logistical functions and identifying areas for improvement
- Proposing strategies to minimize the cost or time required to transport goods

WORK ENVIRONMENT

Immediate Physical Environment

Office settings predominate. However, given the supervisory nature of the role, managers may be required to visit manufacturing and shipping facilities on a regular basis. The majority of logisticians work full time and they sometimes work overtime to ensure that operations stay on schedule.

Plant Environment

Logisticians work in almost every industry. Some logisticians work in the logistical department of a company, and others work for firms that specialize in logistical work, such as freight-shipping companies.

Human Environment

Logisticians routinely interact with fellow management staff and subordinate employees. Like all managers, they must be effective leaders who can communicate singular messages and motivate their staff.

Transferable Skills and Abilities

Communication Skills
- Speaking effectively
- Writing concisely

Interpersonal/Social Skills
- Cooperating with others
- Working as a member of a team

Organization & Management Skills
- Performing duties that change frequently
- Organization –and management skills; making decisions

Research & Planning Skills
- Developing evaluation strategies

The job can be stressful because logistical work is fast-paced. Logisticians must ensure that operations stay on schedule, and they must work quickly to solve any problems that arise. Some logisticians travel to manufacturing plants or distribution centers.

Technological Environment

Logisticians use software systems to plan and track the movement of products. They operate software programs designed specifically to manage logistical functions, such as procurement, inventory management, and other supply chain planning and management systems.

EDUCATION, TRAINING, AND ADVANCEMENT

High School/Secondary

High school students can best prepare for a career as a transportation manager by completing coursework in algebra, calculus, geometry, trigonometry, biology, chemistry, physics, and computer science. Advanced mathematical and computer coursework can provide a good foundation for future work in logistics. Participation in extracurricular activities such as volunteerism and sports can also help students develop the leadership and motivational qualities that can be an important asset for careers in management.

Suggested High School Subjects
- Applied Math
- Business
- Business Math
- College Preparatory

- English
- Government

Famous First

The first bus rapid transit system began operation in California in 1973. The El Monte Busway, an 11-mile stretch of road between downtown Los Angeles and El Monte, California, was originally planned to be used only by express buses making only two stops, at California State College in Los Angeles and the Los Angeles County–USC Medical Center. Transit officials estimated that a bus on the dedicated busway could complete the trip in 19 minutes, as compared to 35 to 45 minutes of driving time in the auto lanes during peak traffic periods, and the El Monte station was provided with a parking lot and feeder bus lines to encourage commuters to take the bus rather than driving.

Source: "Transportation." *Famous First Facts*, Salem, 2016. *Salem Online*, https://online.salempress.com

Postsecondary

Logisticians may qualify for some positions with an associate's degree. However, due to complex logistics and supply chains, companies prefer to hire workers who have at least a bachelor's degree. Many logisticians have a bachelor's degree in business, systems engineering, or supply chain management.

Bachelor's degree programs often include coursework in operations and database management, and system dynamics. In addition, most programs offer courses that train students on software and technologies commonly used by logisticians, such as radio-frequency identification (RFID).

Some employers allow applicants to substitute work experience in place of a specific degree. Previous work experience in a field related to logistics, supply chains, or business can be beneficial. Some gain work experience while working in a logistical support role, such as dispatchers and clerks or while serving in the military. Experience allows a worker to learn about production and supply chain processes.

Related College Majors:
- Business Administration & Management, General
- Marketing Management & Research

Adult Job Seekers

Logisticians work long hours, particularly during periods of the year such as the holiday season when demand for products is high and a high volume of shipping takes place. Even under normal circumstances, the breadth of responsibility required of the role requires a great deal of dedication and time, with frequent late work evenings and weekends required. Managers must also be on-call on a routine basis to assist in troubleshooting and dealing with discrepancies among staff members. The extensive experience and education required to be a successful logistician may make it a difficult job for older professionals or those in a period of employment transition.

Professional Certification and Licensure

Although not required, certification can demonstrate professional competence and a broad knowledge of logistics. Logisticians can obtain certification through American Production and Inventory Control Society (APICS) or the International Society of Logistics (SOLE). To become certified, a logistician typically needs to meet education and work experience requirements and pass an exam.

There are several certifications available from the Defense Acquisition University (DAU). These certifications are required for Department of Defense acquisitions.

Additional Requirements

Logisticians must be skilled multitaskers who can effectively keep detailed records and manage multiple projects simultaneously. The leadership-oriented aspect of the position requires professionals who can motivate large staffs to complete complex tasks on schedule and within budget. Logisticians need strong communication skills to collaborate with colleagues and do business with suppliers and customers. They must develop, adjust, and carry out logistical plans as well as find ways to reduce costs and improve efficiency.

Logisticians must know the needs of their customers in order to coordinate the movement of materials between suppliers and customers. They gain this knowledge through listening to the customer and applying their knowledge of the products and systems to provide what is required.

Logisticians must be able to keep detailed records and simultaneously manage several projects in a fast-paced environment. They must handle unforeseen issues, such as delivery problems, and adjust plans as needed to resolve the issues.

Fast Fact

There are 149 ports located in the US. South Louisiana, Houston, New York/New Jersey, and Long Beach often hit the top of the list when ranked by tonnage or TEUs (twenty-foot equivalent units).

Source: https://www.thelogisticsoflogistics.com

EARNINGS AND ADVANCEMENT

Earnings depend on the size of the employer, the type of goods handled and the employee's qualifications and experience. Nationally, the median annual wage for logisticians was $74,600 in May 2018. The lowest 10 percent earned less than $44,440, and the highest 10 percent earned more than $119,950.

The majority of logisticians work full time and they sometimes work overtime to ensure that operations stay on schedule. They may receive paid vacations, holidays, and sick days; life and health insurance; and retirement benefits. These are usually paid by the employer.

Median annual wages, May 2018

Logisticians: $74,600

Business operations specialists: $67,120

Total, all occupations: $38,640

Note: All Occupations includes all occupations in the U.S. Economy.
Source: U.S. Bureau of Labor Statistics, Occupational Employment Statistics

EMPLOYMENT AND OUTLOOK

Logisticians held about 148,700 jobs in 2016. The largest employers of logisticians were as follows:

Manufacturing	25%
Federal government	20%
Professional, scientific, and technical services	17%
Management of companies and enterprises	10%
Wholesale trade	9%

Employment is expected to grow about as fast as the average for all occupations through the year 2026, which means employment is projected to increase 7 percent. Employment growth will be driven by the need for logistics in the transportation of goods in a global economy.

The performance of the logistical and supply chain process is an important factor in a company's profitability. Companies rely on logisticians to manage the movement of their products and supplies. Supply and distribution systems have become increasingly complex as they continue to try to gain more efficiencies at minimal cost. Employment is expected to grow as companies need more logisticians to move products more efficiently, solve problems, and identify areas for improvement. However, this growth may be limited by mergers of third-party logistics companies.

Overall job opportunities should be good because of employment growth and the need to replace the logisticians who are expected to retire or otherwise leave the occupation. Prospects should be best for candidates who have previous experience using logistical software or doing logistical work for the military.

Percent change in employment, Projected 2016–26

Business operations specialists: 9%

Total, all occupations: 7%

Logisticians: 7%

Note: All Occupations includes all occupations in the U.S. Economy.
Source: U.S. Bureau of Labor Statistics, Occupational Employment Statistics

Related Occupations
- Production Coordinator
- Transportation, Storage, and Distribution Managers

Related Military Occupations
- Transportation Manager
- Transportation Specialist

Conversation With...
CHRISTOS RALLIS
Senior Program Manager
Amazon Logistics
Seattle, WA
Transportation and Logistics, 5 years

1. What was your individual career path in terms of education/training, entry-level job, or other significant opportunity?

As a freshman at Lehigh University, I enrolled as an accounting major primarily because I thought that would offer the best career opportunities after graduation. About four months in, I took an intro to supply chain management course. At that time—2009—startups were really blossoming into the spotlight and I realized the accounting majors who ran big corporations were an older generation. I didn't have to follow that career path. I could target something that appealed to me more, and I realized that was supply chain management. I switched my major and earned my BS in logistics, materials, and supply chain management.

As graduation approached, I found myself with offers from a few different industries. I narrowed it down to manufacturing and transportation. In the end I chose manufacturing because I thought the aerospace industry sounded more exciting than transportation. I worked for an aerospace supplier for nearly four years. Unfortunately, it was a slow-moving company, and I was looking for a change. Prior to graduating, one of my undergraduate professors had told me about Massachusetts Institute of Technology's 10-month supply chain program for a Master of Applied Science degree. I had applied and received a scholarship. The program also required two years' work experience, which I had now completed. I decided it was a good time to go back to school.

By the time I entered MIT, a lot had happened in logistics. Two-day and even same-day shipping had become the new norm. My time at MIT gave me a refreshed perspective on the breadth and intricacy of supply chain networks. I realized that transportation wasn't the old game I thought it was and companies like Amazon—and e-commerce in general—were changing the game for customers while forcing the old guard (FedEx, UPS, et al.) to refresh their own strategies. MIT gave me many opportunities to change career paths and I jumped at a role as a network planner within Amazon's logistics group upon graduation.

Now, I do network design: how we will get a package from where it's located to the customer. It's extremely interesting work. We are at a point where all the low-hanging fruit has been picked. You have to be extremely efficient and come up with innovative ways to get products to customers faster.

2. What are the most important skills and/or qualities for someone in your profession?

In a world where you can ask a smart speaker to order virtually anything and expect it to be on your doorstep within 24 hours, transportation networks need to be extremely efficient, flexible, and resilient. The same is true of the people designing those networks. Someone who has a passion for solving complex optimization problems and thrives on ambiguity will excel in transportation and network planning.

3. What do you wish you had known going into this profession?

I wish I had known the opportunities for growth and innovation. There are so many opportunities and roles in the transportation industry that fit many different skillsets or interests.

4. Are there many job opportunities in your profession? In what specific areas?

Yes! As e-commerce continues to grow so does the transportation industry. There are jobs for anyone's interest. At one end of the spectrum are under-the-roof operations. Those jobs are for people who love hands-on, physical environments. Picture leading teams of tens to hundreds of employees stowing, picking, packing, and sorting millions of packages a day. At the other end of the spectrum are modeling and research roles. These roles are meant for those looking to solve the most complex optimization problems on extremely powerful computers. And in the middle of the spectrum are the network planning, capacity planning, and operations integration roles. This is where my role sits and I love it because I get to help optimization teams design their tools, use these tools, and then work with operations to implement new strategies. To me, it's the best of both worlds, but this simplistic breakdown of transportation roles doesn't even scratch the surface of all the unique roles in the industry.

5. How do you see your profession changing in the next five years? How will technology impact that change, and what skills will be required?

For carrier networks there's a lot of focus on extracting every ounce of efficiency out of long-distance paths from shipper to customer. For instance, the loading and unloading of trailers and the sorting of packages continue to improve from advancement in automation. Those benefits carry over to fulfillment networks, where speed reigns supreme. Fulfillment companies strive to shrink their networks by positioning inventory as close to customers as possible and using automation to sort packages, called sortation automation. Most companies are looking to position humans where they can add more value and leave manual processes to machines.

Over the coming years I'm excited to see how last mile transportation that completes delivery continues to develop. That will include automated ground and air drones, and even multimodal solutions that leverage traditional delivery methods—such as vans—with automated methods such as drones or robots.

Autonomous driving is another interesting area to watch. The number of long-haul truck drivers has diminished, and requirements for drivers to automatically log their hours has added pressure to the job. I think we'll soon see technologies such as semiautonomous truck platooning, which is one driver driving a lead truck with one or many automated trucks following what the lead truck does.

Finally, as consumers push companies to be greener, renewable energy in infrastructure and electric vehicles (EVs) will become more prevalent. The challenge in the short term is that most EVs currently are not capable of withstanding typical daily requirements. Also, maintaining EVs requires a much different infrastructure than currently exists to handle maintenance and meet the need for charging stations.

6. **What do you enjoy most about your job? What do you enjoy least about your job?**

   I love that I get to be hands-on in today's operations and also help design optimization tools to create tomorrow's logistics network. It's a great way to learn how to tackle problems that require quick action and calculated risks as well as problems that require deep analysis and foresight. As exciting and rewarding as this is, there is never an off switch. Professionals in this field are always on call because customers expect their packages 24/7/365. As I said, you need to be resilient and, as in any profession, ensure that you balance work and personal life.

7. **Can you suggest a valuable "try this" for students considering a career in your profession?**

   For those interested in the math and optimization side, start by working on linear programming and traveling salesman problems, which you can find on the internet. For those interested in field operations, the best experience is hands-on. Consider a summer job in a logistics hub for Amazon, FedEx, or UPS. I even know some vice presidents who started their careers picking and packing Amazon boxes. Truly the best way to understand transportation networks is to see them firsthand. If you're short on time, Amazon offers tours of many of their buildings so you can see the action live in an hour or two.

MORE INFORMATION

National Industrial Transportation League (NITL)
1700 N. Moore Street, Suite 1900
Arlington, VA 22209
703.524.5011
info@nitl.org
www.nitl.org

The BWI Business Partnership, Inc.
1302 Concourse Drive, Suite 105
Linthicum Heights, MD 21090
410.859.1000
www.bwipartner.org

Transportation Management Association of San Francisco (TMASF)
180 Montgomery Street, Suite 2360
San Francisco, CA 94104
415.392.0210
tmasfconnects.org

John Pritchard/Editor

Material-Moving Machine Operators

Snapshot

Career Cluster(s): Manufacturing
Interests: Heavy equipment, working with your hands, working outdoors
Earnings (Median Pay): $35,850 per year
Employment & Outlook: As Fast as Average Growth Expected

OVERVIEW

Sphere of Work

Material-moving machine operators drive and maintain small industrial trucks and material handlers. Industrial machine operators also use several other types of small-engine and electronic vehicles, including pallet jacks, e-cars, and scissor lifts, in industrial and warehouse settings. Forklift operators are key contributors to the efficiency of warehouses and factories, possessing the ability to move large loads of cargo and inventory without assistance. Misuse of forklifts and other small

industrial vehicles can cause great danger to both operators and their coworkers, making adherence to safety procedures an integral part of the job.

Work Environment

Material-moving machine operators, including forklift operators, work in a variety of commercial and industrial settings, in industries such as manufacturing, transportation, warehousing, construction, and contracting. Forklift drivers and material-moving machine vehicle operators also work in mining, farming, and food manufacturing. Shipping and materials transport is one of the largest industries that employ forklift drivers. While some material-moving machine operators use a forklift as a primary facet of their job, others use the forklift and other vehicles as a supplement to other duties.

Profile

Interests: Things
Working Conditions: Work Inside, Work both Inside and Outside
Physical Strength: Heavy Work
Education Needs: On-the-Job Training, High School Diploma or GED, High School Diploma with Technical Education
Licensure/Certification: Required
Physical Abilities Not Required: n/a
Opportunities for Experience: Part-Time Work
Holland Interest Score: RCE

* See Appendix A

Occupation Interest

Material-moving machine operators come from a variety of professional backgrounds. In the staff hierarchy of warehousing and manufacturing facilities, material-moving machine operators traditionally have seniority over entry-level employees and laborers. Many have worked their way up from entry-level positions in warehousing, storage, or materials handling. Other workers utilize the position as a way to gain experience to become better candidates for future warehouse-supervisor or facilities-management vacancies.

A Day in the Life—Duties and Responsibilities

Material-moving machine operators use machinery to transport various objects. Some operators move construction materials around building sites or excavate earth from a mine. Others move goods around a warehouse or onto container ships.

Material-Moving Machine Operators

Duties

Material-moving machine operators typically do the following:

- Set up and inspect material-moving equipment
- Control equipment with levers, wheels, or foot pedals
- Move material according to a plan or schedule
- Signal and direct workers to load, unload, and position materials
- Keep a record of the material they move and where they move it to
- Make minor repairs to their equipment

In warehouses, most material-moving machine operators use forklifts and conveyor belts. Wireless sensors and tags are increasingly being used to keep track of merchandise, allowing operators to locate them faster. Some operators also check goods for damage. These operators usually work closely with hand laborers and material movers.

Many operators work for underground and surface mining companies. They help to dig or expose the mine, remove the earth and rock, and extract coal, ore, and other mined materials.

In construction, material-moving machine operators remove earth to clear space for buildings. Some work on a building site for the entire length of the construction project. For example, certain material-moving machine operators help to construct high-rise buildings by transporting materials to workers who are far above ground level.

All material-moving machine operators are responsible for the safe operation of their equipment or vehicle.

The following are examples of types of material-moving machine operators:

Conveyor operators and tenders control conveyor systems that move materials on an automatic belt. They move materials to and from places such as storage areas, vehicles, and building sites. They monitor sensors on the conveyor to regulate the speed with which the conveyor belt moves. Operators also may check the shipping order and determine the route that materials take along a conveyor.

Crane and tower operators use tower and cable equipment to lift and move materials, machinery, or other heavy objects. From a control station, operators can extend and retract horizontal booms, rotate the superstructure, and lower and raise hooks attached to cables at the end of their crane or tower. Operators usually are guided by workers on the ground who use hand signals or who transmit voice signals through a radio. Most crane and tower operators work at construction sites or major ports, where they load and unload cargo. Some operators work in iron and steel mills.

Dredge operators excavate waterways. They operate equipment on the water to remove sand, gravel, or rock from harbors or lakes. Removing these materials helps to prevent erosion and maintain navigable waterways, and allows larger ships to use ports. Dredging also is used to help restore wetlands and maintain beaches.

Excavating and loading machine and dragline operators use machines equipped with scoops or shovels. They dig sand, earth, or other materials and load them onto conveyors or into trucks for transport elsewhere. They may also move material within a confined area, such as a construction site. Operators typically receive instructions from workers on the ground through hand signals or through voice signals transmitted by radio. Most of these operators work in construction or mining industries.

Hoist and winch operators, also called derrick operators, control the movement of platforms, cables, and cages that transport workers or materials in industrial operations, such as constructing a high-rise building. Many of these operators raise platforms far above the ground. Operators regulate the speed of the equipment on the basis of the needs of the workers. Many work in manufacturing, mining, and quarrying industries.

Industrial truck and tractor operators drive trucks and tractors that move materials around warehouses, storage yards, or worksites. These trucks, often called forklifts, have a lifting mechanism and forks, which make them useful for moving heavy and large objects. Some industrial truck and tractor operators drive tractors that pull trailers loaded with material around factories or storage areas.

Underground mining loading machine operators load coal, ore, and other rocks onto shuttles, mine cars, or conveyors for transport from a mine to the surface. They may use power shovels, hoisting engines equipped with scrapers or scoops, and automatic gathering arms that move materials onto a conveyor. Operators also drive their machines farther into the mine in order to gather more material.

WORK ENVIRONMENT

Immediate Physical Environment

Material-moving machine operators work in a variety of environments, including warehouses, shipping facilities, factories, trade centers, ports, and manufacturing facilities. Commercial and industrial settings predominate. They also work in and around construction sites and select retail facilities.

Transferable Skills and Abilities

Communication Skills
- Reading well
- Writing concisely

Organization & Management Skills
- Paying attention to and handling details
- Performing routine work

Technical Skills
- Working with machines, tools, or other objects

Human Environment

Forklift operation and other material-moving machine operation requires strong collaboration, organization, and communication skills. Professionals in this field interact with fellow workers on a near-constant basis, communicating the location, amount, and type of materials that need to be transported.

Technological Environment

In addition to being able to use forklifts and other small motorized vehicles, material-moving machine operators must possess the ability to use shipment-tracking software, inventory-processing systems, and various hand tools such as utility knives, skid steers, and mobile stairs.

EDUCATION, TRAINING, AND ADVANCEMENT

High School/Secondary

High school students can best prepare for a career in materials transport with courses in geometry, chemistry, physics, and introductory computer science. English and writing courses help students prepare for the communication and problem-solving aspects of the occupation.

Suggested High School Subjects
- Applied Math
- Auto Service Technology
- Diesel Maintenance Technology
- Driver Training
- English

Related Career Pathways/Majors

Manufacturing Cluster
- Logistics & Inventory Control Pathway

Famous First

The first steam shovel was invented in 1838 by William S. Otis of Philadelphia, PA, who obtained a patent on February 24, 1839, on a crane for excavating and removing earth. It was first used on the Western Railroad in Massachusetts.

Source: "Business and Industry." *Famous First Facts*, Salem, 2016. *Salem Online*, https://online.salempress.com

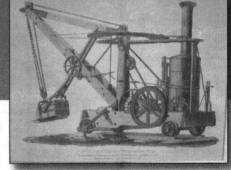

Postsecondary

Postsecondary course work is not a prerequisite for a career as a forklift operator. Although most material-moving machine operators are trained on the job in less than a month, the amount of time spent in training will vary with the type of machine. Some machines, such as cranes and towers, are more complex than others, such as industrial trucks and forklifts. Learning to operate a forklift or an industrial truck in warehouses, for example, may take only a few days; training to operate a crane for port operations may take several months. Most workers are trained by a supervisor or another experienced employee.

During their training, material-moving machine operators learn a number of safety rules, many of which are standardized through the Occupational Safety & Health Administration (OSHA) and the Mine Safety and Health Administration (MSHA). Employers must certify that each operator has received the proper training. Operators who work with hazardous materials receive further specialized training.

The International Union of Operating Engineers (IUOE) offers apprenticeship programs for heavy-equipment operators, such as excavating machine operators or crane operators. Apprenticeships combine paid on-the-job training with technical instruction.

Adult Job Seekers

Forklift operators can work first, second, or third shifts depending on their industry of employment. Materials handlers in the construction industry traditionally work normal business hours, while those employed in the shipping, manufacturing, or warehousing industry may work at all hours of the day and weekends when necessary. The potentially sporadic nature of shifts may make the job less than ideal for enrolled students or workers with families or young children.

Professional Certification and Licensure

A number of states and several cities require crane operators to be licensed. To get a license, operators typically must complete a skills test in which they show that they can control a crane. They also must pass a written exam that tests their knowledge of safety rules and procedures. Some crane operators and industrial truck and tractor operators may obtain certification, which includes passing a written exam.

Certification by the OSHA is required for the operation of all powered industrial trucks, including forklifts, tractors, lift trucks, motorized hand tools, and other industrial vehicles powered by combustion engines or electronic motors. Certification can be earned on the job after instruction by a certified trainer or through external courses at training schools or vocational training programs. Most states require certification to be updated every two years.

Additional Requirements

Forklift operators must possess the patience and organization necessary to move potentially hazardous heavy loads with extreme caution. Misuse and abuse of forklifts and other small motorized industrial machinery is a common cause of on-the-job accidents and fatalities each year. Crane operators and excavating machine operators usually have several years of experience working as construction equipment operators, hoist and winch operators, or riggers and signalers.

Fast Fact

The first known construction cranes were invented by the Ancient Greeks and were powered by men or beasts of burden, such as donkeys.

Source: https://en.wikipedia.org

EARNINGS AND ADVANCEMENT

Earnings depend on the type, geographic location and union affiliation of the employer and the employee's experience. The median annual wage for material-moving machine operators was $35,850 in May 2018. The lowest 10 percent earned less than $25,270, and the highest 10 percent earned more than $56,780. Annual earnings can be reduced due to the amount of time work can be limited by bad weather.

Forklift operators may receive paid vacations, holidays, and sick days; life and health insurance; and retirement plans benefits. These are usually paid by the employer.

Median annual wages, May 2018

Total, all occupations: $38,640

Material-moving machine operators: $35,850

Material-moving workers: $28,570

Note: All Occupations includes all occupations in the U.S. Economy.
Source: U.S. Bureau of Labor Statistics, Occupational Employment Statistics

EMPLOYMENT AND OUTLOOK

Overall employment of material-moving machine operators is projected to grow 6 percent from 2016 to 2026, about as fast as the average for all occupations. Job prospects are expected to be favorable. Many job openings should be created by the need to replace workers who leave these occupations.

Employment of industrial truck and tractor operators is projected to grow 7 percent from 2016 to 2026, about as fast as the average for all occupations. Employment of this occupation is concentrated in warehouse environments. The demand for warehousing will continue to grow as more consumers choose to purchase products online. However, employment growth may be tempered for industrial truck and tractor operators as more warehouses begin using automated machinery to improve their operations. This equipment increases the efficiency of operators, allowing warehouses to employ fewer of them.

Employment of excavating and loading machine and dragline operators is projected to grow 8 percent from 2016 to 2026, about as fast as the average for all occupations. Many of these operators work in the construction industry, where projected growth will drive job growth in this occupation.

Employment of crane and tower operators is projected to grow 9 percent from 2016 to 2026, about as fast as the average for all occupations. As global shipping increases, more of these operators will be needed at ports to load and unload large cargo ships. However, increasing automation at ports may moderate growth. Employment of crane and tower operators also will be driven by growth in the construction industry, which employs about two in five of these workers. Employment of crane and tower operators is projected to grow 14 percent in construction.

Employment of conveyor operators and tenders is projected to show little or no change from 2016 to 2026. Employment growth will be limited as more warehouses use equipment such as high-speed conveyors, high-speed sorting systems, and robotic pickers. This equipment increases the efficiency of operators and tenders, allowing warehouses to employ fewer of them.

Employment of hoist and winch operators is projected to show little or no change from 2016 to 2026. Like crane and tower operators, they will be needed at ports to help load and unload cargo, but employment growth for this occupation may be limited by port automation.

Employment of underground mining loading machine operators is projected to decline 4 percent from 2016 to 2026, largely because of an expected employment decline in coal mining, an industry in which many of these workers are employed.

Employment of dredge operators is projected to grow 5 percent from 2016 to 2026, about as fast as the average for all occupations. In order to improve traffic on waterways and promote their recreational use, dredging of various water areas, including canals, lakes, rivers, and harbors, will be necessary. Demand for dredging of various water areas will drive employment growth of these workers.

Percent change in employment, Projected 2016–26

Total, all occupations: 7%

Material-moving machine operators: 7%

Material-moving workers: 6%

Note: All Occupations includes all occupations in the U.S. Economy.
Source: U.S. Bureau of Labor Statistics, Occupational Employment Statistics

Related Occupations
- Bulldozer Operator
- Freight, Stock & Material Mover
- Lumber Production Worker
- Ship Loader

Conversation With . . .
JESSICA FARRELL

Vice President of Sales
Union Machinery
Union, MO
Forklift Sales, 13 years

1. What was your individual career path in terms of education/training, entry-level job, or other significant opportunity?

I went to East Central College, which is in Union, MO, where I grew up. My mom worked there, so I went for free. Since I didn't know what to study, my dad recommended business and that's what I did. I really gravitated toward sales. I like to get along with people, and I can talk to people and persuade them. I saw all these girls who sold pharmaceuticals and they seemed so glamorous. I thought that's what I would do after I graduated, but I didn't get that chance. I took a job doing collection calls and absolutely hated it, then applied for a sales assistant job at Union Machinery, a company that sells forklifts. I didn't know what a forklift was, but when I met my boss, we hit it off. He said, "I like your attitude; I'll teach you." Now I tell everybody we hire, "I was literally born to sell forklifts. I didn't know it until now." I love it.

My boss is nearing retirement, so I'm buying the company with two other investors, one woman and one man. I'm totally into girl power. We also have a woman mechanic on staff. I'm excited that our new partnership is going to be majority woman-owned. This potentially gives us a lot of ways into new markets, such as government contracts that require giving minority-owned businesses a first-choice pick.

Our clientele, really, is blue collar men. Being a girl helps because that gets you in the door. But it stops right there. I've earned their respect, and that's what you've got to do. It took a while for me to prove I know a lot about forklifts.

I teach forklift training classes. If we didn't have forklifts, there's be nothing in stores. They cost money and they don't make any money, but they are necessary. If we didn't have them, we couldn't move products. They're heavy pieces of equipment that can be dangerous; a smaller one is 9,000 pounds. People die on forklifts if they don't take safety precautions.

They're used mostly by manufacturers. St. Louis has lots of manufacturers' warehousing, and the new thing now is tall spec buildings meant for warehousing. People have decided to go up instead of out because real estate is expensive. Some of the racking systems used inside go 30 feet in the air. St. Louis is a hub for a lot of places to ship out goods.

Our company also moves equipment for people. Manufacturers get big machines in, sometimes multiple pieces that can be 50 feet long. We uncrate it, put the piece of equipment together, get our 40,000-pound capacity forklift, bring their machine in, and drop it where they want it. We have trailers that can carry our forklifts.

2. **What are the most important skills and/or qualities for someone in your profession?**

   In sales, a great personality goes a long way. Also, you need a great memory, intelligence, and a willingness to learn. For example, if I am selling to people who make boxes, I learn how to make boxes. When I'm excited about what they're doing, I might find a better way to sell them a forklift. Everybody loves to talk about what they do. Be a hard worker. Also, operating a forklift requires patience.

3. **What do you wish you had known going into this profession?**

   I wish I had had more confidence in the beginning, but I think that comes with experience. To be honest, I didn't know about this profession, and I still learn technical stuff about forklifts.

4. **Are there many job opportunities in your profession? In what specific areas?**

   There are always job opportunities. Every forklift company needs trained successful salespeople and trained service technicians. For some reason, nobody wants to be a forklift mechanic anymore, even though it's similar to being an auto mechanic. Working with a manufacturer, we came up with a mechanic training program we are introducing to trade schools in our area.

5. **How do you see your profession changing in the next five years? How will technology impact that change, and what skills will be required?**

   Electric forklifts and robotic forklifts are on the rise. We now have robotic forklifts that run day or night in the dark in a warehouse that contains similar items. Everybody is going green, so I definitely see electric on the rise. You save a lot of money. We will need more training for sales and service; we're going to have to be on top of our game to repair electric forklifts. Each manufacturer has different software.

6. **What do you enjoy most about your job? What do you enjoy least about your job?**

   I most enjoy working with people. I like being on the run. I'm always going to see people, learning about something different and solving problems. I like working with the tough cookies; the ones who are hardest to convince will never leave you.

I least enjoy paperwork. I also don't like it when the economy is bad because it's a little discouraging. But you learn to move forward.

7. Can you suggest a valuable "try this" for students considering a career in your profession?

Everyone we interview goes on a "typical day" with me. I take them to see customers who love us, customers with problems, places where we got kicked out. I show them cold calls. I want to show them the real job. Find a forklift company and shadow someone for a day.

MORE INFORMATION

Associated Builders and Contractors (ABC)
4250 N. Fairfax Drive, 9th Floor
Arlington, VA 22203
703.812.2000
gotquestions@abc.org
www.abc.org

Associated General Contractors of America (AGCA)
Director, Construction Education Services
2300 Wilson Boulevard, Suite 400
Arlington, VA 22201
703.548.3118
info@agc.org
www.agc.org

Building Trades Association (BTA)
16th Street, NW
Washington, DC 20006
800.326.7800
info@buildingtrades.com
www.buildingtrades.com

Industrial Truck Association (ITA)
1750 K Street NW, Suite 460
Washington, DC 20006
202.296.9880
www.indtrk.org

International Brotherhood of Teamsters (IBT)
25 Louisiana Avenue, NW
Washington, DC 20001
202.624.6800
www.teamster.org

International Union of Operating Engineers (IUOE)
Director of Research and Education
1125 17th Street, NW
Washington, DC 20036
202.429.9100
www.iuoe.org

National Center for Construction Education and Research (NCCER)
13614 Progress Boulevard
Alachua, FL 32615
888.622.3720
www.nccer.org

John Pritchard/Editor

Material Recording Clerks

Snapshot

Career Cluster(s): Business, Management & Administration, Manufacturing, Marketing, Sales & Service, Transportation, Distribution & Logistics

Interests: Transportation, distribution, warehouse operations, importing and exporting, customer service, business

Earnings (Median Pay): $28,860

Employment & Outlook: Slower than average

OVERVIEW

Sphere of Work

Material recording clerks, also known as shipping and receiving clerks, shipping coordinators, receiving managers, or traffic managers, provide shipping and receiving support to their employers. They may perform a wide variety of tasks, including readying packages for shipment, shipping packages, tracking incoming and outgoing shipments, receiving packages, inventorying receivables, and transporting materials and packages. Shipping

and receiving clerks often work alongside and assist stock clerks and warehouse clerks.

Work Environment

Material recording clerks work in office settings, shipping facilities, and warehouses. Depending on the employer and particular job description, a shipping and receiving clerk may work on a full-time, part-time, or seasonal basis, or as a shift worker. Material recording clerks generally work 40-hour weeks, but holiday, evening, and weekend work may be necessary during periods of increased business.

Profile

Interests: Data, Things
Working Conditions: Work Inside
Physical Strength: Medium Work
Education Needs: High School Diploma or GED, High School Diploma with Technical Education
Licensure/Certification: Usually Not Required
Physical Abilities Not Required: Not Climb
Opportunities for Experience: Military Service, Part-Time Work
Holland Interest Score: REI

* See Appendix A

Occupation Interest

Individuals attracted to the material recording work tend to be physically strong and detail-oriented people. Individuals who excel as exhibit traits such as stamina, organization, dependability, and effective time management. Prospective material recording clerks should enjoy physical work and routines, thrive under pressure, and have a background in warehouse operations, import, export, or transport. Familiarity with computer technologies is also desirable.

A Day in the Life—Duties and Responsibilities

Material recording clerks track product information in order to keep businesses and supply chains on schedule. They ensure proper scheduling, recordkeeping, and inventory control.

Material recording clerks typically do the following:

- Keep records of items shipped, received, or transferred to another location
- Compile reports on various aspects of changes in production or inventory

- Find, sort, or move goods between different parts of the business
- Check inventory records for accuracy

Material recording clerks use computers, tablets, or handheld devices to keep track of inventory. Sensors and tags enable these computers to automatically detect when and where products are moved, allowing clerks to keep updated reports without manually counting items.

Company size greatly influences the daily occupational duties and responsibilities assigned to material recording clerks. In large companies, multiple people and departments perform shipping and receiving tasks, while in smaller companies one person is usually responsible for all shipping and receiving. The level of automation in the shipping and receiving process varies greatly in different organizations and depends on the organization's size and technological environment. The following are examples of types of material recording clerks:

Production, planning, and expediting clerks manage the flow of information, work, and materials within or among offices in a business. They compile reports on the progress of work and on any production problems that arise. These clerks set workers' schedules, estimate costs, keep track of materials, and write special orders for new materials. They perform general office tasks, such as entering data or distributing mail. Expediting clerks maintain contact with vendors to ensure that supplies and equipment are shipped on time.

Shipping, receiving, and traffic clerks keep track of and record outgoing and incoming shipments. Clerks may scan barcodes with handheld devices or use radio frequency identification (RFID) scanners to keep track of inventory. They check to see whether shipment orders were processed correctly in their company's computer system. They also compute freight costs and prepare invoices. Some clerks move goods from the warehouse to the loading dock.

Stock clerks and order fillers receive, unpack, and track merchandise. Stock clerks move products from a warehouse to store shelves. They keep a record of items that enter or leave the stockroom and inspect for damaged goods. These clerks also use handheld radio-frequency identification (RFID) scanners to keep track of merchandise. Order fillers retrieve customer orders and prepare them to be shipped.

Material and product inspecting clerks weigh, measure, check, sample, and keep records on materials, supplies, and equipment that enters a warehouse. They verify the quantity and quality of items they are assigned to examine, checking for defects and recording what they find. They use scales, counting devices, and calculators. Some decide what to do about a defective product, such as to scrap it or send it back to the factory to be repaired. Some clerks also prepare reports, such as reports about warehouse inventory levels.

Duties and Responsibilities

- **Determining method of shipment**
- **Assembling wooden and cardboard containers or selecting preassembled containers**
- **Inserting items into containers**
- **Attaching identification and shipping instructions to containers**
- **Preparing records of merchandise shipped**
- **Posting weight and shipping charges**
- **Maintaining files of shipping records**
- **Verifying receipt of shipments against bills of lading, invoices, or other records**
- **Recording shortages and rejecting damaged merchandise**
- **Routing merchandise to departments**
- **Unpacking and examining incoming shipments**

OCCUPATION SPECIALTIES

Route Returners

Route Returners receive unsold products returned by sales route drivers.

WORK ENVIRONMENT

Immediate Physical Environment

Shipping and receiving clerks work in offices, warehouses, mailrooms, and stockrooms. They may experience temperature extremes, and work settings may be cluttered. Shipping and receiving work tends to be very physical and require extensive walking, lifting, and bending. As a result, shipping and receiving clerks must follow safety precautions to avoid back strain and crush injuries.

Plant Environment

Shipping and receiving clerks working in plant or manufacturing environments provide shipping and receiving support to the business. Shipping and receiving clerks in a plant environment may experience physical risks resulting from production fumes, noise, or plant accidents.

Human Environment

A shipping and receiving clerk's human environment may be social or isolated. Shipping and receiving clerks, depending on their work assignments and the extent of automation within the organization, may interact with colleagues such as stock clerks and traffic clerks, customers, shippers, and supervisors. Experienced shipping and receiving clerks may oversee the work of less experienced clerks or other warehouse employees.

Transferable Skills and Abilities

Communication Skills
- Expressing thoughts and ideas
- Writing concisely

Interpersonal/Social Skills
- Working as a member of a team

Organization & Management Skills
- Following instructions
- Managing time
- Meeting goals and deadlines
- Paying attention to and handling details
- Performing duties that change frequently
- Performing routine work

Research & Planning Skills
- Solving problems

Technical Skills
- Performing scientific, mathematical, and technical work
- Working with machines, tools, or other objects

Technological Environment

Shipping and receiving clerks use adding machines, fax machines, photocopiers, telephones, scales, and postal machines to complete their work. In more automated settings, they also use bar code machines and readers, RFID scanners, sorting systems, robots, computers, internet communication tools, databases, and software designed for labels, purchase orders, character recognition, word processing, and spreadsheets. Depending on the facility, they may also need to operate forklifts, hand trucks, conveyors, or vehicles to move shipments.

EDUCATION, TRAINING, AND ADVANCEMENT

High School/Secondary

High school students interested in pursuing a career as a shipping and receiving clerk should prepare themselves by building good study habits and by studying English, business, computer science, and bookkeeping. Part-time or seasonal work with local businesses may also be beneficial for high school students interested in this career path. High school students may be able to find employment as shipping and receiving clerks directly following graduation.

Suggested High School Subjects
- Bookkeeping
- Business & Computer Technology
- Business Math
- English
- Keyboarding

Related Career Pathways/Majors

Business, Management & Administration Cluster
- Administrative & Information Support Pathway
- Marketing Pathway

Manufacturing Cluster
- Logistics & Inventory Control Pathway

Marketing, Sales & Service Cluster
- Distribution & Logistics Pathway

Transportation, Distribution & Logistics Cluster
- Warehousing & Distribution Center Operations Pathway

Famous First

Widescale use of universal product code (UPC)-barcode technology by a mass merchandiser would take place in 1988 with its introduction in Target stores and distribution centers. It would result in more efficient inventory management through its automation and reduce time spent at the checkout counter.

Source: "Business and Industry." *Famous First Facts*, Salem, 2016. *Salem Online*, https://online.salempress.com

Postsecondary

Formal postsecondary study is not required to become a shipping and receiving clerk. Vocational training in marketing or business may be beneficial for prospective shipping and receiving clerks. As the shipping industry is becoming more automated, additional training in computer technology is also advantageous. Those who obtain an associate's or bachelor's degree may advance more quickly to related managerial positions. Young adults can gain work experience and potential advantage in their future job searches through part-time or seasonal employment in warehouse or mailroom settings.

Adult Job Seekers

Adults seeking employment as shipping and receiving clerks should have a high school diploma or its equivalent. Most employers provide some training for new shipping and receiving clerks. Some senior positions and specialized shipping and receiving jobs require extensive experience and on-the-job training. Many begin their careers as stock clerks, part-time employees, or military shipping and receiving specialists. Advancement in the field is limited; however, some experienced clerks may be promoted to managerial positions. Adult job seekers may benefit from joining professional associations to help with networking and job searching. Professional shipping associations such as the International Air Transport Association generally maintain lists of available jobs.

Professional Certification and Licensure

Professional certification and licensure is not required by law for general shipping and receiving clerks, but may be required as a condition of employment, salary increase, or promotion. Specialized shipping and receiving clerks, particularly those handling dangerous or hazardous goods or materials in the biomedical and pharmaceutical industry, are required by law to complete hazardous materials or dangerous goods training from an accredited program.

Additional Requirements

Individuals who find satisfaction, success, and job security as shipping and receiving clerks will be knowledgeable about the profession's requirements, responsibilities, and opportunities. Integrity and professional ethics are essential qualities in shipping and receiving clerks, as they have access to confidential information and valuable, sometimes hazardous goods and materials. Those who handle dangerous goods must comply with all relevant government regulations.

Fast Fact

Barcodes were originally used to label cars on railroads. In 1974, they moved to supermarkets and have only grown in use ever since.
Source: beltmannlogistics.com

EARNINGS AND ADVANCEMENT

Material recording clerks may advance through ability, training, and work experience. Earnings depend on the geographic location and union affiliation of the employer, the type of industry and the employee's duties. Median annual earnings of material recording clerks was $28,860 in May 2018. The lowest 10 percent earned less than $20,350, and the highest 10 percent earned more than $50,110.

Material clerks may receive paid vacations, holidays, and sick days; life and health insurance; and retirement benefits. These are usually paid by the employer.

Median annual wages, May 2018

Total, all occupations: $38,640

Material recording, scheduling, dispatching, and distributing workers: $32,140

Material recording clerks: $28,860

Note: All Occupations includes all occupations in the U.S. Economy.
Source: U.S. Bureau of Labor Statistics, Occupational Employment Statistics

EMPLOYMENT AND OUTLOOK

There were approximately 3,095,300 material recording clerks employed nationally in 2018. Employment is expected to grow slower than the average for all occupations through the year 2020, which means employment is projected to increase 4 percent.

Although increased use of radio frequency identification (RFID) tags should allow stock clerks to more quickly locate an item or count inventory in some retail stores, stocking shelves and filling orders will still require these workers.

In warehouses, both RFID tags and increased use of other technology, such as handheld devices that read barcodes automatically, allow fewer clerks to do the same amount of work. In addition, use of barcodes, electronic and optical readers, and RFID tags is expected to increase accuracy in shipping, thereby reducing the number of times a product needs to be weighed, checked, or measured.

As retail continues to move from traditional brick-and-mortar stores to online commerce, retailers will seek to automate warehouse operations, including using what are known as "collaborative robots." These new robots can help workers perform tasks and increase efficiency. However, this increased efficiency may reduce the demand for some material recording clerks.

Production, planning, and expediting clerks plan and schedule production and shipment processes, functions that remain difficult to substitute with technology.

Percent change in employment, Projected 2016–26

Total, all occupations: 7%

Material recording clerks: 4%

Material recording, scheduling, dispatching, and distributing workers: 2%

Note: All Occupations includes all occupations in the U.S. Economy.
Source: U.S. Bureau of Labor Statistics, Occupational Employment Statistics

Related Occupations
- Billing Clerk
- Counter & Rental Clerk
- Mail Carrier
- Postal Clerk
- Stock Clerk

Related Military Occupations
- Supply & Warehousing Specialist
- Transportation Specialist

MORE INFORMATION

National Retail Federation
325 7th Street NW, Suite 1100
Washington, DC 20004
800.673.4692
www.nrf.com

Simone Isadora Flynn/Editor

Ship Loader

Snapshot

Career Cluster(s): Manufacturing, Marketing, Sales & Service
Interests: Computers, shipping technology, inventory, machine maintenance, heavy machinery
Earnings (Median Pay): $45,347
Employment & Outlook: Slower Than Average Growth Expected

OVERVIEW

Sphere of Work

Ship loaders, also known as longshoremen and stevedores, work in the shipping industry, performing a variety of tasks related to the transportation of cargo on shipping vessels. Their basic responsibilities include verifying the barge load numbers, operating the loading and unloading equipment, and collaborating with other workers to ensure goods travel securely. Using heavy machinery and handheld scanning technology, ship loaders are able to safeguard a wide range of cargo as they travel to their destination. The job involves a lot of physically demanding tasks and therefore requires stamina.

Work Environment

Ship loaders work in an assortment of environments, including warehouses, wharfs, and docks. Typically, a ship loader will work outside in all kinds of weather. Because of the machinery used and the physical nature of the job, there are several hazards a ship loader needs to be aware of. Sometimes the cargo itself can be hazardous as well. For example, ship loaders need to be cautious when moving liquid cargo such as chemicals, petroleum, or gasoline.

Profile

Interests: Things
Working Conditions: Work Outside
Physical Strength: Medium Work, Heavy Work
Education Needs: On-the-Job Training, High School Diploma or GED
Licensure/Certification: Recommended
Physical Abilities Not Required: Not Hear and/or Talk
Opportunities for Experience: Military Service
Holland Interest Score: RES, RIS

* See Appendix A

Occupation Interest

A career in the shipping industry tends to attract individuals who enjoy physical labor and who do not want to be trapped behind a desk all day. Most ship loaders have had some kind of background in the shipping industry, and many start off as a laborer in a warehouse. Ship loaders have a strong eye for detail and are good at multitasking. They must also be collaborators, as it takes many loaders to get the job done.

A Day in the Life—Duties and Responsibilities

In the ship-loading profession, accuracy and safety are essential. Workers must monitor and verify cargo as it is loaded and unloaded from warehouse to ship. During the loading and unloading process, ship loaders collaborate with other workers to ensure the job is done correctly and safely. They use a variety of technologies, including forklifts, cranes, and x-ray machines. Their daily work involves a lot of physically demanding tasks, such as bending, lifting, and pushing handcarts.

Before the loading of cargo begins, ship loaders verify the count to make sure all scheduled items are being shipped out. Different loading technology is used depending on the cargo being shipped. Commonly used loading technologies include conveyors, mechanical hoists, cranes, and forklifts. The movement of the cargo is monitored constantly during this process. If liquid materials are being shipped, ship loaders weigh the containers to ensure the proper amount gets loaded. They use computers to record the quantity shipped, the weight of the cargo, operating times, and other important information.

When the cargo arrives at its destination, workers on that end perform many of the same duties as when the cargo was first loaded. They make sure the correct amount of cargo has arrived and then use various loading technologies to move the cargo from the ship to the dock, warehouse, or wharf. From there, the cargo is usually loaded onto trucks for delivery to its final destination.

Duties and Responsibilities

- Transporting cargo by hand trucks or tractor
- Operating a crane or winch to load or unload cargo according to signals from other workers
- Guiding loads being lifted to prevent swinging
- Stacking cargo in a transit shed or in the hold of a ship
- Supporting cargo in the ship's hold to prevent shifting during the voyage
- Moving controls to start and stop the flow of grain from the spouts of grain trimmers
- Positioning and fastening hose lines to ships' cargo tanks
- Directing the activities of the cargo gang
- Attaching slings, hooks, or other lifting devices to a winch

WORK ENVIRONMENT

Immediate Physical Environment

Ship loaders work in different dock, wharf, and warehouse environments in all kinds of weather. Warehouses are where much of the inventory control is done, while the loading and unloading occurs at the docks and wharfs. Safety standards must be adhered to at every location.

Transferable Skills and Abilities

Organization & Management Skills
- Performing routine work
- Performing duties that change frequently

Research & Planning Skills
- Developing evaluation strategies

Technical Skills
- Working with your hands
- Working with machines, tools, or other objects

Unclassified Skills
- Using set methods and standards in your work

Work Environment Skills
- Working outdoors

Human Environment

Ship loaders collaborate heavily with others in the shipping industry. Throughout the day, ship loaders will interact with supervisors, machine operators, captains, and fellow ship loaders. Communication is essential to be sure cargo arrives safely and on time.

Technological Environment

Ship loaders use a variety of technology, ranging from handheld tools to large machinery. Throughout the day, ship loaders will use handheld inventory scanners, dollies, conveyors, mechanical hoists, cranes, and other items. Safety gear such as hard hats, gloves, and reflector vests are worn.

EDUCATION, TRAINING, AND ADVANCEMENT

High School/Secondary

Many shipping companies require applicants to have a high school diploma or the equivalent. High school students can prepare for a job as a ship loader with basic courses in mathematics, English, and any computer courses that teach the use of spreadsheets. Because computers are used often in inventory control, a basic understanding of them is important.

Suggested High School Subjects
- Driver Training
- English
- Shop Math

Related Career Pathways/Majors

Manufacturing Cluster
- Logistics & Inventory Control Pathway

Marketing, Sales & Service Cluster
- Distribution & Logistics Pathway

Famous First

Highly skilled shipbuilders and sailors from Phoenicians were the greatest traders in the ancient world from 1000 BCE to 600 BCE. They learned how to navigate and how to use the North Star to sail at night. It is possible that they even sailed as far as Britain and around the southern tip of Africa. To fight off pirates, the Phoenicians designed special warships to accompany their trading fleets. Oarsmen would propel a sharp ramming device at the front of the boat into an enemy's vessel, putting a hole into it that would cause it to sink.

Source: http://www.ushistory.org

Postsecondary

While most shipping companies do not require applicants to have a college education, there are many courses offered by community colleges, technical schools, and vocational schools that would give an individual better knowledge of the profession. Although ship loaders typically receive on-the-job training, many obtain a background in the profession through one of these schools.

Technical and vocational schools provide instruction in a variety of loading-machinery operations, such as cranes and forklifts. Ship loaders cannot use many of these machines until they take a formal class on their operation. These courses provide weeks of formal instruction and hands-on training from experienced instructors. Students are also taught how to maintain these machines and how to comply with safety standards. Completing one of these courses will increase the chances of an individual being hired by a shipping company. Employers are more likely to hire someone with experience with the technology so they do not have to spend time training them. These schools are also a great place to network with others in the industry.

Adult Job Seekers

Individuals considering a career as a ship loader should take into account the amount of time they will have to spend away from personal responsibilities. Individuals with no prior experience in the industry should consider completing a relevant course at a technical or vocational school. These schools sometimes offer job-placement programs that will help individuals transition into their new profession.

Individuals interested in the profession should check if there is a Marine Transport Workers Union in their area. If there is, they can be contacted for more information on a profession as a ship loader.

Professional Certification and Licensure

Ship loaders interested in advancing in the industry should seek out training and certification in the technologies that are commonly used on the job. For example, the National Commission for the Certification of Crane Operators (NCCCO) offers several certification programs. In order to qualify for certification, applicants must be at least eighteen years of age, meet the physical requirements, and pass a written and practical examination. The certification offered by the NCCCO is for loaders already experienced with cranes.

Ship loaders must have forklift certification before he or she can operate one. Forklift classes are offered at many vocational and technical schools, as well as trucking schools. Some employers also offer on-the-job forklift training. Ship loaders can take an online exam offered by the Forklift Academy. Passing the exam gives an individual a permit to operate a forklift, a certificate of achievement, and documentation to provide to employers.

Additional Requirements

Ship loaders should be committed to actively learning new job-related skills for career advancement. They should be dexterous when handling machinery and sufficiently detail oriented to ensure the correct cargo arrives safely.

Fast Fact

The largest ship in the world's fleet can store 18,000 containers, which means it can carry one banana for each European—or more than 745 million bananas.
Source: ocean-insights.com

EARNINGS AND ADVANCEMENT

Earnings of ship loaders depend on the amount of work they have had during the year and whether they operate machinery. Ship loaders also receive a higher pay rate for night, holiday, or overtime work and if they handle hazardous cargo. In 2017, ship loaders had median annual earnings of $40,290.

Unionized ship loaders receive health insurance and are eligible for a pension at age 57.

EMPLOYMENT AND OUTLOOK

There were about 9,000 ship loaders employed nationally in 2018. Employment is expected to grow about as fast as average for all occupations through the year 2026, which means employment is projected to increase 6 to 7 percent. Improvements in material handling equipment and greater use of containerized cargo ships will reduce the need for ship loaders in the future. Yet, as long as goods are carried by ships which use American ports, there will be a need for these workers.

Related Occupations
- Forklift Operator
- Freight, Stock & Material Mover
- Rail Transportation Worker
- Sailor & Deckhand

Related Military Occupations
- Cargo Specialist
- Supply & Warehousing Specialist

MORE INFORMATION

Forklift Academy
5737 Kana Road, Suite 508
Agoura Hills, CA 91301
888.381.2572
www.forkliftacademy.com

Industrial Workers of the World (IWW)
Marine Transport Workers Union
P.O. Box 180195
Chicago, IL 60618
773.728.0996
ghq@iww.org
www.iww.org

International Longshoremen's & Warehousemen's Union (ILWU)
1188 Franklin Street, 4th Floor
San Francisco, CA 94109
415.775.0533
info@ilwu.org
www.ilwu.org

International Longshoremen's Association (ILA)
17 Battery Place, Suite 930
New York, NY 10004
212.425.1200
www.ilaunion.org

Laborers' International Union of North America (LIUNA)
905 16th Street, NW
Washington, DC 20006
202.737.8320
www.liuna.org

Patrick Cooper/Editor

Software Developer

Snapshot

Career Cluster(s): Arts, A/V Technology & Communications, Information Technology

Interests: Computer software technology, math, science, information technology

Earnings (Median Pay): $93,273

Employment & Outlook: Faster Than Average Growth Expected

OVERVIEW

Sphere of Work

Software developers are the creative minds behind computer programs. Some develop the applications that allow people to do specific tasks on a computer or another device. Others develop the underlying systems that run the devices or that control networks. Software designers develop system, utility, and application software, as well as computer games. They also modify existing programs to improve functionality or to meet client needs. On large-scale projects, software designers typically work with a team of professionals that includes software engineers, software architects, and computer

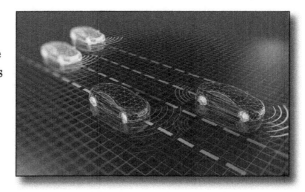

programmers. In these cases, they might be primarily responsible for developing the functional or "front-end" user interface of the program to ensure that it is compatible with a particular platform and related components and that it works reliably and securely. On smaller jobs, software designers might also handle the programming, engineering, and architecture of the program.

Work Environment

Many software designers are self-employed and work at home or in small businesses. Others work for the military, government agencies, or industries such as telecommunications, health care, aerospace, e-commerce, video games, and education. Software designers working for corporations typically work 40-hour weeks, while those who are self-employed may set their own hours. In either case, strict deadlines or unexpected problems may require software designers to work additional hours as needed.

Profile

Interests: Data, Things
Working Conditions: Work Inside
Physical Strength: Light Work
Education Needs: Bachelor's Degree
Licensure/Certification: Recommended
Physical Abilities Not Required: Not Climb, Not Kneel, Not Hear and/or Talk
Opportunities for Experience: Internship, Apprenticeship, Military Service, Part-Time Work
Holland Interest Score: AES, IRE

* See Appendix A

Occupation Interest

People who are attracted to software design careers are analytical and mathematically inclined, with strong problem-solving skills and an aptitude for learning programming languages. They are detail oriented, yet also able to envision the overall design and application of products. Software designers need good communication skills to interact with team members and convey their ideas. Leadership and organizational skills are also important, as is the desire to be knowledgeable about new developments in the industry.

A Day in the Life—Duties and Responsibilities

Most computer programs are born out of a need. Software designers first evaluate that need, usually in consultation with a client, and then conceive of a program to solve the problem. They design computer games, applications for mobile phones, and other highly visible types of software. They also design behind-the-scenes programs known as utilities, which may help users download content from the internet seamlessly, convert files to different formats, protect computers from malware or keylogging, or free up computer disk space when needed. Some software designers develop programs used in business, education, graphic arts, multimedia, web development, and many other fields, as well as programs intended just for other programmers.

Software designers are often responsible for planning a project within budget and time constraints. They must consider compatibility issues, determining the type of platform or multiplatform on which the software will operate and the oldest version on which it will work reliably. They also consider issues such as the maintainability of the software (how often it will need to be updated).

Software designers then devise a schematic of the program that shows its structure, often displayed as a hierarchy consisting of modules. They develop algorithms, which are sets of instructions or steps needed to solve the problems identified by each module. Designers program the code line by line, or supervise other programmers. They test the modules, locate and correct any errors, and then test the program repeatedly until it is secure, user-friendly, and reliable. They might also add graphics and multimedia components or hand that job over to a graphic designer.

Duties and Responsibilities

- Analyzing users' needs and then designing, testing, and developing software to meet those needs
- Recommending software upgrades for customers' existing programs and systems
- Designing each piece of an application or system and planning how the pieces will work together
- Creating a variety of models and diagrams (such as flowcharts) that show programmers the software code needed for an application
- Ensuring that a program continues to function normally through software maintenance and testing
- Documenting every aspect of an application or system as a reference for future maintenance and upgrades
- Collaborating with other computer specialists to create optimum software

WORK ENVIRONMENT

Immediate Physical Environment

Software designers usually work in comfortable offices or from their homes, although some may also travel to meet with clients. They are at some risk for carpel tunnel syndrome, back problems, and eyestrain due to prolonged use of computers.

Human Environment

Software designers typically report to a project manager and are usually members of a development team, along with programmers, systems architects, quality assurance specialists, and others. The designer might also manage the team or oversee the work done by programmers. A high level of communication and cooperation is usually necessary for success. Many designers, however, work alone and are responsible only to their clients.

Transferable Skills and Abilities

Organization & Management Skills
- Paying attention to and handling details
- Organizing information or materials
- Performing routine work

Communication Skills
- Speaking effectively
- Writing concisely

Interpersonal/Social Skills
- Being able to work independently
- Working as a member of a team

Research & Planning Skills
- Creating ideas
- Identifying problems
- Solving problems
- Using logical reasoning

Technological Environment

Software designers use a variety of desktop computers, portable computer devices, video game consoles, and related hardware. They use and interface with various operating systems and database management programs. While software designers do not necessarily do programming, they should be familiar with various computer and markup languages, including C++, Java, ColdFusion, and hypertext markup language (HTML), as well as related compilers and interpreters.

EDUCATION, TRAINING, AND ADVANCEMENT

High School/Secondary

Students should take a strong college-preparatory program that includes English, chemistry, physics, and four years of mathematics, including trigonometry, calculus, and statistics. Computer science or technology, engineering, and electronics courses are also important. Students interested primarily in designing video games or visual-heavy programs should take computer graphics and drawing courses. Other potentially beneficial subjects include psychology, sociology, and business. Participation in technology clubs, science fairs, mathematics competitions, and other related extracurricular activities is encouraged, as is independent study and creation of programs.

Suggested High School Subjects
- Accounting
- Algebra
- Applied Communication
- Applied Math
- Bookkeeping
- Business & Computer Technology
- Business Data Processing
- Calculus
- College Preparatory
- Computer Programming
- Computer Science
- English
- Geometry
- Graphic Communications
- Keyboarding
- Mathematics
- Statistics
- Trigonometry

Related Career Pathways/Majors

Arts, A/V Technology & Communications Cluster
- Visual Arts Pathway

Information Technology Cluster
- Interactive Media Pathway
- Programming & Software Development Pathway

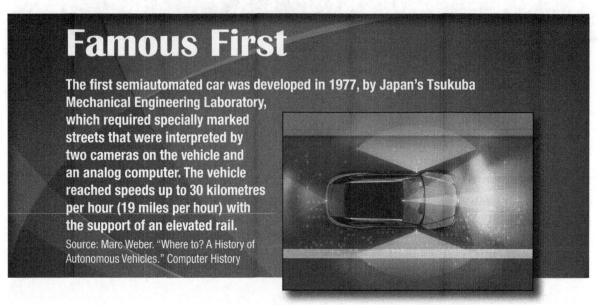

Famous First

The first semiautomated car was developed in 1977, by Japan's Tsukuba Mechanical Engineering Laboratory, which required specially marked streets that were interpreted by two cameras on the vehicle and an analog computer. The vehicle reached speeds up to 30 kilometres per hour (19 miles per hour) with the support of an elevated rail.

Source: Marc Weber. "Where to? A History of Autonomous Vehicles." Computer History

Postsecondary

Although some employers consider job applicants with an associate's degree, most prefer to hire workers with a bachelor's degree or higher in computer science, computer engineering, or a related technical field. Prospective software designers must be familiar with different types of computers and operating systems, systems organization and architecture, data structures and algorithms, computation theory, and other related topics.

Students should focus on classes related to building software to better prepare themselves for work in the occupation. Many students gain experience in software development by completing an internship at a software company while in college. For some positions, employers may prefer that applicants have a master's degree.

Although writing code is not their first priority, developers must have a strong background in computer programming. They usually gain this experience in school. Throughout their career, developers must keep up to date on new tools and computer languages.

Software developers also need skills related to the industry in which they work. Developers working in a transportation, for example, should have knowledge of logistics so that they can understand a transportation company's computing needs.

Related College Majors:
- Computer Engineering
- Computer Engineering Technology
- Computer Maintenance Technology
- Computer Programming
- Computer Science
- Design & Visual Communications
- Educational/Instructional Media Design
- Graphic Design, Commercial Art & Illustration
- Information Sciences & Systems
- Management Information Systems & Business Data Processing

Adult Job Seekers

Adults with a computer science or programming background who are returning to the field can update their skills and knowledge by taking continuing education courses offered by software vendors or colleges. Some courses are available online. Those with family obligations might want to consider self-employment, although regular full-time employment may offer more financial stability. Professional associations may provide networking opportunities, as well as job openings and connections to potential clients.

Advancement is partially dependent on the size of the company and the scale of projects. In large companies, software designers with leadership skills typically move into project management and higher-ranked positions as experience and education warrant. Experienced designers may also establish their own businesses, while designers with advanced degrees may move into college teaching.

Professional Certification and Licensure

There are no mandatory licenses or certifications needed for these positions, although voluntary certification from the Institute of Electrical and Electronics Engineers (IEEE), the Institute for Certification of Computing Professionals (ICCP), and other professional organizations can be especially advantageous for job hunting and networking. Software designers can be certified as Software Development Associates (CSDA) or Software Development Professionals (CSDP) through IEEE or as Computing Professionals (CCP) and Associate Computing Professionals (ACP) through ICCP. Software designers are encouraged to consult prospective employers and credible professional associations within the field as to the relevancy and value of any voluntary certification program.

Additional Requirements

Software designers must have excellent keyboarding skills. Some designers might need a driver's license to travel between job sites.

Software Developer

EARNINGS AND ADVANCEMENT

Earnings for software developers vary depending on the size and location of the employer and the education, experience and certification of the employee. Median annual earnings of applications software developers was $103,620 in May 2018. The lowest 10 percent earned less than $61,660, and the highest 10 percent earned more than $161,290.

The median annual wage for systems software developers was $110,000 in May 2018. The lowest 10 percent earned less than $66,740, and the highest 10 percent earned more than $166,960.

Software developers may receive paid vacations, holidays, and sick days; life and health insurance; and retirement benefits. These are usually paid by the employer.

Median annual wages, May 2018

Software developers, systems software: $110,000

Software developers: $105,590

Software developers, applications: $103,620

Computer occupations: $86,320

Total, all occupations: $38,640

Note: All Occupations includes all occupations in the U.S. Economy.
Source: U.S. Bureau of Labor Statistics, Occupational Employment Statistics

EMPLOYMENT AND OUTLOOK

Software developers held about 1,256,200 jobs nationally in 2016. Employment of software developers is expected to grow much faster than the average for all occupations through the year 2026, which means employment is projected to increase 24 percent or more.

The need for new applications on smartphones and tablets will help increase the demand for applications software developers. These apps, especially ridesharing apps, are especially important in the transportation industry.

The health and medical insurance and reinsurance carriers industry will need innovative software to manage new healthcare policy enrollments and administer existing policies digitally. As the number of people who use this digital platform increases over time, demand for software developers will grow.

Systems developers are likely to see new opportunities because of an increase in the number of products that use software. For example, more computer systems are being built into consumer electronics and other products, including cars, trucks, and buses.

Concerns over threats to computer security could result in more investment in security software to protect computer networks and electronic infrastructure. In addition, an increase in software offered over the internet should lower costs and allow more customization for businesses, also increasing demand for software developers.

Percent change in employment, Projected 2016–26

Software developers, applications: 31%

Software developers: 24%

Computer occupations: 13%

Software developers, systems software: 11%

Total, all occupations: 7%

Note: All Occupations includes all occupations in the U.S. Economy.
Source: U.S. Bureau of Labor Statistics, Occupational Employment Statistics

Related Occupations
- Commercial Artist
- Computer & Information Systems Manager
- Computer Engineer
- Computer Operator
- Computer Programmer
- Computer Security Specialist
- Computer Support Specialist
- Computer Systems Analyst
- Computer-Control Tool Programmer
- Designer
- Graphic Designer
- Information Technology Project Manager
- Network & Computer Systems Administrator
- Network Systems & Data Communications Analyst
- Web Administrator
- Website Designer

Related Military Occupations
- Computer Programmer
- Computer Systems Specialist
- Graphic Designer & Illustrator

Fast Fact

One of the most expensive software in the world, Autodesk Plant Design Suite is a premium product of AutoCAD—one of the most expensive products from AutoCAD—used in modern 3D-plant and structural modeling.

Source: www.rankred.com

MORE INFORMATION

American Institute of Graphic Arts (AIGA)
164 Fifth Avenue
New York, NY 10010
212.807.1990
www.aiga.org

Association for Computing Machinery (ACM)
2 Penn Plaza, Suite 701
New York, NY 10121-0701
800.342.6626
acmhelp@acm.org
www.acm.org

ACM-W scholarships for female students to attend research conferences:
http://women.acm.org/participate/scholarship/index.cfm

The Graphic Artists Guild
32 Broadway, Suite 1114
New York, NY 10004-1612
212.791.3400
pr@gag.org
www.gag.org

Institute for the Certification of Computer Professionals (ICCP)
2400 E. Devon Avenue, Suite 281
Des Plaines, IL 60018-4610
800.843.8227
office@iccp.org
www.iccp.org

Institute of Electrical and Electronics Engineers (IEEE) Computer Society
2001 L Street NW, Suite 700
Washington, DC 20036-4928
202.371.0101
help@computer.org
www.computer.org

A variety of IEEE scholarships, grants, and fellowships:
www.computer.org/portal/web/studentactivities/home

Sally Driscoll/Editor

Taxi Drivers, Ride-Hailing Drivers, and Chauffeurs

Snapshot

Career Cluster(s): Hospitality & Tourism, Transportation, Distribution & Logistics

Interests: Road transportation, urban transportation, hospitality

Earnings (Median Pay): $25,980

Employment & Outlook: As Fast as Average Growth Expected

OVERVIEW

Sphere of Work

Taxi drivers, ride-hailing drivers, and chauffeurs drive people to and from the places they need to go, such as homes, workplaces, airports, and shopping centers. They must be familiar with city streets and locations to take passengers to their destinations.

Work Environment

Taxi drivers and chauffeurs work in towns and cities throughout the world, where they typically navigate their way between airports, business districts, hotels, convention

centers, restaurants, and private residences. A driver may rent his or her vehicle from a fleet company that serves a variety of customers. A chauffeur may work for a single individual or company to whom he or she carries out many different requests. Most chauffeur assignments are prearranged and door-to-door, whereas the taxi driver tends to live for the moment, with each job that comes his or her way a new adventure. Chauffeurs and taxi drivers both work independently and without supervision, answering mostly to their customers rather than to bosses.

Profile

Interests: Data, People, Things
Working Conditions: Work both Inside and Outside
Physical Strength: Light Work, Medium Work
Education Needs: No High School Diploma, On-the-Job Training
Licensure/Certification: Required
Physical Abilities Not Required: Not Climb, Not Kneel
Opportunities for Experience: Part-Time Work
Holland Interest Score: IRE, REC

* See Appendix A

Occupation Interest

Taxi drivers and chauffeurs must be excellent drivers, able to navigate streets during rush hour or poor weather conditions, and be intimately familiar with their cities. Punctuality, flexibility, and an overall sense of responsibility are other key qualifications. While these jobs tend to be portrayed as glamorous, some urban taxi drivers run a high risk of being robbed or assaulted. Drivers sometimes deal with unsavory situations, emergencies, and challenging personalities, although the opportunity to meet celebrities and other interesting people can be enticing.

A Day in the Life—Duties and Responsibilities

Taxi drivers, ride-hailing drivers, and chauffeurs must stay alert and watch the conditions of the road. They have to take precautions to ensure their passengers' safety, especially in heavy traffic or bad weather. Taxi drivers and chauffeurs must also follow vehicle-for-hire or livery regulations, such as where they can pick up passengers and how much they can charge.

Good drivers are familiar with the streets in the areas they serve. They choose the most efficient routes, considering the traffic at that time of day. They know where the most often sought destinations are, such as airports, train stations, convention centers, hotels, and other points of interest. They also know where to find fire and police stations and hospitals in case of an emergency.

The following are examples of types of taxi drivers, ride-hailing drivers, and chauffeurs:

Taxi drivers, also called cabdrivers or cabbies, use a meter to calculate the fare when a passenger requests a destination. Many customers request a cab by calling a central dispatcher who then tells the taxi driver the pickup location. Some drivers pick up passengers waiting in lines at cabstands or in the taxi line at airports, train stations, and hotels. Cabbies drive around the streets looking for passengers in some large cities.

Ride-hailing drivers pick up passengers who seek service through a smartphone app. The fare rate can fluctuate depending on demand; however, passengers are notified if the current fare rate is higher than usual. Passengers pay for rides through a credit card linked to the app. Drivers use their own private vehicles and set their own hours.

Chauffeurs take passengers on prearranged trips. They drive limousines, vans, or private cars. They may work for hire for single trips, or they may work for a person, a private business, or for a government agency. Customer service is important for chauffeurs, especially luxury vehicle drivers. Some do the duties of executive assistants, acting as driver, secretary, and itinerary planner. Other chauffeurs drive large vans between airports or train stations and hotels.

Paratransit drivers transport people with special needs, such as the elderly or those with disabilities. They drive specially equipped vehicles designed to help people with various needs in nonemergency situations. For example, their vehicles may be equipped with wheelchair lifts, and the driver helps a passenger with boarding.

Duties and Responsibilities

- Driving taxicabs, limousines, company cars, or privately owned vehicles to transport passengers
- Picking up passengers and listening to where they want to go
- Helping passengers load and unloading their luggage
- Obeying all traffic laws
- Checking the car for problems and doing basic maintenance
- Keeping the inside and outside of their car clean
- Operating wheelchair lifts when needed
- Keeping a record of miles traveled

WORK ENVIRONMENT

Immediate Physical Environment

The taxi driver or chauffeur is confined to the car, except when taking breaks. Air-conditioning or heat, seats with good support, and a vehicle that is comfortable to maneuver can make the experience mostly pleasant. Sitting for long periods can cause muscular discomfort related to lack of exercise. City traffic and heavy exhaust fumes can also be detrimental to one's health, while breathing in the unpleasant odors present with some customers, such as heavy perfume or the stench of alcohol, can be another negative aspect of the work.

Work hours for taxi drivers, ride-hailing drivers, and chauffeurs vary. Some work part time. Evening and weekend work is common. Some drivers work late at night or early in the morning.

Taxi and ride-hailing drivers work with little or no supervision, and their work schedules are flexible. They can take breaks for a meal or rest whenever they do not have a passenger.

Chauffeurs' work schedules are much more structured. They work hours based on client needs. Some chauffeurs must be ready to drive their clients at a moment's notice, so they remain on call throughout the day.

Transferable Skills and Abilities

Interpersonal/Social Skills
- Cooperating with others
- Working as a member of a team

Organization & Management Skills
- Following instructions
- Organizing information or materials
- Performing routine work

Technical Skills
- Working with data or numbers

Unclassified Skills
- Making minor auto repairs

Work Environment Skills
- Driving a vehicle

Human Environment

For many drivers, contact with customers is the highlight of the job. Conversations may be initiated by either party and may evolve into in-depth discussions about current events or politics. Taxi drivers must be patient, sympathetic, and willing to repeat information about local events or weather several times a day. Drivers must also be comfortable taking directions from the dispatcher, interacting and often competing with other taxi drivers, and exercising tact and patience with other drivers, customers, and pedestrians.

Some drivers contract with a dispatch company that refers passengers and allows the driver to use their service facilities for a fee. Drivers who do not own their taxicab may lease a dispatch company's car as part of the fee. Drivers usually pay for their own expenses such as fuel.

Driving for long periods, especially in heavy traffic, can be stressful for these workers. In addition, they often have to pick up heavy luggage and packages.

Technological Environment

Drivers must be familiar with the basic mechanics of their vehicles, the taximeter, and communications equipment, such as two-way radios or cell phones. The use of ride-sharing apps is increasingly important. GPS (global positioning system) devices, computers, calculators, credit card machines, and other small gadgets may be used as well.

EDUCATION, TRAINING, AND ADVANCEMENT

High School/Secondary

A high school diploma is not always required, although it is desirable. Most employers in the United States expect good English language skills, while knowledge of a second language can also be very useful. Math skills are needed to keep records and make change. Speech communications can give one confidence in relating with the public, and courses in geography will help with map-reading skills. Driver training and auto mechanics courses are vital.

Suggested High School Subjects
- Driver Training
- English
- First Aid Training
- Mathematics

Related Career Pathways/Majors

Hospitality & Tourism Cluster
- Lodging Pathway

Transportation, Distribution & Logistics Cluster
- Transportation Operations Pathway

Famous First

The first driver arrested for speeding was Jacob German, operator of a taxicab for the Electric Vehicle Company, who was arrested on May 20, 1899, by Bicycle Roundsman Schuessler for driving at a "breakneck speed" of 12 miles per hour on Lexington Avenue, New York City. German was booked and jailed in the East 22nd Street station house.

Source: "Transportation." *Famous First Facts*, Salem, 2016. *Salem Online*, https://online.salempress.com

Postsecondary

College courses in business, social sciences, communications, or foreign languages can also be advantageous for drivers, especially those interested in starting their own companies. Regardless of one's educational level, most companies provide on-the-job training that lasts a week or two. A driver should then be ready to tackle the work independently.

Advancement is limited in most places. An experienced driver may be rewarded with the best routes, command a higher salary as a private chauffeur, choose to become a dispatcher, or start his or her own company.

Adult Job Seekers

There are few barriers for adults interested in beginning a new career as a taxi or limousine driver. Drivers can usually find positions that are full- or part-time, work customized hours, or work a shift that fits best with family responsibilities.

Professional Certification and Licensure

All taxi drivers, ride-hailing drivers, and chauffeurs must have a regular automobile driver's license. States and local municipalities set other requirements; many require taxi drivers and chauffeurs to get a taxi or limousine license. This normally requires passing a background check, drug test, and a written exam about regulations and local geography.

Regulations for ride-hailing drivers vary by state and city. Check with your local area for more information.

The Federal Motor Carrier Safety Administration requires limousine drivers who transport 16 or more passengers (including the driver) to hold a commercial driver's license (CDL) with a passenger (P) endorsement. Drivers must pass knowledge and driving skills tests to receive a CDL.

Additional Requirements

Most taxi and limousine companies provide their new drivers with a short period of on-the-job training. This training usually takes from one day to two weeks, depending on the company and the location. Some cities require training by law.

Training typically covers local traffic laws, driver safety, and the local street layout. Taxi drivers also get training in operating the taximeter and communications equipment. Limousine companies, with an emphasis on customer service, usually train their chauffeurs. Ride-hailing drivers receive little to no training beyond how to work the electronic hailing app so they can pick up customers. Paratransit drivers receive special training in how to handle wheelchair lifts and other mechanical devices.

Some cities and states require a driver to be a United States citizen or legal resident. They might test the applicant's proficiency in English. A prospective driver must also be physically fit, as drivers often lift heavy luggage and need to see well. Some cities and states require a medical examination and drug testing prior to licensing.

Fast Fact

A London taxi driver must pass a test to receive his or her license. It typically takes drivers for 2 to 4 years to develop a working knowledge of London's 320 routes in a 6-mile radius of Charing Cross, which includes 25,000 streets and 20,000 landmarks.

Source: https://londontopia.net

EARNINGS AND ADVANCEMENT

Earnings depend on the geographic location of the employer, the number of hours worked, customers' tips and the driver's efforts to seek out customers. The median annual wage for taxi drivers, ride-hailing drivers, and chauffeurs was $25,980 in May 2018. The lowest 10 percent earned less than $19,240, and the highest 10 percent earned more than $40,360.

These wage data include money earned from tips. Taxi drivers and chauffeurs who provide good customer service are more likely to receive higher tips on each fare.

Work hours for taxi drivers, ride-hailing drivers, and chauffeurs vary. Some work part time. Evening and weekend work is common. Some drivers work late at night or early in the morning.
Taxi and ride-hailing drivers work with little or no supervision, and their work schedules are flexible. They can take breaks for a meal or rest whenever they do not have a passenger.

Chauffeurs' work schedules are much more structured. They work hours based on client needs. Some chauffeurs stay on call throughout the day, and must be ready to drive clients at a moment's notice.

Taxi drivers and chauffeurs usually do not receive fringe benefits given to workers of other occupations.

Median annual wages, May 2018

Total, all occupations: $38,640

Motor vehicle operators: $37,130

Taxi drivers and chauffeurs: $25,980

Note: All Occupations includes all occupations in the U.S. Economy.
Source: U.S. Bureau of Labor Statistics, Occupational Employment Statistics

EMPLOYMENT AND OUTLOOK

There were approximately 305,100 taxi drivers, ride-hailing drivers, and chauffeurs employed nationally in 2016. Employment is expected to grow as fast as average for all occupations through the year 2026, which means employment is projected to increase 20 percent to 28 percent. This is due to local and suburban travel increasing as the population grows. Job opportunities may fluctuate from season to season and from month to month.

Percent change in employment, Projected 2016–26

Total, all occupations: 7%

Motor vehicle operators: 5%

Taxi drivers and chauffeurs: 5%

Note: All Occupations includes all occupations in the U.S. Economy.
Source: U.S. Bureau of Labor Statistics, Occupational Employment Statistics

Related Occupations
- Bus Driver
- Truck Driver

Conversation With . . .
BILL MARSH

Black Time Limousine
Haverhill, MA
Driver, 14 years (retired)

1. What was your individual career path in terms of education/training, entry-level job, or other significant opportunity?

Most of my career I worked for a Japanese trading company in the logistics division, handling cargo shipped by ocean and air. I lost the job during an economic downturn in the Japanese economy. During my last several years with the company I was on the board of directors and set up meetings all over the country. As a result, I had a lot of contacts among limousine companies that I hired to drive executives, so I reached out to several of them in the Boston area where I was living at the time.

I drove for six different limousine companies over the course of fourteen years and ended my career driving for Black Tie Limousine. I consider Black Tie the premiere limousine service and was very happy there. My wife had gone back to her job teaching and my new job worked for our family.

2. What are the most important skills and/or qualities for someone in your profession?

You have to be a good driver, a safe driver. You have to be able to communicate well with people. You have customers that request you, so you develop relationships.

You also have to be dependable and get used to working off hours. It's not a 9-to-5 job. I drove a lot of executives to and from the airport and often had to be up by 3 or 5 a.m. Other drivers do a lot of evening events and are out late. Our limo drivers had to be at least 21 years old.

3. What do you wish you had known going into this profession?

Some companies fall short on safety compliance. You read some horror stories in the news, like the limo that caught fire on prom night. Luckily all the teens got out safely.

The best way to find a good company to work for is to ask the doormen at major hotels which ones they think are best. They get to know the limousine companies and drivers who come and go all the time. Ask a lot of questions.

The best companies are located in the major cities, but there are some good regional outfits, too.

4. Are there many job opportunities in your profession?

Yes, there are always job opportunities for drivers. Some drivers are retirees who end up moving away, like I did when I retired. Others are students who graduate from college or grad school and go into other professions. A surprising number of drivers are educated people with professional backgrounds.

It's a good job for students who are 21 or over. There's a lot of downtime—which you are getting paid for—while waiting to drive people back to their hotel or next destination. I got a lot of reading done, but people in college or graduate school can get a lot of studying done.

5. How do you see your profession changing in the next five years? How will technology impact that change and what skills will be required?

The use of GPS already has made the job a lot easier for drivers who don't like using maps. I was very good reading maps and enjoyed using them. GPS also has its limitations. It once directed me over a mountain when I was driving a celebrity. She laughed as she directed me to her driveway. GPS can be wrong sometimes.

Driverless cars could be a huge change in the future. But limousines will always have to have a chauffeur to open doors and handle bags.

6. What do you enjoy most about your job? What do you enjoy least about your job?

The best part was meeting all kinds of great people. I met a lot of celebrities and CEOs—famous, wealthy people, most of whom were down to earth. We'd talk about food and restaurants and about how we both had kids in colleges. I'd pick people up from their private or corporate jets and take them to the Four Seasons or the Ritz. I've driven Carly Simon, Carl Yastrzemksi, and Richard Gere. When the vice premier of China visited, I was part of an entourage of 22 black Lincoln town cars. For one company we drove all the Kenyan runners for the Boston Marathon. We had someone in the car who was a greeter and met them at the airport with a bouquet of flowers. I drove them around all week.

You spend a lot of time with people celebrating major events in their lives. We did a lot of weddings. I had guys who told me they did four weddings on one day. I drove children and families to the airport for Make-A-Wish trips to Disney, and I drove one large group from Ireland around Boston for St. Patrick's Day.

For our job we wore a black suit with a black tie, black vest, and white shirt. Your shoes better be shined and clean. I didn't mind it most of the time, but in the summertime it could be uncomfortably hot.

7. **Can you suggest a valuable "try this" for students considering a career in your profession?**

   See if you like driving. Some people get bored, others like it. You can try delivering pizza— some places require pizza delivery drivers to be 18, but others allow teens to deliver at 16.

MORE INFORMATION

National Association of Taxi Drivers (NATD)
100 W. Hosack, Suite 104
Boerne, TX 78006
800.977.0959
www.joinnatd.org

National Limousine Association (NLA)
49 S. Maple Avenue
Marlton, NJ 08053
800.652.7007
info@limo.org
www.limo.org

The Rideshare Guy
(Blog and podcast)
therideshareguy.com

3200 Tower Oaks Boulevard
Suite 220
Rockville, MD 20852
301.984.5700
info@thetransportationalliance.org
www.tlpa.org

Sally Driscoll/Editor

Urban and Regional Planner

Snapshot

Career Cluster(s): Architecture & Construction, Government & Public Administration, Transportation, Distribution & Logistics
Interests: Public policy, architecture, geography, community services, public planning, community and urban infrastructure
Earnings (Median Pay): $73,050
Employment & Outlook: Faster Than Average Growth Expected

OVERVIEW

Sphere of Work

Urban and regional planners decide how best to use the land and resources of a certain community or region, then develop the plans to do so. Their work may include establishing guidelines for the preservation of ecologically sensitive areas, formulating a strategy to attract new businesses to the region, or helping to draft legislation that will address environmental and social issues, such as public parks and homeless shelters. Planners study different elements of a particular area, including population demographics, employment numbers, and aspects of public infrastructure such as highways and sewer

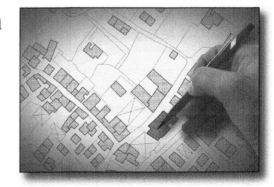

lines, in order to determine the best use of land for the community as a whole.

Work Environment

Urban and regional planners generally work in offices in consulting firms or government organizations. They often spend time in the field, inspecting sites intended for development. Planners work at least 40 hours per week, plus some evenings and weekends when participating in public meetings.

Profile

Interests: Data, People
Working Conditions: Work Inside
Physical Strength: Light Work
Education Needs: Bachelor's Degree, Master's Degree
Licensure/Certification: Recommended
Physical Abilities Not Required: Not Climb, Not Handle, Not Kneel
Opportunities for Experience: Internship, Volunteer Work, Part-Time Work
Holland Interest Score: ESI

* See Appendix A

Occupation Interest

Individuals attracted to urban and regional planning tend to find satisfaction in providing services to others and seeing projects through from start to finish. They are spatially oriented and can visualize how various projects will affect local communities. Planners should have an affinity for math and geographic information systems and be able to use statistical data to solve problems.

A Day in the Life—Duties and Responsibilities

Urban and regional planners identify community needs and develop short- and long-term solutions to improve and revitalize communities and areas. As an area grows or changes, planners help communities manage the related economic, social, and environmental issues, such as planning new parks, sheltering the homeless, and making the region more attractive to businesses.

Urban and regional planners are responsible for the development of a particular area. On a given day, a planner who works for a government organization may help devise plans and policies that will affect community interests like zoning and public utilities, or make recommendations on how officials should respond to development proposals. Planners in private companies may spend their time negotiating with those same officials, conducting feasibility studies on proposed projects, or collecting and analyzing data on current land use. Urban and regional planners often must attend public hearings to address the questions and concerns of the community. Their responsibilities may also include soliciting and selecting proposals from developers, coordinating building plans with consultants and various construction personnel, or reviewing geographical information system maps to determine what services are needed in what areas, which could be anything from more fire hydrants to greater access to public transportation.

When beginning a project, planners often work with public officials, community members, and other groups to identify community issues and goals. Through research, data analysis, and collaboration with interest groups, they formulate strategies to address issues and to meet goals. Planners may also help carry out community plans by overseeing projects, enforcing zoning regulations, and organizing the work of the groups involved.

Urban and regional planners may specialize in areas such as transportation planning, community development, historic preservation, or urban design, among other fields of interest.

Planners often collaborate with public officials, civil engineers, environmental engineers, architects, lawyers, and real estate developers.

Duties and Responsibilities

- Meeting with public officials, developers, and the public regarding development plans and land use
- Administering government plans or policies affecting land use
- Gathering and analyzing data from market research, censuses, and economic and environmental studies
- Conducting field investigations to analyze factors affecting community development and decline, including land use
- Reviewing site plans submitted by developers
- Assessing the feasibility of proposals and identify needed changes
- Recommending whether proposals should be approved or denied
- Presenting projects to communities, planning officials, and planning commissions
- Staying current on zoning and building codes, environmental regulations, and other legal issues

OCCUPATION SPECIALTIES

Recycling Coordinators

Recycling Coordinators develop and implement recycling programs and encourage and assist residents and organizations to participate.

WORK ENVIRONMENT

Immediate Physical Environment

Urban and regional planners prepare and assess data in an office setting, but are usually required to visit various outdoor worksites. While they use computers in their daily activities, they do not spend all day at a desk.

Transferable Skills and Abilities

Communication Skills
- Speaking effectively
- Writing concisely

Interpersonal/Social Skills
- Cooperating with others
- Working as a member of a team

Organization & Management Skills
- Paying attention to and handling details
- Performing duties that change frequently

Research & Planning Skills
- Analyzing information
- Developing evaluation strategies

Technical Skills
- Performing scientific, mathematical, and technical work

Human Environment

Urban and regional planners interact with the public, government workers, peers, and supervisors in person, by phone, and via email. When conducting field investigations, they may work with people such as land developers, public officials, and community representatives. They must cooperate with and adapt to a variety of personalities in a deadline-oriented environment.

Technological Environment

An urban planner's technological environment will generally include computers, global positioning system (GPS) devices, and computer-aided design (CAD) software, as well as software for desktop publishing and map creation.

EDUCATION, TRAINING, AND ADVANCEMENT

High School/Secondary

High school students interested in pursuing a career in urban planning should study math and computer science and should also take classes that help to develop strong communication skills. An internship or part-time job in local government will provide valuable experience.

Suggested High School Subjects
- Algebra
- Applied Biology/Chemistry
- Applied Communication
- Applied Math
- Audio-Visual
- College Preparatory
- Drafting
- Economics
- English
- Geometry
- Government
- Mechanical Drawing
- Political Science
- Social Studies
- Sociology
- Trigonometry

Related Career Pathways/Majors

Architecture & Construction Cluster
- Design/Pre-Construction Pathway

Government & Public Administration Cluster
- Planning Pathway

Transportation, Distribution & Logistics Cluster
- Transportation Systems/Infrastructure Planning, Management & Regulation Pathway

Famous First

The first city carriage service ran along Broadway in New York City from Wall Street to Bleecker Street in what is now Greenwich Village. The proprietor was A. Brower. The first vehicle to run along the route was an open carriage, which was replaced in 1829 by the Sociable, a closed carriage pulled by two horses. It sat on double-deck springs and was so high off the ground that passengers had to climb six steps to get inside. Ten passengers could be accommodated on its long sideways seats. The fare was one shilling.

Source: "Transportation." *Famous First Facts*, Salem, 2016. *Salem Online*, https://online.salempress.com

Postsecondary

Most urban and regional planners have a master's degree from an accredited urban or regional planning program. In 2016, there were 71 programs accredited by the Planning Accreditation Board (PAB) that offered a master's degree in planning. Master's degree programs accept students with a wide range of undergraduate backgrounds. However, many candidates who enter these programs have a bachelor's degree in economics, geography, political science, or environmental design.

Most master's programs have students spending considerable time in seminars, workshops, and laboratory courses, in which they learn to analyze and solve planning problems. Although most master's programs have a similar core curriculum, there is some variability in the courses they offer and the issues they focus on. For example, programs located in agricultural states may focus on rural planning, and programs located in larger cities may focus on urban revitalization.

Bachelor's degree holders can qualify for a small number of jobs as assistant or junior planners. In 2016, there were 15 accredited bachelor's degree programs in planning. Candidates with a bachelor's degree typically need work experience in planning, public policy, or a related field.

Related College Majors:
- City/Urban, Community & Regional Planning
- Urban Studies/Affairs

Adult Job Seekers

Adults looking for urban planning work should have at least a bachelor's degree, and in most cases a master's degree is required. Job seekers can apply directly to local government agencies, private architecture and engineering firms, and technical consultancies for any open positions.

Professional Certification and Licensure

As of 2016, New Jersey was the only state that required urban and regional planners to be licensed. More information is available from the regulatory board of New Jersey. The American Institute of Certified Planners (AICP) offers the AICP certification for planners. To become certified, candidates must meet certain education and experience requirements and pass an exam.

Additional Requirements

Although not necessary for all positions, some entry-level positions require one to two years of work experience in a related field, such as architecture, public policy, or economic development. Many students gain experience through real planning projects or part-time internships while enrolled in a master's planning program. Others enroll in full-time internships after completing their degree.

Urban and regional planners need to have good written and oral communication skills, and must be able to use diplomacy when reconciling different points of view. They should also be flexible, decisive, and good listeners, with an affinity for spatial thinking.

EARNINGS AND ADVANCEMENT

Earnings of urban and regional planners depend on the size of the employer, the size and geographic location of the community in which they work and the individual's education and experience. The median annual wage for urban and regional planners was $73,050 in May 2018. The lowest 10 percent earned less than $45,180, and the highest 10 percent earned more than $114,170.

Most urban and regional planners work full time during normal business hours, and some may work evenings or weekends to attend meetings with officials, planning commissions, and neighborhood groups. Some planners work more than 40 hours per week. Urban and regional planners may receive paid vacations, holidays, and sick days; life and health insurance; and retirement benefits. These are usually paid by the employer.

Median annual wages, May 2018

Social scientists and related workers: $78,650

Urban and regional planners: $73,050

Total, all occupations: $38,640

Note: All Occupations includes all occupations in the U.S. Economy.
Source: U.S. Bureau of Labor Statistics, Occupational Employment Statistics

EMPLOYMENT AND OUTLOOK

Urban and regional planners held about 36,000 jobs in 2016. The largest employers of urban and regional planners were as follows:

Local government, excluding education and hospitals	68%
Architectural, engineering, and related services	12%
State government, excluding education and hospitals	11%
Management, scientific, and technical consulting services	3%
Federal government	2%

Planners work throughout the country, but most work in large metropolitan areas. Employment of urban and regional planners is projected to grow 13 percent from 2016 to 2026, faster than the average for all occupations. Demographic, transportation, and environmental changes will drive employment growth for planners.

Within cities, urban planners will be needed to develop revitalization projects and address issues associated with population growth, environmental degradation, the movement of people and goods, and resource scarcity. Similarly, suburban areas and municipalities will need planners to address the challenges associated with population changes, including housing needs and transportation systems covering larger areas with less population density.

Planners will also be needed as new and existing communities require extensive development and improved infrastructure, including housing, roads, sewer systems, parks, and schools.

However, federal, state, and local government budgets may affect the employment of planners in government, because development projects are contingent on available funds.

Urban and regional planners should expect to face competition for positions. Job opportunities for planners often depend on government budgets and economic conditions. When municipalities and developers have funds for development projects, planners are in higher demand.

Percent change in employment, Projected 2016–26

Urban and regional planners: 13%

Social scientists and related workers: 11%

Total, all occupations: 7%

Note: All Occupations includes all occupations in the U.S. Economy.
Source: U.S. Bureau of Labor Statistics, Occupational Employment Statistics

Related Occupations
- Architect
- City Manager
- Civil Engineer
- Construction Manager
- Economist
- Landscape Architect
- Market Research Analyst
- Social Scientist

Fast Fact

Boston and Washington, DC, suffer the worst traffic congestion in the United States, at a cost of up to $2,291 and $2,161 per driver, with Boston drivers losing up to 164 hours each year and Washington drivers losing 155 hours, compared to a nationwide average of 97 hours.

Source: inrix.com Global Traffic Scorecard

Conversation With...
CAROL RHEA, FAICP
Partner, Orion Planning & Design
President, American Planning Association
Huntsville, AL
Urban Planner, 31 years

1. What was your individual career path in terms of education/training, entry-level job, or other significant opportunity?

Like most planners, I never knew planning existed as a potential career until I was well into college. I earned a bachelor's degree in earth science from the University of North Carolina at Charlotte and went on to earn a master's in geography with a concentration in planning.

My first job was with the Southwest Florida Regional Planning Council, where I worked on regional comprehensive plans as well as community development programs for housing and land use studies, such as the environmental impact of oil and gas leasing on the Outer Continental Shelf. From there, I moved to the North Carolina Division of Community Assistance. We provided consulting services, mainly to governments, but also nonprofits, chambers of commerce, or downtown development programs. One of my major projects was helping translate the state's water protection program to local governments.

I went on to become Director of Planning and Development for Monroe, NC. During this time, I got involved with the North Carolina chapter of the American Planning Association (APA), and became state president. I later was elected to the national board.

After I started my family, I was a consultant for many years. Then one day in 2010 I got an email asking if I'd be interested in joining forces with other talented people who knew each other through APA and creating a firm. Today, Orion Planning + Design has six partners. We work all over the country. I do mostly comprehensive master planning and code work for communities. Codes include zoning codes and subdivision regulations. We often start with a master plan and end with a code plan because codes help implement the plans. We work closely with a community's staff because they need to see this as their plan. We're not just in it for the money; having our plans implemented is the goal.

2. What are the most important skills and/or qualities for someone in your profession?

Number one is the ability to communicate, both orally and written. You need to take large amounts of data and information, determine what's relevant to a community, and convey that to stakeholders such as government staff, residents, and bankers and lawyers. Teamwork is essential. A big part of the job is building bridges and creating avenues of cooperation.

3. What do you wish you had known going into this profession?

I would have gotten a joint planning and law degree. You must gain an understanding of the legal framework involved with codes.

4. Are there many job opportunities in your profession? In what specific areas?

Yes. Historically, planners are in government jobs, but increasingly we're seeing them in nontraditional fields. For example, I know a planner who works with AARP (American Association of Retired Persons), and helped to create their livability index. We'll see demand in health-related jobs because we now understand that the way we build cities directly impacts health. Transportation planning and environmental planning will grow. The federal government has planners at its facilities—including military—around the world. Planning generalists will always be in demand.

5. How do you see your profession changing in the next five years? What role will technology play in those changes, and what skills will be required?

People will increasingly demand 24/7 access to data and public processes. It won't be enough to have a meeting or two or post information on Facebook or websites.

Until now, we've based plans on the 10-year census and estimates, but that will change dramatically. Real-time data-driven plans will be big.

The so-called "sharing economy," including businesses like Uber and Airbnb, is changing the way communities view transportation and land use. Airbnb doesn't lend itself to a strict zoning policy, for example.

As the housing crisis gets bigger, that will drive new ways to create affordability. In California we're seeing three-hour commutes because people can't afford to live close to their jobs. Maybe parking lots will be converted to housing.

Climate change and globalization also will drive planning. More communities are embracing planning for events such as tornados and earthquakes. Globalization means, for example, that a small town in North Carolina watched its main employer, an Alcoa plant, shut down when Russia started flooding the market with aluminum.

6. **What do you enjoy most about your job? What do you enjoy least about your job?**

   I love the variety. I love the people I work with in my firm and my clients; the people we work with are fun and challenge us and really make our days better. I love that planners are passionate and care about communities and people. I also like that I keep my eye on what's happening at a national and global level, but also what's happening on the street.

   I least like dealing with people who are obstructionists for no reason, who don't come to the table with a spirit of cooperation to help their communities.

7. **Can you suggest a valuable "try this" for students considering a career in your profession?**

   Participate in your community's planning process. Go to public meetings. Volunteer. Intern with or shadow a planner so you can see what they do on a daily basis.

   Note: This interview first appeared in *Careers in Sales, Insurance & Real Estate* © 2016.

MORE INFORMATION

American Planning Association (APA)
205 N. Michigan Avenue, Suite 1200
Chicago, IL 60601
312.431.9100
customerservice@planning.org
www.planning.org

Association of Collegiate Schools of Planning (ACSP)
6311 Mallard Trace
Tallahassee, FL 32312
850.385.2054
www.acsp.org

Urban Land Institute (ULI)
1025 Thomas Jefferson Street, NW
Suite 500 West
Washington, DC 20007
202.624.7000
www.uli.org

Susan Williams/Editor

Water Transportation Workers

Snapshot

Career Cluster(s): Agriculture, Food & Natural Resources, Transportation, Distribution & Logistics

Interests: Construction, mechanics, machine technology, welding, maintenance, navigation

Earnings (Median Pay): $54,400

Employment & Outlook: As Fast as Average Growth Expected

OVERVIEW

Sphere of Work

Water transportation workers operate and maintain vessels that take cargo and people over water. The vessels travel to and from foreign ports across the ocean and to domestic ports along the coasts, across the Great Lakes, and along the country's many inland waterways.

Sailors and deckhands work on boats and ships as members of deck crews. Most sailors and deckhands are responsible for cleaning the interiors and exteriors of their boats or ships, maintaining equipment and lifeboats, handling mooring lines and other docking procedures, raising and lowering anchors,

and keeping watch. Deckhands who serve on oceangoing vessels are ranked from entry level to most experienced, as ordinary seamen, able seamen, or boatswains.

Work Environment

Water transportation workers work on many different types of boats and ships. Deepwater vessels include containerships, oil tankers, tall ships, luxury yachts, and cruise ships. Inland vessels include ferries, water taxis, tugboats, barges, and fishing boats. Since vessels cannot operate in frozen water, many of these jobs are seasonal or short term, and the work may involve extended periods away from home. Inland vessels may provide regular working hours and more steady employment than deep-sea vessels. Most positions are team based and require working in close quarters with other sailors and officers.

Profile

Interests: Data, Things
Working Conditions: Work Outside, Work both Inside and Outside
Physical Strength: Light Work, Medium Work, Heavy Work
Education Needs: On-the-Job Training, High School Diploma or GED
Licensure/Certification: Required
Physical Abilities Not Required: N/A
Opportunities for Experience: Internship, Apprenticeship, Military Service
Holland Interest Score: REI, RIE

* See Appendix A

Occupation Interest

People who are attracted to the work performed by water transportation workers are enthusiastic about working in a marine or freshwater environment. As the work is physically demanding, they must be strong and able to tolerate the hard labor involved in transporting people or cargo. They have a strong work ethic and are team players. While most of the work tends to be routine, sailors and deckhands must also be flexible and resourceful, as they are sometimes called upon to perform a variety of additional duties and handle emergencies as they arise. Cleanliness and consideration for others are highly valued, given the close living and working quarters on board many vessels.

A Day in the Life—Duties and Responsibilities

Water transportation workers operate and maintain vessels that take cargo and people over water. The vessels travel to and from foreign ports across the ocean and to domestic ports along the coasts, across the Great Lakes, and along the country's many inland waterways.

The responsibilities and duties assigned to water transportation workers vary by vessel and by individual experience and ranking. Most deckhands, especially ordinary seamen, are responsible for keeping their vessels clean and in good repair. Under sail, deckhands clean portable furniture and permanent seating, maintain the bathrooms, clean portholes, and rinse off or scrub the railings and deck floors. When the boat or ship is docked, they clean and polish the exterior. Deckhands are also usually responsible for maintaining anchors and weighing them when ordered. They care for the rigging, sails, and other gear. On vessels with limited crews, they may be required to assume additional tasks, such as cooking.

Able seamen must also maneuver and maintain lifeboats, a task that includes performing regular safety checks. In the event of an emergency, they might have to guide passengers into the lifeboats. They stand watch when scheduled, checking for other vessels, buoys, icebergs, and other obstacles that might be in the path of the ship or boat. Able seamen and boatswains may also assist in charting the vessel's course and steering under the direction of the mate or captain.

Depending on their work setting, sailors and deckhands may have specialized duties in addition to the tasks described above. Deckhands aboard ferries operate the chains, docking aprons, and gates during dockings and departures. They guide vehicles on and off the ferry, decide on vehicle placement to ensure the weight is evenly balanced, place blocks in front of the wheels when necessary, and may assist passengers or collect fares. Those employed on tall ships are responsible for handling and maintaining the sails. They might also help give educational tours or presentations when docked. Deckhands on privately owned luxury yachts spend much of their time polishing the chrome, catering to guests, cooking meals, and/or organizing scuba diving excursions. Aboard cargo ships, deckhands might be required to rig cargo booms and help load and unload cargo.

Duties

Water transportation workers typically do the following:

- Operate and maintain nonmilitary vessels
- Follow their vessel's strict chain of command
- Ensure the safety of all people and cargo on board

These workers, sometimes called merchant mariners, work on a variety of ships. Some operate large deep-sea container ships to transport manufactured goods and refrigerated cargos around the world. Others work on bulk carriers that move heavy commodities, such as coal or iron ore, across the oceans and over the Great Lakes. Still others work on both large and small tankers that carry oil and other liquid products around the country and the world. Others work on supply ships that transport equipment and supplies to offshore oil and gas platforms.

Workers on tugboats help barges and other boats maneuver in small harbors and at sea. Salvage vessels that offer emergency services also employ merchant mariners. Cruise ships also employ water transportation workers, and some merchant mariners work on ferries to transport passengers along shorter distances.

A typical deep-sea merchant ship, large coastal ship, or Great Lakes merchant ship employs a captain and a chief engineer, along with three mates, three assistant engineers, and a number of sailors and marine oilers. Smaller vessels that operate in harbors or rivers may have a smaller crew. The specific complement of mariners is dependent on U.S. Coast Guard (USCG) regulations. Also, there are other workers on ships, such as cooks, electricians, and general maintenance and repair workers.

The following are examples of types of water transportation workers:

Captains, sometimes called masters, have overall command of a vessel. They have the final responsibility for the safety of the crew, cargo, and passengers. Captains typically do the following:

- Steer and operate vessels
- Direct crew members
- Ensure that proper safety procedures are followed
- Purchase equipment and supplies and arrange for any necessary maintenance and repair Oversee the loading and unloading of cargo or passengers
- Keep logs and other records that track the ship's movements and activities
- Interact with passengers on cruise ships

Mates, or deck officers, direct the operation of a vessel while the captain is off duty. Large ships have three officers, called first, second, and third mates. The first mate has the highest authority and takes command of the ship if the captain is incapacitated. Usually, the first mate is in charge of the cargo and/or passengers, the second mate is in charge of navigation, and the third mate is in charge of safety. On smaller vessels, there may be only one mate who handles all of the responsibilities. Deck officers typically do the following:

- Alternate watches with the captain and other officers
- Supervise and coordinate the activities of the deck crew
- Assist with docking the ship
- Monitor the ship's position, using charts and other navigational aides
- Determine the speed and direction of the vessel
- Inspect the cargo hold during loading, to ensure that the cargo is stowed according to specifications
- Make announcements to passengers when needed

Pilots guide ships in harbors, on rivers, and on other confined waterways. They are not part of a ship's crew but go aboard a ship to guide it through a particular waterway that they are familiar with. They work in places where a high degree of familiarity with local tides, currents, and hazards is needed. Some, called harbor pilots, work for ports and help many ships that come into the harbor during the day. When coming into a commercial port, a captain will often have to turn control of the vessel over to a pilot, who can safely guide it into the harbor. Pilots typically do the following:

- Board an unfamiliar ship from a small boat in the open water, often using a ladder
- Confer with a ship's captain about the vessel's destination and any special requirements it has
- Establish a positive working relationship with a vessel's captain and deck officers
- Receive mooring instructions from shore dispatchers

Sailors, or deckhands, operate and maintain the vessel and deck equipment. They make up the deck crew and keep all parts of a ship, other than areas related to the engine and motor, in good working order. New deckhands are called ordinary seamen and do the least complicated tasks. Experienced deckhands are called able seamen and usually make up most of a crew. Some large ships have a boatswain, who is the chief of the deck crew. Sailors typically do the following:

- Stand watch, looking for other vessels or obstructions in their ship's path and for navigational aids, such as buoys and lighthouses
- Steer the ship under the guidance of an officer and measure water depth in shallow water
- Do routine maintenance, such as painting the deck and chipping away rust
- Keep the inside of the ship clean
- Handle mooring lines when docking or departing
- Tie barges together when they are being towed
- Load and unload cargo
- Help passengers when needed

Ship engineers operate and maintain a vessel's propulsion system, which includes the engine, boilers, generators, pumps, and other machinery. Large vessels usually carry a chief engineer, who has command of the engine room and its crew, and a first, second, and third assistant engineer. The assistant engineer oversees the engine and related machinery when the chief engineer is off duty. Small ships might have only one engineer. Engineers typically do the following:

- Maintain a ships' mechanical and electrical equipment and systems
- Start the engine and regulate the vessel's speed, following the captain's orders
- Record information in an engineering log
- Keep an inventory of mechanical parts and supplies
- Do routine maintenance checks throughout the day
- Calculate refueling requirements

Marine oilers work in the engine room, helping the engineers keep the propulsion system in working order. They are the engine room equivalent of sailors. New oilers usually are called wipers, or pumpmen, on vessels handling liquid cargo. With experience, a wiper can become a Qualified Member of the Engine Department (QMED). Marine oilers typically do the following:

- Lubricate gears, shafts, bearings, and other parts of the engine or motor
- Read pressure and temperature gauges and record data
- Perform daily and periodic maintenance on engine room machinery
- Help engineers with repairs to machinery
- Connect hoses, operate pumps, and clean tanks
- Assist the deck crew with loading or unloading of cargo, if necessary

Motorboat operators run small, motor-driven boats that carry only a few passengers. They provide a variety of services, such as fishing charters, tours, and harbor patrols. Motorboat operators typically do the following:

- Check and change the oil and other fluids on their boat
- Pick up passengers and help them board the boat
- Act as a tour guide, if necessary

OCCUPATION SPECIALTIES

Ordinary Seamen

Ordinary Seamen scrub decks, paint, clean personnel quarters, and perform general maintenance work.

Able Seamen

Able Seamen are expected to have a knowledge of all parts of the ship and be able to operate all gear and deck equipment.

Quartermasters

Quartermasters may be required to be certified by the USCG as able seamen. They steer the ship and maintain visual communications with other ships.

Boat Loaders

Boat Loaders transfer liquid cargo, such as petroleum, gasoline, and heating oil from and onto barges and tankers. They may also tend winches and chutes to load boats and barges with iron ore at ore docks.

WORK ENVIRONMENT

Immediate Physical Environment

Water transportation workers work outside in harsh environments. Their work is physically demanding. Emotional issues related to being away from home are common among mariners. Sailors and deckhands are in some danger of slipping, machine accidents, injuries due to fires and collisions, or falling overboard and drowning.

Water transportation workers usually work for long periods and can be exposed to all kinds of weather. Many people decide that life at sea is not for them because of difficult conditions onboard ships and long periods away from home. However, companies try to provide pleasant living conditions aboard their vessels. Most vessels are air-conditioned and include comfortable living quarters. Many also include entertainment systems with satellite TV and internet connections, and meals may be provided.

Workers on deep-sea ships can spend months at a time away from home. Workers on supply ships have shorter trips, usually lasting for a few hours or days. Tugboats and barges travel along the coasts and on inland waterways, and crews are usually away for two to three weeks at a time. Those who work on the Great Lakes have longer trips, around two months, but often do not work in the winter, when the lakes freeze. Crews on all vessels often work for long periods, seven days a week, while aboard.

Ferry workers and motorboat operators usually are away only for a few hours at a time and return home each night. Many ferry and motorboat operators service ships for vacation destinations and have seasonal schedules.

Transferable Skills and Abilities

Interpersonal/Social Skills
- Being able to remain calm
- Cooperating with others
- Working as a member of a team

Organization & Management Skills
- Handling challenging situations
- Performing duties that change frequently
- Performing routine work

Human Environment

Depending on the size of the vessel, sailors and deckhands report to a boatswain, mate, or captain. They may work alone or with any number of other deckhands. If transporting passengers, a deckhand might enjoy some level of interaction with the guests. Sailors and deckhands who work on oceangoing ships, tugboats, and other vessels that require overnight or long-term stays generally share cabins with other workers.

Technological Environment

Sailors and deckhands use mops, brooms, wire brushes, disinfectants, and scraping tools for cleaning and employ various hand and power tools for repairing items. Other basic tools and supplies include water pumps, winches for hoisting ropes, davits for raising and lowering lifeboats, cargo-handling machinery, rigging apparatuses, fishing nets and ropes, semaphores, and blinker lights.

EDUCATION, TRAINING, AND ADVANCEMENT

High School/Secondary

A high school diploma or its equivalent is required for most positions. Over a dozen high schools offer a specialized curriculum created by the U.S. Maritime Administration, but a vocational or academic program from a traditional high school provides adequate preparation as well. Courses in woodworking, metalworking, welding, or construction teach valuable skills and the safe use of tools. English, math, health, and history courses are also important. Foreign language proficiency may be useful for working in a particular region of the United States or for international travel.

Suggested High School Subjects
- English
- Machining Technology
- Shop Math
- Shop Mechanics
- Welding

Related Career Pathways/Majors

Agriculture, Food & Natural Resources Cluster
- Natural Resources Systems Pathway

Transportation, Distribution & Logistics Cluster
- Transportation Operations Pathway

Famous First

The first Great Lakes vessel was *Le Griffon*, a two-masted armored square-rigger built in 1679 by the explorer Robert Cavelier, Sieur de La Salle, at Cayuga Creek, near the Niagara River in New York. The keel was laid on January 26, 1679, and its first voyage was made on August 7. It was of 60 tons burden and sailed Lake Erie and Lake Michigan. It sank on September 18, 1679, in a gale in Mackinaw Strait and is believed to be resting in Mississagi Strait, Manitoulin Island, Canada.

Source: "Transportation." *Famous First Facts*, Salem, 2016. *Salem Online*, https://online.salempress.com

Postsecondary

Most entry-level sailors and deckhands are taught on the job, although those interested in working aboard deep-water vessels will need to take a brief basic training program in first aid, safety, personal survival techniques, and firefighting to meet the International Maritime Organization's Standards of Training, Certification, and Watchkeeping for Seafarers (STCW) requirement. Other training necessary for advancement is available through USCG–approved programs held at maritime academies, community colleges, vocational schools, and other training centers. Tall ships and other educational ships and boats frequently offer unpaid internships or apprenticeships.

Employers may prefer to hire workers who have earned a bachelor's degree from a merchant marine academy. The academy programs offer a bachelor's degree and a Merchant Mariner Credential (MMC) with an endorsement as a third mate or third assistant engineer. Graduates of these programs also can choose to receive a commission as an ensign in the U.S. Naval Reserve, Merchant Marine Reserve, or USCG Reserve.

Adult Job Seekers

Adults who meet the basic educational and physical requirements should be able to compete with younger job seekers. Prior custodial, mechanical, or military experience might be especially advantageous for those switching to a maritime career. Some training is offered online and courses can be taken at night school. Union membership can be a helpful means of finding employment. Candidates can also apply directly to shipping companies.

Professional Certification and Licensure

Mariners who work on ships traveling on the open ocean require the Standards of Training, Certification, and Watchkeeping (STWC) endorsement. Regional USCG offices provide this training, and it includes topics such as first aid and lifeboat safety. The STWC training must be completed every five years. Mariners who work on inland waterways and the Great Lakes are excluded from the STWC endorsement.

Most mariners also must have a Merchant Mariner Credential (MMC), which they can apply for at a USCG regional examination center. Entry-level employees, such as ordinary seamen or wipers, do not have to pass a written exam. However, some have to pass physical, hearing, and vision tests, and all must undergo a drug screening, in order to get their MMC. They also have to take a class on shipboard safety. The MMC must also be renewed every five years.

Pilots are licensed by the state in which they work. The USCG licenses pilots on the Great Lakes. The requirements for these licenses vary, depending on where a pilot works.

All sailors and deckhands who work aboard U.S. merchant marine vessels greater than one hundred gross register tons (domestic tonnage) must obtain a MMC from the Coast Guard and a Transportation Worker Identification Credential (TWIC) from the Department of Homeland Security. Applicants must be at least 16 years old to be considered for entry-level positions as ordinary seamen. They must also speak English, prove citizenship or permanent resident status, pass drug tests, and meet other qualifications. Those who are at least 18 years old and meet specified work experience requirements are eligible for the able seaman ranking. STCW certification is required for positions involving interactions with passengers.

Advancement is dependent on experience and training, determined in part by the USCG and the STCW requirements. Generally, one attains certification as an ordinary seaman and then progresses through the other seaman ranks. Each ranking typically offers additional compensation, prestige, and opportunities for supervising those with lower rankings. With additional education and experience, one can move into other positions, such as ship engineer, mate, or officer. These positions typically require a bachelor's degree.

Additional Requirements

Ordinary seamen, wipers, and other entry-level mariners get on-the-job training for six months to a year. The length of training depends on the size and type of ship and waterway they work on. For example, workers on deep-sea vessels need more complex training than those whose ships travel on a river.

Mariners might need a U.S. passport. Some jobs require a driver's license, fishing license, scuba diving certification, or other credentials. All sailors and deckhands should have excellent swimming skills.

EARNINGS AND ADVANCEMENT

Earnings depend on the type of vessel and the job assignments and experience of the employee. Median annual earnings of water transportation workers were $54,400 in May 2018.

Water transportation workers typically progress from lower level positions to higher level ones, making work experience an important requirement for many jobs. A ship engineer, for example, might need experience as a marine oiler, and mates may have previously worked as sailors. In some cases, workers gain the needed hands-on experience as part of their education program.

After obtaining their MMC, crewmembers can apply for endorsements that may allow them to move into more advanced positions.

Wipers can get an endorsement to become a Qualified Member of the Engine Department (QMED) after six months of experience by passing a written test.

It takes three years of experience and the passing of a written test for an ordinary seaman to become an unlimited able seaman. However, several able seaman endorsements below the level of unlimited are available after six months to one year of experience, depending on the type of ship the seamen work on.

Able seamen can advance to become third mates after at least three years of experience in the deck department. This experience must be on a ship similar to the type they hope to serve on as an officer. They also must take several training courses and pass written and onboard exams to receive the third-mate's endorsement on their MMC. The difficulty of these requirements increases with the complexity and size of the vessel. Similarly, QMEDs can receive an endorsement as a third assistant engineer after three years of experience in the engine room and upon completion of a number of training and testing requirements. Experience and testing requirements increase with the size and complexity of the ship.

Officers who graduate from a maritime academy receive an MMC with an endorsement of a third mate or third assistant engineer, depending on the department in which they are trained.

To move up each step of the occupation ladder, from third mate/third assistant engineer, to second mate, to first mate, and then to captain or chief engineer, requires 365 days of experience at the previous level. A second mate or second assistant engineer who wants to move to first mate/first assistant engineer also must complete a 12-week training course and pass an exam.

> **Fast Fact**
>
> Pirates would often hide much of their crew below the deck. Ships that displayed crew openly on the deck were thought to be honest merchant ships, known as "above board."
>
> Source: www.tradeonlytoday.com/

EMPLOYMENT AND OUTLOOK

There were approximately 86,300 water transportation workers employed nationally in 2016. Employment in water transportation occupations is expected to grow as fast as average for all occupations through the year 2026, which means employment is projected to increase 8 percent. Job growth will stem from increasing tourism and growth in offshore oil and gas production. Employment will also increase in and around major port cities due to rapidly increasing international trade. Domestic waterways employment is expected to grow due to the U.S. Department of Transportation's Maritime Administration (MARAD) Marine Highways initiatives to develop and expand freight and passenger water transportation.

Fluctuations in the demand for bulk commodities, such as petroleum products, iron ore, and grains, is a key factor influencing waterborne employment. When demand for these commodities is high, the need for water transportation workers goes up; when demand slows, so does the need for workers.

The use of larger vessels that can carry more cargo may also limit employment growth. Nevertheless, these workers will continue to be needed as federal laws and subsidies ensure that there always will be a fleet of merchant ships with U.S. flags. Keeping a fleet of merchant ships is considered important for the nation's defense.

Riverboat cruises have gained in popularity, and this trend may lead to more opportunities for workers on inland rivers such as the Mississippi or Ohio River. However, most oceangoing cruise ships go to international destinations, and these ships generally do not employ U.S. workers.

Demand for motorboat operators will be driven by growth in tourism and recreational activities, where they are primarily employed.

Related Occupations
- Ship Loader

Related Military Occupations
- Seaman

Conversation With . . .
SHEILA LUCEY

Harbormaster
Town of Nantucket
Nantucket, MA
Harbormaster, 6 years

1. **What was your individual career path in terms of education/training, entry-level job, or other significant opportunity?**

    After I graduated from high school, I enlisted in the U.S. Coast Guard and did 24 years. I was a boatswain mate, which means we drove boats. I was stationed at a lot of small boat stations and worked closely with harbormasters. During my last year in the Coast Guard, I was in charge of Coast Guard Station Brant Point on Nantucket, which is an island off the coast of Cape Cod. A job for assistant harbormaster became available, so I decided to retire from the Coast Guard and apply. I had that job for five years, and became harbormaster in 2012.

    I grew up in South Boston, which overlooks Boston Harbor. I never spent time on boats until I went into the Coast Guard, but we used to go to the beach all the time. I wouldn't say I grew up "on the water," but I grew up close to the water.

2. **What are the most important skills and/or qualities for someone in your profession?**

    You have to have good management skills and administrative skills. You need to have boat-handling skills. And you have to be able to work with all different types of people. You can run into a lot of conflict because there are so many different rules. You have local rules as far as moorings and the town pier and things like that. Then you get into boating and people trying to do dangerous things that you have to talk them out of it. There's basic enforcement of wake regulations and speed limits on the water. And nobody likes being told what to do, especially when they're out boating and trying to have a good time. Sometimes you've got to be the person that comes along and tells them they can't do what they want to do.

3. **What do you wish you had known going into this profession?**

    I think the Coast Guard was a really good segue into being harbormaster. I had a lot of experience dealing with all the things I deal with now, but now it's on a smaller, local scale. I do wish I was a little bit better at the computer end of things. I can do anything I want with a boat, but I have a hard time sometimes with the computer.

4. Are there many job opportunities in your profession? In what specific areas?

For the most part, harbormasters work for municipalities and communities that are coastal communities, so you're limited by geography. In some places, like Alaska, people who are actually dock masters are called harbormasters. They work for private companies, such as boat basins. If you want to be a harbormaster, you could start in a private marina and work your way up. You could also start in safe boating education.

5. How do you see your profession changing in the next five years? What role will technology play in those changes, and what skills will be required?

Technology plays a huge, huge part. GPS (global position system) has come into play. Boats have become very computerized. We handle 2,200 moorings and used to handwrite them on cards, but now we use computer programs to manage it.

6. What do you enjoy most about your job? What do you enjoy least about your job?

What I enjoy most about my job is that it's outside most of the time. We're active even in the winter because there are people still commercial fishing and commercial scalloping. Pretty much anything that happens on the water, we're relied upon. Obviously we rely heavily on the Coast Guard to take care of the big stuff, but we try to take care of anything inside the harbor so that they can save their assets to help people offshore.

I also enjoy working with people and the fact that there's something different every day. You never know what will happen. A few weeks ago, a sewer line failed and raw sewage was flowing into the harbor. Separate from that, we ended up having a little bit of a diesel sheen, so we had to set booms and take care of all that with the help of the fire department. I just really like that it's exciting.

What I enjoy least is that you can't make everybody happy and they let you know it quite a bit. There are days when it's blowing 60 and raining sideways or snowing sideways and you need to be outside helping somebody who just didn't pay attention to the warnings or didn't heed the warnings. That can be frustrating.

7. Can you suggest a valuable "try this" for students considering a career in your profession?

Apply with the local harbormaster. We always have a lot of staff on in the summer time. We have a dock staff, we run a pump-out program, and we hire high school kids and young college kids all the time. We go from a full-time staff of three to a full-time staff of 50 in the summer—that's including the lifeguards. But even the lifeguards here on Nantucket get to take a look at what the harbormaster does. If somebody's stuck in shallow water, we might need someone to go in and swim, and the lifeguards have such good first aid training that we take them with us on the boats. We try to expose the kids to everything just in case there's an interest.

Note: This interview first appeared in *Careers Outdoors* © 2018.

MORE INFORMATION

Inlandboatmen's Union
1711 W. Nickerson, Suite D
Seattle, WA 98119
206.284.6001
www.ibu.org

Sailors' Union of the Pacific (SUP)
450 Harrison Street
San Francisco, CA 94105
415.777.3400
www.sailors.org

Seafarers International Union (SIU)
5201 Auth Way
Camp Springs, MD 20746
301.899.7355
www.seafarers.org

Paul Hall Center for Maritime Training and Education
45705 Locust Grove Drive
Piney Point, MD 20674301.994.0010
www.seafarers.org/paulhallcenter/phc.asp

United States Coast Guard (USCG)
National Maritime Center
100 Forbes Drive
Martinsburg, WV 25404
888.427.5662
www.uscg.mil/nmc

Information about STCW policies:
www.uscg.mil/nmc/stcw_policies.asp

Information about Merchant Mariner Credentials:
www.uscg.mil/nmc/faq/merchant_mariners_credentials.asp

Sally Driscoll/Editor

What Are Your Career Interests?

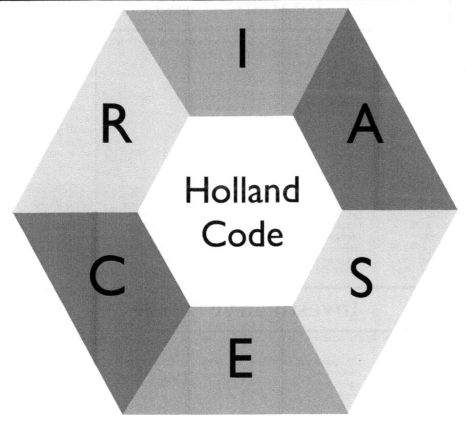

This is based on Dr. John Holland's theory that people and work environments can be loosely classified into six different groups. Each of the letters above corresponds to one of the six groups described in the following pages.

Different people's personalities may find different environments more to their liking. While you may have some interests in and similarities to several of the six groups, you may be attracted primarily to two or three of the areas. These two or three letters are your "Holland Code." For example, with a code of "RES" you would most resemble the Realistic type, somewhat less resemble the Enterprising type, and resemble the Social type even less. The types that are not in your code are the types you resemble least of all.

Most people, and most jobs, are best represented by some combination of two or three of the Holland interest areas. In addition, most people are most satisfied if there is some degree of fit between their personality and their work environment.

The rest of the pages in this booklet further explain each type and provide some examples of career possibilities, areas of study at MU, and co-curricular activities for each code. To take a more in-depth look at your Holland Code, take a self-assessment such as the SDS, Discover, or a card sort at the MU Career Center with a Career Specialist.

This hexagonal model of RIASEC occupations is the copyrighted work of Dr. John Holland, and is used with his permission. The Holland Game is adapted from Richard Bolles' "Quick Job Hunting Map." Copyright 1995, 1998 by the MU Career Center, University of Missouri-Columbia.

Realistic *(Doers)*

People who have athletic ability, prefer to work with objects, machines, tools, plants or animals, or to be outdoors.

Are you?		Can you?	Like to?
practical	independent	fix electrical things	tinker with machines/vehicles
straightforward/frank	ambitious	solve electrical problems	work outdoors
mechanically inclined	systematic	pitch a tent	be physically active
stable		play a sport	use your hands
concrete		read a blueprint	build things
reserved		plant a garden	tend/train animals
self-controlled		operate tools and machine	work on electronic equipment

Career Possibilities
(Holland Code):

Air Traffic Controller (SER)	Dental Technician (REI)	Laboratory Technician (RIE)	Property Manager (ESR)
Archaeologist (IRE)	Farm Manager (ESR)	Landscape Architect (AIR)	Recreation Manager (SER)
Athletic Trainer (SRE)	Fish and Game Warden (RES)	Mechanical Engineer (RIS)	Service Manager (ERS)
Cartographer (IRE)	Floral Designer (RAE)	Optician (REI)	Software Technician (RCI)
Commercial Airline Pilot (RIE)	Forester (RIS)	Petroleum Geologist (RIE)	Ultrasound Technologist (RSI)
Commercial Drafter (IRE)	Geodetic Surveyor (IRE)	Police Officer (SER)	Vocational Rehabilitation
Corrections Officer (SER)	Industrial Arts Teacher (IER)	Practical Nurse (SER)	Consultant (ESR)

Investigative *(Thinkers)*

People who like to observe, learn, investigate, analyze, evaluate, or solve problems.

Are you?		Can you?	Like to?
inquisitive	intellectually self-confident	think abstractly	explore a variety of ideas
analytical	Independent	solve math problems	work independently
scientific	logical	understand scientific theories	perform lab experiments
observant/precise	complex	do complex calculations	deal with abstractions
scholarly	Curious	use a microscope or computer	do research
cautious		interpret formulas	be challenged

Career Possibilities
(Holland Code):

Actuary (ISE)	Chemical Engineer (IRE)	Geologist (IRE)	Physician, General Practice (ISE)
Agronomist (IRS)	Chemist (IRE)	Horticulturist (IRS)	Psychologist (IES)
Anesthesiologist (IRS)	Computer Systems Analyst (IER)	Mathematician (IER)	Research Analyst (IRC)
Anthropologist (IRE)	Dentist (ISR)	Medical Technologist (ISA)	Statistician (IRE)
Archaeologist (IRE)	Ecologist (IRE)	Meteorologist (IRS)	Surgeon (IRA)
Biochemist (IRS)	Economist (IAS)	Nurse Practitioner (ISA)	Technical Writer (IRS)
Biologist (ISR)	Electrical Engineer (IRE)	Pharmacist (IES)	Veterinarian (IRS)

Appendix A: Holland Code

Artistic *(Creators)*

People who have artistic, innovating, or intuitional abilities and like to work in unstructured situations using their imagination and creativity.

Are you?		Can you?	Like to?
creative	original	sketch, draw, paint	attend concerts, theatre, art exhibits
imaginative	introspective	play a musical instrument	read fiction, plays, and poetry
innovative	impulsive	write stories, poetry, music	work on crafts
unconventional	sensitive	sing, act, dance	take photography
emotional	courageous	design fashions or interiors	express yourself creatively
independent	complicated		deal with ambiguous ideas
Expressive	idealistic		
	nonconforming		

Career Possibilities (Holland Code):

- Actor (AES)
- Advertising Art Director (AES)
- Advertising Manager (ASE)
- Architect (AIR)
- Art Teacher (ASE)
- Artist (ASI)
- Copy Writer (ASI)
- Dance Instructor (AER)
- Drama Coach (ASE)
- English Teacher (ASE)
- Entertainer/Performer (AES)
- Fashion Illustrator (ASR)
- Interior Designer (AES)
- Intelligence Research Specialist (AEI)
- Journalist/Reporter (ASE)
- Landscape Architect (AIR)
- Librarian (SAI)
- Medical Illustrator (AIE)
- Museum Curator (AES)
- Music Teacher (ASI)
- Photographer (AES)
- Writer (ASI)
- Graphic Designer (AES)

Social *(Helpers)*

People who like to work with people to enlighten, inform, help, train, or cure them, or are skilled with words.

Are you?		Can you?	Like to?
friendly	cooperative	teach/train others	work in groups
helpful	generous	express yourself clearly	help people with problems
idealistic	responsible	lead a group discussion	do volunteer work
insightful	forgiving	mediate disputes	work with young people
outgoing	patient	plan and supervise an activity	serve others
understanding	kind	cooperate well with others	

Career Possibilities (Holland Code):

- City Manager (SEC)
- Clinical Dietitian (SIE)
- College/University Faculty (SEI)
- Community Org. Director (SEA)
- Consumer Affairs Director (SER)
- Counselor/Therapist (SAE)
- Historian (SEI)
- Hospital Administrator (SER)
- Psychologist (SEI)
- Insurance Claims Examiner (SIE)
- Librarian (SAI)
- Medical Assistant (SCR)
- Minister/Priest/Rabbi (SAI)
- Paralegal (SCE)
- Park Naturalist (SEI)
- Physical Therapist (SIE)
- Police Officer (SER)
- Probation and Parole Officer (SEC)
- Real Estate Appraiser (SCE)
- Recreation Director (SER)
- Registered Nurse (SIA)
- Teacher (SAE)
- Social Worker (SEA)
- Speech Pathologist (SAI)
- Vocational-Rehab. Counselor (SEC)
- Volunteer Services Director (SEC)

Enterprising *(Persuaders)*

People who like to work with people, influencing, persuading, leading or managing for organizational goals or economic gain.

Are you?
self-confident
assertive
persuasive
energetic
adventurous
popular

ambitious
agreeable
talkative
extroverted
spontaneous
optimistic

Can you?
initiate projects
convince people to do things your way
sell things
give talks or speeches
organize activities
lead a group
persuade others

Like to?
make decisions
be elected to office
start your own business
campaign politically
meet important people
have power or status

Career Possibilities (Holland Code):

Advertising Executive (ESA)
Advertising Sales Rep (ESR)
Banker/Financial Planner (ESR)
Branch Manager (ESA)
Business Manager (ESC)
Buyer (ESA)
Chamber of Commerce Exec (ESA)

Credit Analyst (EAS)
Customer Service Manager (ESA)
Education & Training Manager (EIS)
Emergency Medical Technician (ESI)
Entrepreneur (ESA)

Foreign Service Officer (ESA)
Funeral Director (ESR)
Insurance Manager (ESC)
Interpreter (ESA)
Lawyer/Attorney (ESA)
Lobbyist (ESA)
Office Manager (ESR)
Personnel Recruiter (ESR)

Politician (ESA)
Public Relations Rep (EAS)
Retail Store Manager (ESR)
Sales Manager (ESA)
Sales Representative (ERS)
Social Service Director (ESA)
Stockbroker (ESI)
Tax Accountant (ECS)

Conventional *(Organizers)*

People who like to work with data, have clerical or numerical ability, carry out tasks in detail, or follow through on others' instructions.

Are you?
well-organized
accurate
numerically inclined
methodical
conscientious
efficient
conforming

practical
thrifty
systematic
structured
polite
ambitious
obedient
persistent

Can you?
work well within a system
do a lot of paper work in a short time
keep accurate records
use a computer terminal
write effective business letters

Like to?
follow clearly defined procedures
use data processing equipment
work with numbers
type or take shorthand
be responsible for details
collect or organize things

Career Possibilities (Holland Code):

Abstractor (CSI)
Accountant (CSE)
Administrative Assistant (ESC)
Budget Analyst (CER)
Business Manager (ESC)
Business Programmer (CRI)
Business Teacher (CSE)
Catalog Librarian (CSE)

Claims Adjuster (SEC)
Computer Operator (CSR)
Congressional-District Aide (CES)
Cost Accountant (CES)
Court Reporter (CSE)
Credit Manager (ESC)
Customs Inspector (CEI)
Editorial Assistant (CSI)

Elementary School Teacher (SEC)
Financial Analyst (CSI)
Insurance Manager (ESC)
Insurance Underwriter (CSE)
Internal Auditor (ICR)
Kindergarten Teacher (ESC)

Medical Records Technician (CSE)
Museum Registrar (CSE)
Paralegal (SCE)
Safety Inspector (RCS)
Tax Accountant (ECS)
Tax Consultant (CES)
Travel Agent (ECS)

BIBLIOGRAPHY

Abbott, Malcolm, and C.J. Bamforth. *The Early Development of the Aviation Industry: Entrepreneurs of the Sky*. New York: Routledge, 2019.

Blanchard, Olivier, and Daniel Newman. *Human/Machine: The Future of Our Partnership with Machines*. London: Kogan Page Ltd., 2019.

Campbell, Harry. *Rideshare Guide: Everything You Need to Know about Driving for Uber, Lyft and Other Ridesharing Companies*. New York: Skyhorse Publishing Company, Inc., 2018.

Coyle, John Joseph., et al. *The Management of Business Logistics: A Supply Chain Perspective*. Mason, OH: South-Western/Thomson Learning, 2006.

Daganzo, Carlos. *Logistics Systems Analysis*. New York: Springer, 2010.

Fallon, Michael. *Self-Driving Cars: The New Way Forward*. Minneapolis: Twenty-First Century Books, 2019.

Federal Aviation Commission. *How to Become a Pilot: The Step-by-Step Guide to Flying*. Rockville, MD: R. Reginald/Borgo Press, 1991.

Freedman, Jeri. *Coding Careers in Transportation*. New York: Cavendish Square Publishing, LLC, 2020.

Greek, Joe. *A Career in Transportation and Warehousing*. New York: Rosen Publishing, 2019.

Lawrence, Robert. *How to Become an Airline Pilot: Achieve Your Dream without Going Broke*. Robert Lawrence Inc., 2018.

Leisy, Craig A. *Transportation Network Companies and Taxis: The Case of Seattle*. New York: Routledge, 2019.

Lipson, Hod, and Melba Kurman. *Driverless: Intelligent Cars and the Road Ahead*. Cambridge, MA: The MIT Press, 2017.

Morkes, Andrew. *Drone Pilots*. Broomall, PA: Mason Crest, 2020.

Murphy, Paul R., and A. Michael Knemeyer. *Contemporary Logistics*. New York: Pearson, 2018.

Orr, Tamra. *A Career as an Aircraft Mechanic and Service Technician*. New York: The Rosen Publishing Group, Inc., 2019.

Reeb, Tyler. *Empowering the New Mobility Workforce: Educating, Training, and Inspiring Future Transportation ... Professionals*. New York: Elsevier, 2019.

Rushton, Alan, et al. *The Handbook of Logistics and Distribution Management*. London: Kogan Page, 2017.

Sarkar, Suman. *The Supply Chain Revolution: Innovative Sourcing and Logistics for a Fiercely Competitive World*. New York: McGraw-Hill, 2017.

Thompson, Clive. *Coders: The Making of a New Tribe and the Remaking of the World.* New York: Penguin Press, an Imprint of Penguin Random House, 2019.

Torchinsky, Jason, and Beau Boeckmann. *Robot, Take the Wheel: The Road to Autonomous Cars and the Lost Art of Driving.* New York: Apollo Publishers, 2019.

Walden, Joseph L. *The Forklifts Have Nothing to Do!: Lessons in Supply Chain Leadership.* IUniverse, 2003.

Watson, Jack, and Danielle Thorne. *So You Want to Be a Commercial Airline Pilot: Here's the Info You Need.* Ocala, FL: Atlantic Publishing Group, Inc., 2017.

Watson, Stephanie. *What Is the Future of Self-Driving Cars?* Washington, DC: ReferencePoint Press, 2017.

INDEX

A

able seamen 379, 383, 384
aerodynamics 27, 34
aerodynamists 30
aeronautical design engineers 30
aeronautical drafters 31
aeronautical engineers 28
aeronautical project engineers 31
aeronautical research engineers 30
aeronautical test engineers 30
aerospace engineers 27, 28, 31, 32, 36, 37
Aerospace Industries Association (AIA) 35, 42
agricultural aircraft pilots 77
air conditioning technicians 92
Aircraft Electronics Technician (AET) 66
Aircraft Maintenance Professionals Society (AMT) 73
aircraft maintenance supervisors 62
aircraft mechanics 58, 62, 65, 71
aircraft mechanics airframe 65
aircraft mechanics powerplant 65
Aircraft Owners and Pilots Association (AOPA) 88
air crew member 69, 84
airframe and powerplant (A&P) mechanics 60
airline and commercial pilots 74
Airline Dispatchers Federation (ADF) 196
Air Line Pilots Association, International (ALPA) 88
airplane navigator 84
airplane-patrol pilots 77
airplane pilot 84
Air Traffic Collegiate Training Initiative (AT-CTI) program 49
Air Traffic Control Association (ATCA) 54, 57
air traffic controllers 43, 44, 45, 47, 48, 50, 51, 52
air traffic controller training 53
air traffic control manager 53
air-traffic control specialists, center 46
air-traffic control specialists, station 47
air-traffic control specialists, tower 46
Air Transport Association of America (ATAA) 210
air transportation workers 52, 82, 205, 206
Amalgamated Transit Union (ATU) 117
ambulance dispatchers 194, 195
American Bus Association (ABA) 117
American Institute of Aeronautics and Astronautics (AIAA) 35, 42
American Institute of Certified Planners (AICP) 370
American Institute of Graphic Arts (AIGA) 348
American Planning Association (APA) 374, 377
American Production and Inventory Control Society (APICS) 292
American Public Transportation Association (APTA) 117
American Society for Engineering Management (ASEM) 268
American Society for Photogrammetry and Remote Sensing (ASPRS) 126, 132
American Society for Quality (ASQ) 268
American Society of Safety Engineers (ASSE) 268
American Trucking Associations (ATA) 236
angledozer operators 161
animator 248
architect 265
architecture 338, 343, 363, 370
art and design workers 246, 247
asphalt spreader operators 160
Associate Computing Professionals (ACP) 344
Associated Builders and Contractors (ABC) 173, 315
Associated General Contractors of America (AGCA) 315
Association for Computing Machinery (ACM) 145, 156, 348

Association for the Advancement of Cost Engineering International (AACEI) 268
Association for Women in Aviation Maintenance (AWAM) 73
Association of Collegiate Schools of Planning (ACSP) 377
Association of Flight Attendants (AFA) 204, 210
Association of Information Technology Professionals (AITP) 145, 156, 286
Association of Public-Safety Communications Officials International (APSCOI) 196
Association of Technology, Management, and Applied Engineering (ATMAE) 268
Association of Women Industrial Designers (AWID) 252
astronautical engineering 27, 28
auto collision technology 94
automobile dealers 97
Automotive Aftermarket Industry Association (AAIA) 102
automotive body repairer 98
automotive & heavy equipment mechanic 98
automotive service advisor 98
Automotive Service Association (ASA) 102
automotive service attendant 98
automotive service technicians 96, 97
automotive technicians 90, 91, 93, 95, 96, 100
Automotive Youth Education Services (AYES) 102
auto retrofitters 92
auto service technology 94, 109, 227, 306
aviation 39, 51, 54, 55, 56, 61, 65, 66, 69, 70, 71, 75, 78, 80, 84, 85, 86, 197, 198, 201
aviation systems 65
Aviation Technician Education Council (ATEC) 73
avionics maintenance technology 65
avionics technicians 60, 61, 65, 66, 68
A/V technology 243, 337, 342

B

billing clerk 326
blueprint reading 33, 64, 79, 94, 243, 259
boat loaders 384
brake repairer technicians 92
Building Trades Association (BTA) 173, 315

bulldozer operator 159, 162, 164, 165, 166
bus and truck mechanics 11, 12, 13
bus driver 232, 358
bus drivers, school 112
bus drivers, transit and intercity 112
business operations specialists 294, 296
Bus Rapid Transit (BRT) systems 113
BWI Business Partnership, Inc., The 300

C

cabbies 351
cabdrivers 351
CAD training 244
CAID software 240, 242
captains 200, 331
cargo and freight agents 3, 4, 17, 18
cargo specialist 335
cartographers 118, 119, 120, 121, 123, 125, 126, 127, 128, 129
cartographic drafters 123
cartography 124, 125, 126
ceramic engineer 38
charter bus drivers 106
charter bus industry 12
chauffeurs 349, 350, 351, 353, 357
chief controllers 47
chief information officers (CIOs) 273
chief technology officers (CTOs) 274
city manager 373
civil engineer 129, 373
cleaners 213
combat engineer 169
commercial airplane pilots 77
commercial and industrial designers 246, 247
commercial artist 347
commercial designers 237
commercial dispatchers 187, 188
commercial driver's license (CDL) 110, 111, 166, 218, 228, 355
communications professionals 187
computer-aided design and drafting (CADD) 40, 240, 247
computer-aided design (CAD) 240, 367
computer-aided industrial design (CAID) 239
computer-aided manufacturing (CAM) software 32
computer-control tool programmer 143, 347

computer engineer 143, 155, 282, 347
computer engineering 271, 343
computer & information systems manager 143, 155, 282, 347
computer network architect 143, 155, 282
computer operator 143, 347
computer programmer 144, 155, 282, 347
computer security specialist 347
computer software technology 337
computer support specialist 143, 155, 282, 347
computer systems analyst 143, 282, 347
computer systems officer 155, 282
computer systems specialist 144, 155, 347
computer technology 127, 133, 152, 322
Computing Research Association (CRA) 156
concrete paving machine operators 160
construction education services 173, 315
construction equipment operation 164
construction equipment operators 157, 158, 159, 162, 166, 167, 168
construction laborer 169, 221
construction manager 373
construction trades workers 168
control and valve installers and repairers 14, 15, 168
conveyor operators 303
copilots 74, 82, 84
Core77 252
counter & rental clerk 326
couriers 3, 23, 24
crane and tower operators 304
crane operators 307
crawler-tractor operators 161
customer service representatives 24

D

database administrator 143, 155, 282
database management 217, 271, 291, 341
day haul or farm charter bus drivers 107
deckhands 378, 379, 380, 382, 383, 385, 386, 387, 389
deep sea, coastal, and Great Lakes water transportation 9
Defense Acquisition University (DAU) 292
delivery services 180, 181, 182
delivery truck drivers 175, 179, 181, 182
Department of Defense 44, 292

Department of Homeland Security 389
derrick operators 304
designated airworthiness representatives (DARs) 61
designer 238, 239, 245, 246, 339, 340
diesel engine specialists 11, 12, 13
diesel maintenance technology 109, 227, 306
diesel service technician 69, 98
dispatchers 47, 187, 188, 189, 190, 191, 193, 194, 195, 196
drafting, general 35
dredge operators 304
driver/sales workers 174
driver training 109, 216, 227, 306, 332, 354

E

economist 373
educational/instructional media design 343
electrical & electronics engineer 38
emergency dispatchers 187, 188, 189
energy conservation & use technician 264
engineering and scientific programmers 136
engineering design 35
engineering, general 261
engineering/industrial management 261
engineering technician 129
engineering technology 152, 343
engineers in training (EITs) 35
environmental design 369
environmental health & safety officer 264
excavating machine operators 307, 308
executive pilots 77
experimental aircraft mechanics 62

F

FAA Certificate of Demonstrated Proficiency 203
farm equipment mechanic 98
Federal Aviation Admininstration (FAA) 203
Federal Communications Commission (FCC) 66
federal flight deck officers. 78
federal law enforcement officers 78
Federal Motor Carrier Safety Administration (FMCSA) 108, 117, 236
field-map editors 122

field service engineers 30
fine-grade-bulldozer operators 161
first aid training 201, 395
first-line supervisors/managers 22, 23
flexible packaging association (FPA) 186
flight attendants 197, 198, 200, 202, 203, 204, 205, 206
flight attendant training 202
flight engineers 82, 84
flight operations specialist 53
forklift academy 334, 336
freight, stock & material mover 169, 182, 311, 335
freight transportation arrangement 17
front-end technicians 92
fundamentals of engineering (FE) exam 35

G

garbage collector drivers 226
gas compressor 14, 15
gas plant operators 14, 15
gas pumping station operators 14, 15
gaugers 14, 15
general and operations managers 10
general education development (GED) 163, 191
general freight trucking 11
general manager & top executive 282
general retailing & wholesaling operations & skills 193
geodetic surveyors 122
geologist 129
geomatics 125
geophysicist 129
GIS technology 121, 125
global positioning system (GPS) 123, 165, 227, 367
Graphic Artists Guild, The 348
graphic communications 342
graphic design, commercial art 343
graphic designer 248, 347
ground passenger transportation 3, 12
ground passenger transportation subsector 12

H

hand laborers 211
hand packers and packagers 214
heating & cooling mechanic 98
heavy and tractor-trailer truck drivers 223
heavy equipment service technician 69, 98, 169
heavy truck drivers 226
highway maintenance worker 169
hoist and winch operators 304
Homeland Security Act of 2002 78
Human Factors and Ergonomics Society (HFES) 268

I

IEEE Computer Society (IEEE) 145
IER 119, 147
illustration 343
illustrator 347
industrial arts 32, 63, 178, 216, 243
industrial design 244
industrial designers 237, 239, 240, 241, 242, 245, 246, 247
Industrial Designers Society of America (IDSA) 252
industrial engineering 253, 254
industrial engineers 253, 254, 255, 256, 257, 258, 261, 262, 263, 264
industrial hygienist 264
industrial/manufacturing engineering 261
industrial/manufacturing technology 244
industrial truck and tractor operators 304
Industrial Truck Association (ITA) 173, 315
Industrial Workers of the World (IWW) 336
information sciences & systems 140, 152, 278, 343
information security analyst 143, 155, 282
information technology (IT) professionals 134
information technology managers 280
Inlandboatmen's Union 396
inland water transportation 9
Inspection Authorization (IA) 66
Inspection authorized (IA) mechanics 61

Institute for Certification of Computing Professionals (ICCP) 344
Institute for Operations Research and the Management Sciences (INFORMS) 268
Institute for the Certification of Computer Professionals (ICCP) 145, 156, 348
Institute of Electrical and Electronics Engineers Computer Society 156
Institute of Electrical and Electronics Engineers (IEEE) 344, 348
Institute of Industrial Engineers (IIE) 261, 268
Institute of Packaging Professionals (IPP) 186
intercity bus drivers 104, 106, 108
International Brotherhood of Teamsters (IBT) 117, 186, 204, 222, 229, 236, 315
International Longshore and Warehouse Union (ILWU) 222
International Longshoremen's Association (ILA) 336
International Maritime Organization 387
International Municipal Signal Association (IMSA) 196
International Society of Logistics (SOLE) 292
International Society of Women Airline Pilots (ISWAP) 88
International Union of Operating Engineers (IUOE) 307, 315
interurban and rural bus transportation 12
IT directors 274, 280
IT project management 271, 276, 278, 279
IT project managers 270, 271, 272, 275, 278, 279
IT security manager 280

J

Junior Achievement and Future Business Leaders of America 259

K

keyboarding 139, 277, 321, 342

L

laborers 211, 212, 213, 214, 217, 219, 220, 221, 302, 303

Laborers' International Union of North America (LIUNA) 173, 186, 222, 336
land surveyors 122
LIDAR systems 120
light-imaging detection and ranging (LIDAR) 120
light truck or delivery services drivers 180, 181
local messengers 24
local transit bus drivers 106
locomotive engineers 8, 9
lodging pathway 354
logisticians 287, 289, 290, 291, 292, 293, 294, 295, 296
logistics 140, 188, 217, 279, 283, 285, 288, 290, 291, 292, 295, 297, 299, 343, 359
long-haul truck driver 224, 230
longshoremen 328
lumber production worker 221, 311

M

machine feeders and offbearers 214
machine maintenance 328
machining technology 64, 94, 178, 259, 387
mail carrier 326
maintenance, installation & repair pathway 64, 94
maintenance/operations pathway 163
management analyst & consultant 155
management information systems 274
management information systems (MIS) directors 274
management pathway 277
manufacturing engineers 257
manufacturing production process development pathway 33, 260
mapmakers 118, 120
mapping manager 129
marine engineer 264
marine highways initiatives 391
marine oilers 381
marine surveyors 122
Marine Transport Workers Union 333, 336
Maritime Administration (MARAD) 391
marketing management & research 292
material movers 211, 212, 213, 214, 215, 217, 218, 219, 220, 221, 303

material-moving machine and vehicle
operators 22, 23
material-moving machine operators 214, 302,
303, 305, 307, 309, 310
material-moving workers 219, 221, 309, 311
material recording clerks 316
mates 381, 382, 390
mathematician 129, 143, 155
mechanical drafting 35
mechanical drawing 124, 243, 260, 368
mechanical engineering 342
medical records administrator 282
Merchant Mariner Credential (MMC) 388
Merchant Marine Reserve 388
messengers 3, 23, 24
metals technology 94
Mid-Atlantic Professional Truck Drivers
Association (MAPTDA) 236
Mine Safety and Health Administration
(MSHA) 307
mine surveyors 122
mining & geological engineer 129
mobile-lounge drivers 107
motorboat operators 384
motorcoach drivers 106
motor vehicle dispatchers 190
motor vehicle operators 112, 181, 182, 231,
232, 357, 358

N

National Academies of Emergency Dispatch
(NACD) 196
National Action Council for Minorities in
Engineering (NACME) 269
National Aeronautics and Space
Administration (NASA) 35, 42
National Air Traffic Controllers Association
(NATCA) 50, 57
National Association of Programmers (NAP)
145
National Association of Taxi Drivers (NATD)
362
National Automotive Technicians Education
Foundation (NATEF) 102
National Center for Aerospace &
Transportation Technologies (NCATT) 66

National Center for Construction Education
and Research (NCCER) 164, 173, 315
National Commission for the Certification of
Crane Operators (NCCCO) 333
National Council of Examiners for Engineering
and Surveying (NCEES) 126, 132
National Industrial Transportation League
(NITL) 300
National Institute for Automotive Service
Excellence 95, 102
National Limousine Association (NLA) 362
National Maritime Center 396
National Oceanic and Atmospheric
Administration (NOAA) 34
National Post Office 22
National Retail Federation 327
National School Transportation Association
(NSTA) 117
National Society of Black Engineers (NSBE)
269
National Society of Professional Surveyors
(NSPS) 130, 132
naval architect 264
navigation 29, 60, 61, 74, 76, 121, 125, 138,
224, 227, 378, 382
navigators 77
network & computer systems administrator
144, 155, 282, 347
Network Professional Association (NPA) 286
network systems & data communications
analyst 347
network systems pathway 151
Next Generation Air Transportation System
(NextGen) 53
nonscheduled air transportation 67
nonscheduled carriers 3
North American Aerospace Defense Command
49

O

Occupational Safety & Health Administration
(OSHA) 307
Office of Communications 210
Office of Personnel Management (OPM) 50
operating engineers 160, 167
operations research analyst 144, 155, 264, 282
operations specialties managers 281

order fillers 318
ordinary seamen 379, 380, 382, 388, 389

P

packer/packager 221
Paperboard Packaging Council (PPC) 186
paratransit drivers 351, 356
Paul Hall Center for Maritime Training and Education 396
Petroleum pump system operators 14, 15
photogrammetrists 118, 120, 125
photography 242
physical labor 170, 329
physical science 124, 260
pile-driver operators 160, 167
pilots 43, 45, 46, 47, 56, 63, 74, 75, 76, 78, 79, 80, 81, 82, 83, 84, 86, 87, 184, 189, 382, 388
pipeline transportation 3, 14
pipeline transportation of crude oil 14
pipeline transportation of natural gas 14
pipeline transportation subsector 14
Planning Accreditation Board (PAB) 369
political science 259, 369
postal clerk 326
postal service 37, 67
postal service clerks 22, 23
postal service mail carriers 22, 23
postal service subsector 22
postmasters 22, 23
principles and practice of engineering 35, 262
product designers 237, 288
production coordinator 195, 296
Professional Aviation Maintenance Association (PAMA) 65, 73
professional engineering (PE) 35
Professional Truck Driver Institute (PTDI) 236
programming & software development pathway 139, 151, 277, 342
public planning 363
public policy 363
public safety 121

Q

Qualified Member of the Engine Department (QMED) 383, 390
quality assurance specialists 340
quality-control engineers 257
quartermasters 384

R

radar & sonar operator 84
radiator technicians 92
radio dispatchers 190
radio frequency identification (RFID) 318, 325
radio transceiver 187
railcar repairers 8, 9
railroad brake, signal, and switch operators 8, 9
railroad conductors 8, 9
railroad workers 2
rail-track laying and maintenance equipment operators 8, 9
rail transportation 221, 335
rail transportation subsector 8
rail transportation worker 221, 335
receiving managers 316
reclamation workers 62
recycling coordinators 366
refinery operators 14, 15
refuse and recyclable material collectors 214, 218
reservation and transportation ticket agents 3, 4, 16
reservation & ticket agent 195
ride-hailing drivers 349
Rideshare Guy, The 362
road transportation 349
roustabout 221
route returners 319

S

safety engineers 257, 268
sailors 54, 332, 378, 379, 380, 381, 383, 386, 387, 389, 390, 396
Sailors' Union of the Pacific (SUP) 396

scarifier operators 161
scenic and sightseeing transportation 3, 15
scenic and sightseeing transportation, land 15
scenic and sightseeing transportation subsector 15
scenic and sightseeing transportation, water 15
scheduled air transportation 67
school and employee bus transportation 12
school bus drivers 103, 105, 111, 112, 113
scraper operators 161
Seafarers International Union (SIU) 396
seaman 389, 390
Service Employees International Union (SEIU) 196
service technicians 64, 65, 67, 68, 96, 97, 98, 313
ship engineers 383
ship loader 221, 311, 328, 392
shipping and receiving clerks 316, 320, 321
shipping coordinators 316
shipping industry 178, 322, 328, 329, 331
shipping technology 328
shop math 94, 178, 332, 387
shop mechanics 94, 178, 260, 387
Sky Shield 49
small engine mechanic 98
social scientist 373
Society of Automotive Engineers International (SAE) 42
Society of Hispanic Professional Engineers (SHPE) 269
Society of Women Engineers (SWE) 269
software designers 337, 338, 339, 340, 341, 344
Software Development Associates (CSDA) 344
Software Development Professionals (CSDP) 344
software publishers 142, 143
space operations officer 38, 84
specialized freight trucking 11
special operations force 53
special operations officer 84
standard driver's license (SDL) 227
Standards of Training, Certification, and Watchkeeping (STWC) 388
stevedores 328
stock clerk 182, 326

stress analysts 30
supply chain management 256, 287, 291, 297
supply & warehousing specialist 326, 335
support activities for air transportation 52, 67
support activities for rail transportation 17
support activities for road transportation 17
support activities for transportation 3, 17
support activities for transportation subsector 17
support activities for water transportation 17
surveying, mapping & drafting technician 129
surveyors 118, 119, 120, 122, 123, 126, 130, 131, 132
survey party chiefs 123
survey technicians 123
systems architects 146, 340
systems engineering 32, 40, 291

T

tamping equipment operators 160
tank-truck drivers 226
taxi and limousine service 12
taxicab starters 190
taxi drivers 349, 362
technical education 90, 163, 224, 302, 317
Technology Student Association (TSA) 269
test pilots 77
time-study engineers 257
tourism 103, 110, 209, 349, 354
tractor-trailer-truck drivers 226
trade/industrial education 94
traffic clerks 318, 320
traffic managers 316
transit and ground passenger transportation 3, 12
transit drivers 106
Transportation Communications International Union (TCIU) 222
transportation design 238
transportation engineering 254
Transportation engineering 254
transportation maintenance manager 69
transportation management 288
Transportation Management Association of San Francisco (TMASF) 300
transportation management professionals 288
transportation managers 288

Transportation Security Administration (TSA) 203, 229, 236
transportation specialist 206, 232, 296, 326
transportation, storage, and distribution managers 296
Transportation Worker Identification Credential (TWIC) 389
transport engineering 254
Transport Workers Union of America (TWUA) 204, 210
travel clerks 3, 4, 16
truck, bus & other commercial vehicle operation 111, 217, 228
truck driver 224, 228, 229, 230, 233
truck drivers, heavy and tractor-trailer 11, 12, 17, 18
truck drivers, light or delivery services 11, 12, 24
truck transportation 3, 11
truck transportation subsector 11
tune-up technicians 92

U

underground mining loading machine operators 311
United Construction Workers (UCW) 173
United Motorcoach Association (UMA) 117
United States Coast Guard (USCG) 396
United States Geospatial Intelligence Foundation 126
United Transportation Union (UTU) 117
University & College Designers Association (UCDA) 252
urban and regional planners 363, 364, 365, 367, 370, 371, 372, 373
Urban Land Institute (ULI) 377
urban studies/affairs 370

urban transit systems 113
urban transportation 349
USCG Reserve 388
U.S. Coast Guard (USCG) 381
U.S. Department of Transportation 210, 236, 391
U.S. Maritime Administration 386
U.S. Naval Reserve 388

V

value engineers 31
vehicle and mobile equipment mechanics 97, 98
vehicle driver 114, 232
visual arts pathway 243, 342
vocational training 308
volunteer work 271, 364

W

waiter/waitress 206
warehousing 178, 216, 260, 322, 326, 335
warehousing and storage subsector 25
water transportation 378
water transportation subsector 9
water transportation workers 378
web administrator 144, 155, 282, 347
web developer 144, 155, 282
website designer 347
welding 64, 94, 387
Wide Area Augmentation System (WAAS) 48
woodshop 178, 243

Y

yardmasters 8, 9